ACCOUNTING, MANAGEMENT CONTROL AND BUSINESS ORGANISATION

Accounting, Management Control and Business Organisation

An institutionalist perspective

W.B. SEAL
Sheffield Hallam University

Avebury

Aldershot · Brookfield USA · Hong Kong · Singapore · Sydney

Published by
Avebury
Ashgate Publishing Limited
Gower House
Croft Road
Aldershot
Hants GU11 3HR
England

Ashgate Publishing Company
Old Post Road
Brookfield
Vermont 05036
USA
Reprinted 1995

British Library Cataloguing in Publication Data

Seal, W. B.
  Accounting, Management Control and
  Business Organisation: An Institutionalist
  Perspective
  I. Title
  658.15

Typeset by
The Graphics Unit
Sheffield Hallam University
Sheffield S1 1WB
England

ISBN 1 85628 503 0

Printed and bound by Athenæum Press Ltd.,
Gateshead, Tyne & Wear.

Contents

Acknowledgements

I would like to thank Tony Lowe and Mo Yamin for their help and encouragement over the years it has taken to develop the ideas in this book. I would also like to thank Mike Bromwich for his comments. I have benefited from the support of my Head of Department, Keith Harrison at Sheffield Hallam University. In the latter connection, I would like to thank Mel McClellan for helping me with the graphics and layout of the book.

Some of the material in chapters four and seven has already appeared in my articles in the *Cambridge Journal of Economics* and the *British Accounting Review*, respectively. I would like to thank the publishers of those journals for giving me permission to reproduce this material. I would also like to thank the following publishers and editors for allowing me to make selective use of their material (the details of the sources are listed in the bibliography) - Ray Ball, Sage publications, Harcourt Brace Jovanovich, Blackwell, Academic Press, Elsevier Science Publishers, Cambridge University Press, Pergamon Press, Administrative Science Quarterly, American Accounting Association, Harvard University Press, American Economic Association, Prentice Hall International, Oxford University Press, University of Chicago Press, Lloyds Bank Economic Bulletin and Harvard Business School Press.

Introduction

The context of the book

Although the 'Anglo' economies such as the US and UK have evolved different economic institutions and face different economic problems, there are some commonalities. For example, both economies are characterised by large stock markets, active markets for control and powerful accounting professions. Both economies are facing the growing challenge not only from East Asian manufacturing competition but also a dramatic growth in direct investment from that region. However, the most relevant commonality from the viewpoint of this book is that both nations share a neoclassical economics tradition that has failed to provide theoretical guidance to help policy makers respond to the new challenges. For example, neoclassical theory cannot show whether 'deindustrialisation' or the construction of foreign owned simple assembly style operations (screw-driver firms) is 'good' or a 'bad' from a national economic development perspective.

This intellectual void is increasingly being filled by approaches which stem from business related disciplines. Thus Porter (1990) and Kaplan (1983) have both addressed national economic challenges from their own particular academic perspectives. This book is in this tradition as it develops an institutionalist theory of the firm by drawing on accounting and management control literatures. I submit that this approach offers fresh insights on the new economic challenges facing the 'Anglo' economies.

The main problematic of the book

Accounting, management control and economics:a reinterpretation

The purpose of this book is to investigate the role of accounting and management control in the creation of national wealth. The problematic is thus firmly located in the economics domain. This focus is important because there are an increasing number of perspectives which see accounting as an essentially social institution which must therefore be looked at through the spectacles of social theory. The approach in this book does not deny the importance of the social but rather offers an *economic* explanation for the development of *social institutions*.[1]

The book may be more narrowly located within the economics domain since it is concerned with issues of *production*, particularly that branch of the subject usually called the *theory of the firm*. This focus is important because there is a large financial economics/capital markets literature which implicitly focuses on the *exchange* aspect of economic activity (Lev and Ohlson, 1982). There are, of course, existing subjects specialisms which are concerned with the economics and accounting of production. Thus there is a whole branch of economics known as *Industrial Economics* which subsumes the theory of the firm. Similarly, there is a body of knowledge usually called *management accounting* which offers prescriptions for reporting, analysing and controlling productive activity, traditionally in manufacturing industry but increasingly also in service industries. Yet, it is precisely this *separation* of perspectives and specialisation of disciplines which has stimulated the approach presented in this book.

The 'Uncongenial Twins Paradigm'

Another substantial, predominantly normative, 'economics and accounting' literature is concerned with comparing and contrasting accountants' and economists' approaches to income measurement and asset valuation. While some of these works have become classics [Harcourt and Parker (1969); Hicks (1946)], the debate usually ends in a 'truce' based on the recognition that economists and (especially financial) accountants are operating in different worlds. Different problems inevitably beget different paradigms.

Many academics in both disciplines have been satisfied with the *status quo*. However, my contention in this book is that the orthodox economics approach does not satisfactorily address its own agenda let alone contribute solutions to problems in other disciplines such as accounting! In order to illustrate the aim of the book, I would label the traditional approach the 'Uncongenial Twins

Paradigm' after a well known paper by Boulding (1962). Boulding examined the paradox of how two disciplines such as economics and accounting could share much terminology but very little else. While Boulding's work has deservedly become a classic and his argument for peaceful coexistence between the two subjects based on an 'agreement to differ' principle probably reflects the past relationship between the two subjects, there are a number of both practical and theoretical reasons for arguing that this separation is becoming less sustainable.

Firstly, there have been major advances in the theory of the firm tracing their ancestry to Coase's classic $(1937)^2$ article which asked the question 'Why do firms exist?'. As will be examined in greater length throughout the book, other researchers such as Williamson, Ouchi and Aoki have all offered their own answers to this question. Often called the 'New Institutional Economics'(Langlois, 1986), most of these new theories of the firm emphasise *organisational* and *contractual* rather than the *engineering/monopoly* perspectives which dominated the old industrial economics. Some economists would agree with the new emphasis on contractual relationships but would reject the Coasian choice between markets and firms. Thus *agency theorists* argue that the firm is a 'legal fiction', merely a 'nexus of contracts'(Jensen and Meckling, 1976). While agency theory has become the dominant theory in management accounting research, I will argue that the non-agency versions of institutional economics offer superior frameworks for modelling management accounting problems.

Secondly, there have been developments in accounting based on making management accounting more aware of its organisational and competitive context. New subdisciplines such as *Management Control* and *Strategic management accounting* have begun to address Johnson and Kaplan's (1987) criticism that conventional management accounting had become 'irrelevant'. These researchers argued that because of a *practical* preoccupation with the financial reporting and because of a *theoretical* base in marginalist/optimising models drawn from Neoclassical production theory, management accounting was offering information/solutions which weakened, rather than strengthened the competitive position of American industry. While as we shall see in later chapters, their critique has its own problems, the impact of their book indicated a loss of confidence in the old *pot-pourri* of codified practice and applied neoclassical theory.

In short, if these advances are combined there is no longer any validity in the 'Uncongenial Twins paradigm'. Indeed, there is much to be gained from a new *synthesis*. Thus, following Williamson's terminology, we can derive a much richer theory of the firm if we develop the measurement branch of transaction cost economics. This, in my view, is the great contribution of

Ouchi's 'organisational failures framework'. This model explicitly introduces issues of *organisational control* into the comparative institutional choice paradigm. As well as a richer theory of the firm that shows how management control theory can be used to explain economic phenomena, there are promising new management control prescriptions.

In this book, I have concentrated on exploring the explanatory possibilities of the theory since it is more consistent with the aims of the book as stated above. Yet, before I explain how I have approached this task, I feel that some mention of the prescriptive potential of these new synthesis is appropriate. The traditional prescriptions of management accounting based on neoclassical perspectives offered optimal solutions to problems based on *given* organisational and behavioural constraints. Thus the economic order quantity model suggested solutions to both inventory management problems. However, as Kaplan (1983) and others have pointed out, the really spectacular gains come from radical changes such as 'just-in time' manufacturing which abolishes rather than optimises inventory. However, this possibility can only be realised if managers examine a number of institutional factors such as the external boundaries of firm, contractual relationships with suppliers and internal working practices. All these factors are ignored by conventional neoclassical economics but are the central concerns of transaction cost/organisational failures models.

Some major themes in the book

Accounting as an economic institution

To many economists, the great intellectual achievement of neoclassical economics is the theory of general equilibrium. Supremely formal, it is essentially 'institution-free'. From this perspective then, the explanation and treatment of institutions such as accounting must be rather *ad hoc*. There are, however, critics who suggest that rather than being at the heart of economic enquiry , it should be seen as a limiting, special case. Thus, from an institutionalist perspective, the problem of 'incomplete markets', which general equilibrium theorists recognise as the 'achilles heel' of their enterprise, is not an awkward special case but a general condition which can only be remedied through institutional means.

The institutionalist position is neatly summarised by Langlois (1986) who argues that institutions have 'an informational support function' (p. 237). If this is true of institutions, *in general*, then it would seem to be even more true for an institution such as accounting which is explicitly concerned with the provision and communication of economic information. It is perhaps surprising therefore that few[3] have directly posed the question 'Why do we have accounting?' in the same spirit as Coase's seminal question 'Why do we have firms?'

Both these questions are parallel sub-themes in this book. Coase's question has stimulated much of the literature on the firm that I have drawn on. With respect to the 'origin of accounting theme', some of the economic interpretations that I have offered have been tempered by an acceptance of the social theory position that, although both accounting and firms are economic institutions, accounting is a more universal institution with more elements of the 'social' than the firm.

Institutional economics: agency versus transaction cost theory

Recent developments in institutional economics offer a number of theoretical alternatives- principal-agent theory, the 'positive theory of agency' and transaction cost economics. Some argue that some of the differences between the last two schools are merely terminological. I submit that there is not only a substantive difference between positive agency and transaction cost economics but that the latter offers a hitherto largely unrealised potential as a theoretical framework for analysing accounting and management control issues. Firstly, transaction cost economics distinguishes between a 'governance' branch and a 'measurement' branch. Both these branches offer institutionalist solutions to the general problem of incomplete contracts. Secondly, individuals are assumed to be *bounded rational*. As Simon (1978) has argued, rationality may be seen in 'process' as well as the more traditional 'product' terms typical of neoclassical economics. This less demanding concept of rationality is much easier to relate to the world of institutions such as accounting where rationality of procedure rather than rationality of outcome is the only feasible objective.

Natural selection theory, accounting and management control

Critics of the new institutional economics have frequently accused it of 'panglossian' theorising (Tinker, 1988). While this is certainly true of many of the seminal works, I submit that the tendency to argue that 'everything is for the best' or that institutions evolve purely to fulfil *functional* purposes may be corrected by a more explicit analysis of selection processes. Much of the book is concerned with an extensive exploration of economic theories of natural selection. The novelty of the approach has resulted in a critical perspective on business organisation. It has also led to a new perspective on economic selection theory seeing it in terms of 'information flows' as well as the more traditional 'resource flows' (Aldrich, 1979). Competition takes place not only in the traditional markets for products and factors of production but also in the 'market for control'. In the latter domain, the book argues that accounting and management control play both passive and proactive roles.

Since the book is primarily concerned with an economic approach, it is important that there is a mechanism for linking economic behaviour by firms to the wider economy. In the traditional theory of supply the output and pricing decisions of individual firms in an industry can be physically aggregated. Institutionalist theory does not produce such specific input/output relationships. It sees the economy in terms of populations of firms with specific organisational characteristics. One role of selection theory is thus to provide the link between the individual firm and the wider economy. The theory cannot predict the output of specific products but it can suggest how changes in organisational practices may have an impact on broad categories of economic activity. Thus, if it is argued that advanced manufacturing industry requires certain types of firm structure and processes and these are driven out by environmental pressures, then we have the organisational explanation of 'deindustrialisation' presented in this book.

Organisational control processes as explanatory theory

This explanation is an example of how management control can be used as part of an explanatory economic theory. Indeed, although I have earlier described management control as a subdiscipline of management accounting, it might be argued that the relationship should be reversed. Thus if the problematic is organisational/managerial control then there may be a variety of possible structures and processes. From this perspective, management accounting is the subdiscipline. Indeed, the significance of management accounting as an organisational control device cannot be taken for granted since, as Ouchi (1977; 1980) has pointed out in his 'Organisational Failures Framework', *behaviour control* is sometimes more appropriate than *output control*.

The book actually moves management control away from its origins in the management science literature towards a broader explanatory social paradigm. Radical thinkers in the 'labour process' tradition would probably claim that they have been offering such a paradigm for many years. Indeed, while the book draws on the some of the insights of these theorists, it also shows that a process theory of the firm subsumes investment as well as labour control issues.

6

Another advantage stemming from a management control perspective on the firm is that it sheds new light on company decentralisation. In the older 'hierarchical decomposition' model pioneered by Williamson (1970;1975), there was an emphasis on company structures and divisionalisation. In the approach presented in this book, the divisionalised company is looked at in a far more critical light. International comparisons and longitudinal studies have shown it to be culturally specific, organisationally unstable and even destructive of basic core competencies.

Some further applications

As well as offering a new theory of deindustrialisation and a critical perspective on the divisionalised company, the theory is applied to other topics which are difficult to analyse using conventional neoclassical theory. Thus the book presents a theory of the 'warehouse and screw-driver' firm which confronts the issue of the *locus of control* of the productive process. This is particularly relevant in the UK which seems to be basing its current industrial policy on encouraging inward, particularly, Japanese, investment.

This policy is clearly based on an implicit theory of 'management failure' by UK owned companies. Some of this failure is described in terms of 'short-termism' and an inability to develop new products. The management control model of the firm suggests a reinterpretation which focuses on the problems of *financial control styles* rather than the illusive concepts of 'incorrect' discount rates and/or 'truncated' cash flows. The much admired Japanese management practices and the 'Johnson and Kaplan' thesis are also located within the new theory (Johnson and Kaplan, 1987).

Much of the empirical material in the book consists of what economists call 'stylised facts'. These are data which are generally accepted by informed observers. The contribution of the book is to offer a new interpretation of these facts. There is also some original empirical data. This is offered in order to illustrate the empirical possibilities of the theory rather than as a significant addition to existing data. Unlike much of the data used in conventional economic analysis, case study material is often the only source of data. It is both time consuming to collect and difficult to generalise from. However, there are also examples of more conventional empirical work using capital market data to test hypotheses about internal management practices.

A chapter by chapter description of the book

As a guide to understanding the structure of the book , the reader is referred to figure I which relates the main themes of the book to some of the main schools of economic thought. As can be seen, a preferred route is indicated leading to a new synthesis and some specific applications. The numbers indicate the chapters in which particular parts of the research agenda are addressed.

The sequence of chapters generally follows the 'actual route' indicated in the figure. The main exception is chapter two. It would perhaps have been neater to move from the arguments in chapter one to those in chapter three. However, this would be ignoring the actual paths of both the accounting and industrial economic literatures which, as I have already explained, have developed on *parallel* rather than converging lines. Thus the insights of the Austrians were not absorbed into the 'old' engineering model of industrial economics. Similarly, accounting was used an *exogenous source of data* rather than being seen as part of the 'contracting technology' of the firm (Ball, 1989).

Chapter *one* looks at alternative economic approaches to uncertainty in economic life. It initially considers the Austrian approach which argues that general equilibrium theory begins from a faulty premise concerning the nature of the economic problem. With the introduction of uncertainty into economic life a number of theoretical responses have been proposed such as *complete contingent markets* and *rational expectations*. These approaches preserve the general equilibrium framework. Alternative responses to uncertainty see a solutions in institutional developments such as money, firms, and laws. The chapter highlights the asymmetry of influence between the two disciplines. Thus there is little in the *economics* literature on the role of accounting in the economic life in contrast to the extensive influence of economics on the accounting literature. It is argued too many economists assume the existence of markets and then consider how agents cope with uncertainty instead of starting from a more fundamental position which puts markets on the same playing field as other institutions.

Chapter *two* demonstrates many features of the 'Uncongenial Twins paradigm'. The 'old' industrial economics made extensive use of Structure-Conduct-Performance (S-C-P) models which combined a traditional engineering/monopoly perspective on the firm with an equally traditional *normative* accounting literature. The function of accounting was to provide data with which to test S-C-P theories even though it was recognised (via the normative accounting literature) that the data were not always appropriate for that purpose. In fact, Demsetz's critique of the use of accounting data to support S-C-P theories is one starting point for the 'new industrial economics'

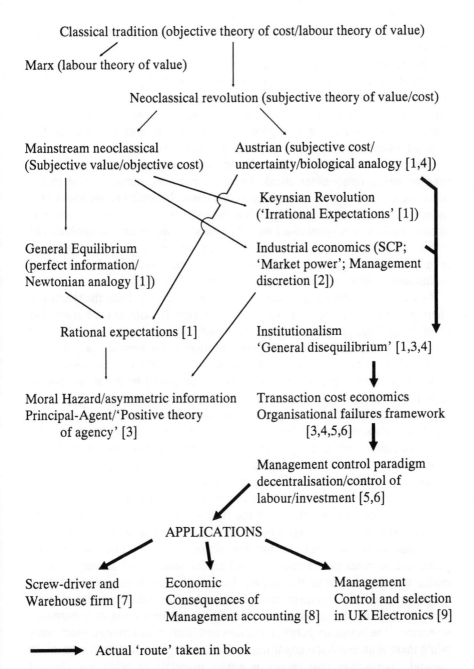

Classical tradition (objective theory of cost/labour theory of value)

Marx (labour theory of value)

Neoclassical revolution (subjective theory of value/cost)

Mainstream neoclassical
(Subjective value/objective cost)

Austrian (subjective cost/
uncertainty/biological analogy [1,4])

Keynsian Revolution
('Irrational Expectations' [1])

General Equilibrium
(perfect information/
Newtonian analogy [1])

Industrial economics (SCP;
'Market power'; Management
discretion [2])

Rational expectations [1]

Institutionalism
'General disequilibrium' [1,3,4]

Moral Hazard/asymmetric information
Principal-Agent/'Positive theory
of agency' [3]

Transaction cost economics
Organisational failures framework
[3,4,5,6]

Management control paradigm
decentralisation/control of
labour/investment [5,6]

APPLICATIONS

Screw-driver and
Warehouse firm [7]

Economic
Consequences of
Management accounting [8]

Management
Control and selection
in UK Electronics [9]

Actual 'route' taken in book

Figure 1   **Diagram showing the themes developed in the book and their relation to existing schools of economic thought (numbers refer to chapters in which topics are primarily covered)**

which explains the firm in *efficiency*[4] rather than *monopoly* terms (Demsetz, 1974).

The chapter also looks at managerialist theory. This subdivision of industrial economics assumes that, given a degree of oligopoly in the product market and a separation of ownership and control, a degree of managerial discretion may develop. In this approach both the capital market and the market for control become important constraints. In addition, attention is focused on the operation of managerial labour markets and the determinants of executive remuneration. Generally speaking, technical efficiency is still seen as being non-problematical. There is, however, some interest in the reporting of profit which in a managerialist model become endogenous to the theory. Thus, in early managerialist theory, the role of information is introduced in a very specialised way. The issue is one of the *manipulation* of information by , for example, managers 'under-reporting' profit. The problem is not one of cognition which was only considered in the͏ so-called 'behavioural' (that is, 'not economic') theories of the firm.

As has already been explained, chapter *three* picks up from the themes in chapter one rather more than those in chapter two. It looks at the burgeoning contracting literature(Principal- agent,'positive agency' and transaction cost economics) which has as its starting point problems of uncertainty, asymmetric information, impacted information and so on. While some antecedents of contracting theory (particularly agency) can be traced to the managerialist 'problem', transaction cost economics begins with the Coase's (1937) question "Why do firms exist?" The chapter reviews the various 'paradigm wars' which characterise so much of this literature. Some of these wars are waged within the economics literature (for example, agency versus transaction cost economics) while sometimes they spill over into the accounting literature (for example, critiques of the 'positive accounting' paradigm).

I argue that given that my aim in this book is to integrate accounting and management control in a theory of the firm, the choice does not rest on the details of the various paradigms but rather on the implied 'way of thinking'. It is on this basis that I submit that transaction cost economics is generally preferable to other contractual approaches. Its behavioural assumptions are easier to reconcile with the largely implicit behavioural assumptions of accounting and management control. It recognises that contracts may be 'incomplete' and that transactions thus require the protection of governance structures. The boundary between markets and firms is an active research issue while there is an explicit recognition of the role of a 'measurement branch'. In general, transaction cost theory is easier to relate to other branches of organisational theory such as contingency theory. Finally, we have an emerging paradigm known as the 'Organisational failures framework' which has already made some impact in the accounting and management control literature.

One feature of all the theories of new institutional economics is that the selection processes which they all rely on have been under-researched. Thus in chapter *four*, I review economic selection processes, in general, as well as looking at the role of accounting in these processes. A theory is presented which shows how the firm must reconcile differential survival traits in the different markets which comprise its environment. This may be difficult because the practices which lead to success in the *product* market such as 'clan' type organisational traits may be threatened by conflicting traits which lead to success in the market for control. It is argued that the latter environment encourages financial control techniques which may be quite inappropriate for product innovation and 'continuous improvement' manufacturing.

The firm is seen in 'process' rather than production function terms. This perspective is further developed in chapters *five* and *six* which explicitly introduce the systems methodology of the management control literature. From this point of view, the firm is seen as a 'learning' entity employing feedback and servo mechanisms. Systems models have a reputation of being either vacuous or technocratic. Yet a systems perspective is different from the conventional theory of the firm which is a 'production function to which a maximand- profit- has been assigned' (Putterman, 1988, p.247). Under capitalism, ownership and control are inseparable- the firm must be managed by the capitalist or the system will lose it alleged efficiency properties. Radical economists such as Marglin (1974;1984) have long argued that close supervision of production by capitalist was at the heart of the factory system and that a 'rentier class is a class ripe for expropriation' [(1984) p. 105]. The corollary of this argument is that just as control theory can explain industrialisation, it can just as effectively explain 'deindustrialisation'!

Chapter *six* is particularly concerned with 'hierarchical decomposition'. Here the link between control theory and economic theories of decentralisation/divisionalisation has already been made by Williamson. However, although he establishes a case for decentralisation, his theory does not pursue the cybernetic approach to its logical limits. If the M-form corporation *is* just an internal capital market then it is in danger of total decomposition! The chapter explores both theoretical and empirical evidence which suggests that the M-form lacks the universal efficiency properties that Williamson has claimed for it. International comparisons show that large corporations in some capitalist economies have other forms of governance which involve bank control and a more explicit role for the personnel function. These are both characteristics of what Aoki (1990b) has called his 'J-firm'. The chapter further explores other aspects of this model such as 'quasi-hierarchy' and horizontal information flows.

The bulk of the theoretical development of the book takes place in the first six chapters. The remaining chapters are more applied. Chapter *seven* analyses the concept of the 'warehouse and screw-driver ' firm. Since some would argue that it is easy to identify such firms in terms of low value added, I have reviewed the literature on value added. I submit that the real characteristic which needs to be measured (or pursued) is 'organisational rent' rather than value added.

In chapter *eight* an 'economic consequences ' approach is used to evaluate critics of modern management accounting such as Kaplan and Johnson (Kaplan, 1983;1984 and Johnson and Kaplan, 1987). Kaplan's wide ranging critique includes problems such as short-termism and conflicts between managerial incentives and economic wealth generation. Part of the controversy generated by his work stems from his bold claim that there is a link between the microeconomic calculations performed by management accounting and national economic competitiveness. Since my whole book is concerned with developing precisely that idea it would perhaps be surprising if I failed to support much of the 'Kaplan ' thesis.

My main criticism is that the term 'economic calculation' has far wider connotations than Kaplan suggests. It is not just a matter of 'missing measurements' (such as introducing Activity Based Costing). Similarly, if he is proposing a 'Japanese Cure' as some of his critics suggest (Ezzmel, et al., 1990), and if this is viewed as a matter of *institutional reform* rather than *culture transformation,* then such reforms would be perceived as being extremely threatening to existing UK and US financial institutions and cultures.

The potentially radical nature of the 'Japanese Cure' is further illustrated in chapter *nine* in the context of an analysis of the UK electronics industry. The theoretical model employed is an extension of the natural selection theory presented in chapter four. The main theoretical elaboration involves a consideration of Aldrich's (1979) 'rational selection ' model. This theory is based on increasing the element of managerial discretion to include aspects of strategic choice. The chapter pushes the purely *economic* selection model to its limits. Any further relaxation of competitive pressures would probably involve the explicit introduction of *socially constructed* institutionalist theory (Dimaggio and Powell, 1983). As mentioned at the beginning of this chapter, while social theory has been increasingly and effectively introduced into the accounting literature, it is beyond the scope of this book.

Concluding remarks

This final reiteration of the focus of the book fulfils a vital role in methodological clarification. I agree with Boland (1982) that methodological pluralism is preferable to hegemony and that the choice of problem should determine the methodological approach rather than vice versa. Thus although many disciplinary boundaries are crossed in this book, the economic perspective is informed by an almost 'classical' concern with the 'wealth of nations'.

Another classical outcome is that although I have not intended to explore distributional issues, I have found that, especially in the context of management control, it is often difficult to separate distributional from efficiency objectives. Perhaps this is an example of how 'unintended consequences' can affect the researcher as well as the institutional phenomena under investigation!

Footnotes

1. The meaning of 'institution' in this book is based on the notion of a set of rules and routines around which economic activities such as production and exchange can take place. It is not concerned explicitly with the institutions of accounting such as professional bodies. Schotter (1981) proposes that '(A) social institution is a regularity in social behavior that is agreed by all members of society, specifies behavior in specific recurrent situations, and is either self-policed or policed by some external authority' (p. 11).

2. Coase has explained (1990) how his early academic experience was in accounting and commerce rather than economics and that this influenced much of his economics research.

3. Although as we shall see later, Ball (1989) presents a 'Coasian' approach integrating a theory of the firm with an interpretation of accounting and auditing.

4. The definition of the term 'efficiency' is fraught with ambiguities. Following Jensen's (1983) suggestion, I employ the concept as heuristic device to aid theory construction rather than as the extremely precise concept found in theoretical welfare economics.

1 Imperfect information, equilibrium and economic institutions

In this chapter I consider alternative economic approaches to uncertainty in economic life. Since it begins from a starting point of ignorance, I initially consider the Austrian approach. There are of course other responses to uncertainty such as Complete Contingent Markets and Rational Expectations. These approaches preserve the general equilibrium framework. Alternative responses to uncertainty see a solution in the development of institutions such as money, firms and even accounting. I have not found an extensive analysis of the role of accounting in the economics literature even in the works which have focused on matters of uncertainty and information. I have therefore turned to the accounting literature to find sporadic attempts to relate accounting to both the firm and to problems of economic information.

The neo-classical world of the conventional undergraduate course presents not only a formidable and elegant model of the economy in the shape of general equilibrium theory but an almost overwhelming psychological 'gestalt'. The aim of this chapter is not to repeat familiar criticisms of neo-classical economics or, more especially, general equilibrium theory. It is rather more concerned in trying to escape from a gestalt that *begins* by presenting the economic world in terms of certainty and purpose and which therefore treats uncertainty as an awkward complication of the basic theory.

There may be no sinister plot behind the conventional ordering. It may just be a matter of easier teaching. For example, Alchian (1950) hints at the pedagogical power of the conventional approach in his plea for a different order or priorities:

> It is straightforward, if not heuristic, to start with complete uncertainty and nonmotivation and then add elements of foresight and motivation in

the process of building an analytical model. The opposite approach, which starts with certainty and unique motivation, must abandon its basic principles as soon as uncertainty and mixed motivations are recognised (p. 221).

Alchian's position is related to the Austrian critique of mainstream economics which argues that uncertainty and ignorance lie at the heart of the economic problem and that assuming them away fundamentally distorts the theoretical agenda. In the past decade these arguments have experienced something of a revival. It could, however, be argued that Austrian thinking or 'rhetoric', as Ricketts puts it (Ricketts, 1987), has been more triumphant in the political/policy sphere than in the world of academic economics. Uncertainty is undoubtedly now taken more seriously by academic economists but, as will be discussed later, it has been coralled into a 'rational expectations' pound leaving mainstream neoclassical theory not only largely intact but, in the macroeconomic sphere, freshly resurgent!

The first section of the chapter examines the implications of Austrian thinking for *all* planning systems including firms in a market economy. It is argued that the issues of ignorance and idiosyncratic knowledge which have been discussed in the literature of comparative systems do not simply disappear just because the bureaucratic/administrative system is one of many in a market economy. Or, to put it another way, the Austrian critique is as challenging for *management scientists* as it is for state planners.

The next section looks at the more recent literature on economic uncertainty. In terms of the subject matter of the book, I had thought that since one remedy for uncertainty would be to increase information and that since one of the aims of accounting is to provide economic information, then, logically, the literature on uncertainty and information would provide a theoretical link between economic and accounting paradigms. As it turned out, it has proved difficult to establish a direct link along these lines. As discussed below, the tendency among economists is to take a 'passive' approach to information, modelling how existing knowledge is used rather than 'actively' seeking more or better information. This is the basis of the ubiquitous rational expectations theory.

There *is* a link between accounting and economics but it is a less direct than I first thought. Accounting is an *institution* and thus a fundamental theoretical requirement is to establish a role for *institutions in general* in an economic paradigm. The firm is also an institution. Yet, as many economists from Coase (1937) onwards have noted, the economic rationale of the firm is neither immediately obvious nor a matter of general agreement. Given the ever expanding debate on the origin and raison d'etre of firms, it is high time that the economic rationale of accounting is investigated along similar lines.

1.   An Austrian perspective

1.1   Ideology and paradox in Austrian thinking

The ideological reputation of Austrian thinking rests on its well known critique of central planning and government intervention in economic policy. Planners, it is argued, do not have the economic knowledge either to optimally allocate resources nor even to smooth out short-term fluctuations in activity. Lack of information scuppers efficient economic calculation in all varieties of socialism, market or otherwise (see Hayek, 1945, and Mises, 1949). Markets with private property rights are seen as devices which reveal, disseminate and economise on economic information. Yet, within this viewpoint lies a paradox, for it is this same tradition which stresses uncertainty and ignorance that has provided a powerful rationale for that sometimes gigantic planning system - the firm.

Another paradox of the Austrian school is that while the whole position is based on the problem of uncertainty and ignorance, the solution is rarely if ever seen in terms of actively seeking information or developing information systems. Indeed, as discussed below, economic statistics, techniques such as econometrics, even accounting data are all viewed with the greatest suspicion.

1.2   Subjectivism and cost

One of the defining characteristics of the Neoclassical revolution in economic thinking was the stress on a subjective rather than objective theory of value. The Austrians took this subjectivism into their philosophy both of knowledge and of social science. It is beyond the scope of this book to fully review the Austrian position. Of rather greater relevance is the problem that a thoroughgoing subjectivism creates for the economist, the management scientist and even the accountant. For example, Barry (1979) suggests that the adoption of subjectivism raises the following question:

> It is true that in a crucial sense ignorance precludes the successful implementation of the massive centralised economic planning associated with socialist regimes; but can the doctrine ... provide sufficient justification for Hayek's rejection of a wide range of planning policies and institutions which fall short of a socialist economy? (p. 11).

As will be argued later in this chapter, it is a form of 'constitutional ignorance' that actually justifies a number of institutions including firms.

To the economist, a particular conundrum is the subjective nature of cost. The well known concept of opportunity cost - the value of next best alternative - can only be revealed as a result of 'genuine real-life competition between resource owners' (Barry, 1988, p. 59). In this extreme subjectivist world, orders to subordinates in the firm are as 'empty', 'artificial' and 'politically fabricated' as the orders to managers in central planning. In other words, an awkward question remains unanswered - since markets are suspended within firms, how do managers manage in an Austrian world? The responses to this question are varied. As we shall see in later chapters, one answer may be to structure firms along participatory rather than hierarchical lines. Another, more in the Austrian tradition, may be to 'unbundle' the firm.

Buchanan (1969) argues that many economists simultaneously embrace a subjectivist and objectivist notion of cost. He contrasts the two concepts of cost as follows:

> In the strict neoclassical model, costs are distinguished sharply from foregone profits because they are not tied *directly* to choice. Costs are objectively measurable outlays, approximated by the value of alternate product. ... Costs, to the extent that they are objective and, hence, externally measurable by an outsider who stands apart from the choice process, provide the basis for a predictive hypothesis about prices (p. 43).

He goes on to propose a formidable list of characteristics attributable to the London-Austrian conception of cost; it is 'borne exclusively by the decision maker'; it 'only exists in the mind of the decision-maker'; it is forward looking; it can never be realised; it cannot be measured; it can be 'dated at the moment of decision or choice' (p. 43). Indeed, given these characteristics, it is perhaps not surprising that so many economists and management scientists can pay lip service to the notion of opportunity cost and then swiftly move on to more objective manifestations! The professional motivation is obvious - few are prepared to marginalise their contribution to practical affairs by adhering to such a self-denying doctrine. Many have seen it as a convenient stick with which to set about socialism and central planning but then are reluctant to accept the implied limitations on managerial competence within the capitalist/free enterprise firm. I will argue throughout this book that the deep insights of the Austrians can usefully be applied to those mini-planning systems called firms.

The problems of management raised by the subjective view of cost are discussed in a collection of papers written by authors based or linked with the L.S.E. in the middle of this century (Buchanan, 1973). For example, Wiseman

(1973) argues that the profit maximising 'rule' of equating marginal cost and marginal revenue was non operational due to the subjective nature of cost:

> Uncertainty creates conditions in which it is expected that the mechanisms of profit maximisation in competitive markets will function imperfectly and will required positive government action to support it. But the final check on efficiency is still the bankruptcy court, and the difficulties about the interpretation of the marginal cost price equation are unimportant to its functioning (p. 235).

Wiseman opts for a survivalist approach arguing that while markets cannot check on the marginal 'rule', they can deliver their verdict on the easily observable 'net revenue rule'. Thus the similarity between the *state* as a planning system and the *firm* as a planning system must not be overstated. Unlike the decision rules in the planned economy, the firm's decision rules must, typically, pass the *ex post* profitability test even if they cannot be checked *ex ante*. Or, as will be seen in chapter four, competitive markets can have a rationality which transcends the rationality or lack of rationality of individual economic agents. Wiseman's views also reflect a typically Austrian position that the context in which decisions are taken, in terms of incentives and penalties, is rather more important than the technical aspects of the choice itself. As will be shown later (and especially in chapter three), it is this view that informs the approach to accounting theory offered by the contractarian paradigms such as Agency and Transaction cost theory.

1.3   Developments of Austrian theory: rational expectations versus institutional economics

The Austrian (or L.S.E!) contribution to analysing uncertainty may also be traced in the development of modern expectations theory. The work of Lachmann (1956) shows the link between Austrian theorising on the centrality of uncertainty and ignorance and the integrating function of markets, particularly the stock market. In his review of the 'rational expectations' literature, Kantor (1979) states that 'Lachmann anticipates some of the flavour of rational expectations' (p. 1428). This is a generous attribution given the dominance of 'rational expectations' thinking in modern, and especially financial, economics.

Before this important development is reviewed it must be stressed that there is nothing inevitable about moving from Austrian thinking through rational expectations to a modern Neoclassical position. Indeed, the chapter will trace an alternative 'institutionalist' development of Neo-Austrian[1] thought. The alternative 'pathways' followed in this book may be illustrated expectations to a modern Neoclassical position. Indeed, the chapter will trace an alternative 'institutionalist' development of Neo-Austrian[1] thought. The alternative 'pathways' followed in this book may be illustrated diagrammatically in a sort of 'family tree' drawn in figure 1.1. As can be seen, the Neo-Austrian line tends to 'fork' - one strand leading to Rational expectations and thereby reconciliation with mainstream Neoclassical theory while another strand merges with behavioural and Keynesian traditions. It is this latter strand that is emphasised in this book and which, as will be discussed in chapter three, forms the basis for choosing *transaction cost* rather than *principal-agent* versions of institutional economics.

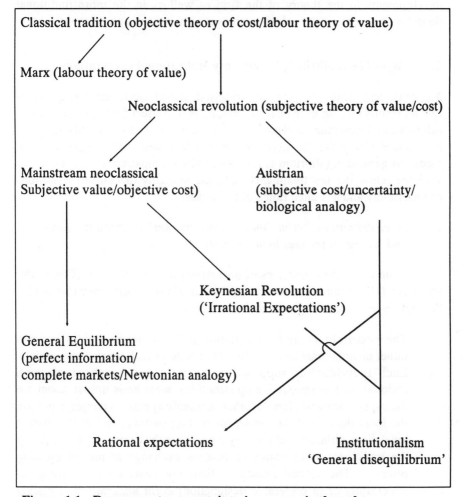

Figure 1.1 Responses to uncertainty in economic thought

The main elements of rational expectations thinking and their role in mainstream neoclassical economics are well known and extensively covered in the literature. Less well known is the alternative strand pursued in this book which synthesises some of the more 'idiosyncratic' approaches to economics such as behaviouralism and Keynesianism. From a mainstream perspective, these approaches have been presented as more or less interesting special cases. Indeed, in the case of Keynesianism, a literature grew up precisely in order to show that Keynes' theories may have been empirically interesting but were ultimately based on special assumptions such as 'money illusion'. As will be seen below, the success of the neoclassical counter revolution has affected developments in the theory of the firm as well as in the more traditional domains of expectations analysis such as macroeconomic and finance theory.

2.   General equilibrium, uncertainty and rational expectations

Modern economic theory cannot be criticised on the basis of naive suggestions that its results rely on unrealistic assumptions of perfect foresight or costless information. Uncertainty and costly information *have* been explicitly analysed but in such a way that the normative power and theoretical elegance of the theory of general equilibrium is left essentially unimpaired. However, as we shall see below, the new treatments are based on highly specialised definitions of uncertainty and a limited range of responses.

2.1   Some definitions: 'event' uncertainty, 'market' uncertainty; 'passive' and 'active' responses to uncertainty

In their survey of the economics of uncertainty and information Hirschleifer and Riley (1979) introduce some useful distinctions. Firstly, they distinguish between *event* uncertainty and *market* uncertainty:

> The modern literature on uncertainty and information divides into two rather distinct branches. The first branch deals with *market uncertainty*. Each individual is supposed to be fully certain about his own endowment and productive opportunities; what he is unsure about are the supply-demand offers of other economic agents. In consequence, on the individual level the search for trading partners and at the market level disequilibrium and price dynamics take the centre stage - replacing the traditional assumptions of costless exchange at market clearing prices ... The second branch of literature deals with *technological uncertainty* or (a preferable designation) *event uncertainty* ... market

uncertainty concerns the *endogenous variables* of the economic system, event uncertainty the *exogenous* data (p. 1376-77).

This seemingly innocuous distinction is vital in understanding the different treatments of uncertainty represented in figure 1.1. Event uncertainty is more tractable in the sense that traditional economic models may be employed. It may also be regarded as the form of uncertainty 'that is always with us'. In other words, *any form* of economic system must face many aspects of exogenous uncertainty. This is, by definition, not true of endogenous uncertainty which is generated by the institutional arrangements. Thus, as will be argued later, the institutionalist response to uncertainty is based on the ability to reduce market uncertainty. A tentative array of responses is illustrated in Table 1.1.

Table 1.1
Different combinations of uncertainty and modes of analysis

	Event Certainty	Event Uncertainty
Market Certainty	General Equilibrium	CCM/Portfolio theory
Market Uncertainty	Planning	Rational expectations/ 'New Institutionalism'

Hirschleifer and Riley's (HR) second distinction is between the *economics of uncertainty* which they define as a generally passive adaptation to uncertainty and the *economics of information* which may be seen as an attempt to overcome uncertainty by active search. The first category of analysis is concerned with the literature on topics such as *adverse selection* and *moral hazard* which are associated with the theory of insurance and are beyond the scope of this book. The second category, on the other hand, is central to the concerns addressed and will be looked at in some detail.

The literature on Complete Contingent Market regimes (CCM) and the so-called stock market economy is of some if rather limited relevance to the themes developed in this book. Since it will be argued later that a further extension of the so-called *disequilibrium* literature is fruitful then a brief survey of attempts to incorporate uncertainty into general equilibrium theory is necessary. In other words, it is only be pushing the formal model to its limits that we can fully appreciate the role of less formal approaches and in particularly the significance of *incomplete markets*.

Shubik (1988) effectively summaries the CCM approach and points to its implications thus:

> Suppose trade is in M commodities and for T time periods. Furthermore, suppose that during any period the economy can randomly be in any one of K states. We may invest a host of time-dated contingent goods such as "wheat in 1991, if the sun shines". We may regard the economy has having MKT goods. If we permit trading between all pairs of time-dated contingent goods we require $\dfrac{MKT\,(MKT-1)}{2} \sim \dfrac{(MKT)^2}{2}$ markets.

> The use of money cuts down the number of markets to $(MKT - 1)$, but even this number is enormous in comparison to what exists. Any attempt to model trade with uncertainty through time as a playable game reveals the difficulties encountered in trust, accounting, clearing, and documenting ownership claims in futures markets (p. 36).

Neo-Austrian arguments that the stock market represent a forum for forward trading have been formally analysed by Arrow (1964) and Diamond (1967). Once again, Shubik pays these models 'backhanded' compliments:

> As soon as we add production, fiduciary decision making, control, differential information, or insufficient numbers of securities to cover the generation of all lotteries, the promise of great generality evaporates. Yet in return, it is precisely here that a major opportunity for a reconciliation of law and economic theory appears. The law is process-oriented and institutional; much of microeconomic theory is equilibrium oriented and noninstitutional (p. 37).

This opportunity to reconcile institutionalism with economic theory is certainly one which will be grasped in this chapter and throughout the book. Before this is attempted, we must look at the 'rational expectations' approach to uncertainty which, in view of its influence on both theory and policy, certainly cannot be briefly dismissed as a 'useful limiting case'.

2.2 Rational expectations

While the CCM approach to uncertainty can be portrayed as a theoretically elegant but empirically empty escape route for general equilibrium economics, the rational expectations approach has had a far-reaching impact on both empirical work and on policy making in the UK in the past decade. In particular, the policy dominance of the New Classical theory in macroeconomics and a generally *laissez-faire* industrial policy can all be intellectualised in terms of rational expectations thinking. The literature is reviewed (sympathetically) by Kantor (1979) who credits Lachmann with anticipating the ideas of Muth who is generally regarded as the founding father (Muth, 1960, 1961). Lachmann admits that his insights on the stock exchange as a market in "continuous futures" would sound 'rather platitudinous and might be hardly worth mentioning were it not for the fact that it differs from the Keynesian theory of the Stock Exchange which is now so much *en vogue*' (Lachmann, 1956, p. 68). In fact, it is this debate with Keynesian views of expectations that informs much of the theoretical and policy debate.[2] As we shall see later, Keynesian ideas are also important in a disequilibrium perspective on institutions.

The rational expectations paradigm is particularly dominant in discussions of informational efficiency or the Efficient Markets Hypothesis (EMH). As Jensen (1978) puts it with typical vigour:

> In the literature of finance, accounting, and the economics of uncertainty, the Efficient Market Hypothesis is accepted as a fact of life, and a scholar who purports to model behaviour in a manner which violates it faces a difficult task of justification (p. 96).

A sound logical base and, in the case of the EMH, a substantial weight of empirical testing, means that naive critics of the concept are easily dealt with. For example, rational expectations does not imply perfect foresight. As Kantor puts it:

> ... It is however incorrect to assume that rational expectations regards errors in forecasts as insignificant or absent. The implication of rational expectations is rather that forecast errors are not correlated with anything that could be profitably known when the forecast was made. Or, in other words, *while markets may be wrong, they are not wrong without good reason* (p. 1430).

Or as Arrow (himself no great friend of rational expectations) puts it:

> It is the weaker form of this hypothesis that has become widely current. If we recognise that forecasting must be uncertain, that we can never know the future in detail, then the requirement of perfect foresight cannot hold literally. However, we can ask that foresight be accurate on the average (p. 159).

Rational expectations (RE, henceforth) theory has, however, some far from naive critics in the shapes of Arrow, Simon and Shubik, amongst others. Yet, even these sophisticated critics cannot always agree on the precise areas of vulnerability. For example, there seems to be some disagreement over the RE view on 'second-guessing' which is a central component of Keynesian criticism of the stock market. Compare, Shubik's definition of RE with Simon's criticism. Shubik (1988) writes:

> A formal definition requires an almost Talmudic piling up of special assumptions. In essence, however, the idea is that intelligent individuals will take into account all second guessing so that their expectations include guesses about the guesses of others, and vice versa. If all parties are equally intelligent and industrious and have the same basic information, then their guesses should all be consistent (p. 50).

Contrast this with Simon (1978):

> For situations where the rationality of an action depends upon what others (who are also striving to be rational) do again, no consensus has been reached as to what constitutes optimal behaviour ... (p. 9) ... The so-called "rational expectations" models ... ignore potential coalitions and attempted mutual outguessing behaviour (p. 10).

On the same page in a footnote Simon takes a very 'Keynesian' position arguing that 'a rational person would be well advised, if he know that all others were following the "rational expectations" or "consistent expectations" rule to recalculate his own behaviour on that assumption'. Simon's main criticism of RE is that it represents the traditional economics concern not to 'replace substantive criteria of rationality with procedural criteria, but rather to find substantive criteria broad enough to extend the concept of rationality beyond the boundaries of static optimisation under certainty' (Simon, 1978 p. 10). He argues that an alternative response is to emphasise 'procedural rationality'. As we shall see in the next section, this is another way of developing an 'institutionalist' solution.

3.   Disequilibrium, information and accounting

3.1   The firm as an institutional response to uncertainty and disequilibrium

As we have already seen, general-equilibrium theory services as a useful limiting case from which to develop a more institutional form of economics.

Similarly, the concept of rationality discussed in terms of procedural versus substantive rationality may also serve as a departure point. Whatever the starting point, a similar set of concepts tends to feature in the discussion - decision making under uncertainty, adaptation, *bounded rationality*, *process* versus *product* in decision making and (not always explicitly) *evolutionary* theory.

Drawing on these concepts, a number of writers have sought to 'deduce' a role for institutions by starting with a critique of general equilibrium theory. Langlois (1986) points out the immense strain on the individual agent's cognitive powers implied by general equilibrium theory. Institutions reduce these demands. As he puts it:

> (I)nstitutions have an informational support function. They are, in effect, interpersonal stores of coordinative knowledge: as such, they serve to restrict at once the dimensions of the agent's problem-situation and the extent of the cognitive demands place on the agent (p. 237).

Loasby's discussion of the origin of the firm also starts from a critique of general equilibrium theory and draws on many of Simon's ideas. Surely, no-one has explained the origin of the firm more pithily:

> In conditions of perfect knowledge, the theory of the firm is very simple: there are no firms (1976, p. 70).

As many writers have found, it is somewhat easier to explain the *existence* of firms than it is to suggest the *boundaries* between markets and hierarchies or the limits to the firm. As Demsetz (1969) emphasised, in a thoroughgoing comparative institutional approach, it is not sufficient to merely identify market failure - some knowledge of alternative institutional arrangements must be acquired. In the context of the firm versus market debate, this means that a theory of how firms *internally allocate* resources must be compared with the generally better known properties of the market.

Even agreement on a chosen model of the market may be contentious. Loasby (1976), for example, favours a Keynesian rather than a 'rational' view of expectation formation. In contrast, Shubik (1988) argues that it is possible to reconcile acceptance of rational expectations perspective with an incomplete markets explanation of institutions. For example, it is perfectly plausible to believe that in the case of small trades of thickly traded stocks the EMH is good approximation of reality. This does not mean that we can apply the same theory to the takeover situation when large blocks of stock and a few players are the norm. It is in the latter case that institutional factors become important.[3]

Loasby's interpretation of Keynes reflects that of Leijonhufvud (1968) in its emphasis on disequilibrium problems. Rational expectation theorists are generally dismissive of Leijonhufvud's ideas. For example, according to Kantor, disequilibrium analysis 'ran into the dead end of ad hoc assumptions and indeterminate outcome' (p. 1428). It is perhaps true that the heady excitement of the Keynesian counter revolution did quickly subside in the macroeconomic literature for reasons that are not altogether clear. Indeed, Kantor is not alone in his cryptic association of disequilibrium theory and intellectual anarchy. Even disequilibrium theory, in the sense of analysing situations *between* equilibria, requires a notional, if unattainable, concept of equilibrium. What it does reject is a rigid adherence to the method of *comparative statics* which, by definition, rules out a consideration of the *path* between equilibrium positions.[4] Abandonment of comparative statics may mean that some tractability is lost. But as the Transaction Cost literature illustrates, it does not inevitably lead to *ad hoc* assumptions.

It is regrettable, perhaps, that Leijonhufvud and others who had the supreme insight to visualise the economy in terms of *servo-mechanisms* and *signalling problems* then failed to draw on the abundant system control literature. At least part of the intention of this book is to remedy this omission.[5]

3.2   Institutional economics and disequilibrium economics

I submit that some of the so-called 'New Institutional economics' can be interpreted as part of a 'disequilibrium tradition' in the sense that it emphasises 'process' rather than 'product' rationality and admits incomplete contracts. However, this interpretation is probably more true of the *transaction cost* rather than *agency* version of the new paradigm.[6]

Williamson (1985) usefully distinguishes between the transaction cost approach and the agency approach. They are both contractarian paradigms but represent different traditions (see figure 1.1). In agency, the firm is viewed as a 'nexus of contracts'. Attention is focussed on the formal structure of these contracts with relatively little concern with either compliance problems or the formally 'imperfect' or 'incomplete' contracts which characterise, or are even the essence of hierarchical/internal organisation. In spite of his affection for legal citations and terminology, Williamson's view of the firm comes over as a much more organic, adaptive construct with a behavioural dimension that has been so effectively developed by others such as Ouchi (see later chapters).

To Williamson, the transactions cost approach does not try and resolve all problems in the *ex ante* bargaining state. In his view, 'the *ex post support institutions of* contract *matter*' (1985, p. 29, Author's italics). It is in this function that the measurement branch would seem to play a particularly crucial role. Williamson has not developed this theme in subsequent published work. Indeed, there is some evidence to suggest that he would prefer to minimise the difference between transaction cost theory and agency theory' (see, for example, Williamson, 1988). Clearly, theoretical fudge can increase the number of horses that can be ridden.[7]

3.3 Institutional economics and accounting

The aim of this chapter (and book!) is not simply to argue for a reconciliation between institutional and general equilibrium economics. It has the further objective of examining and explaining the role of the particular institution of *accounting* in economic life. Accounting does not only play a *general* institutional role of stabilising expectations, it is self evidently concerned with more active responses to uncertainty. In the new institutional economics, the firm and accounting are *codeterminous* institutions - the rise of the firm as a solution to incomplete contracts is codeterminous with the development of accounting. Ball (1989) makes this point very effectively arguing that:

> Accounting and auditing are institutional phenomena, so it is reasonable to assume that they derive many of their properties from the nature of firms as economic institutions. Progress in understanding accounting and auditing, at all levels of abstraction from broad conception of their economic function through to an understanding of the reasons for specific accounting and auditing techniques, seems likely to require a theory of the firm that views institutional phenomena as its domain ... (p. 1).
> ... accounting techniques such as standard costing are one of the reasons for the firm's very existence, providing a repetitive, low cost means of contracting that allows it to survive as an intermediary. Under this view, the firm, its products and its quasi-pricing technologies are joint inventions. The historical sequence is not necessarily proof of economic causality (p. 29).

There are many possible definitions of accounting. Antle recently stated that '(A)ccounting institutions are the institutions that surround the production and dissemination of financial information both across and within organisations' (1989, p. 103). This definition contains the key words 'institution' and 'information' which link the domains of economics and accounting in a way that is consistent with the arguments presented in this chapter.

4.   Economic information and accounting

The above discussion establishes a *raison d'etre* for both the institutions of the firm and of accounting within a theoretically consistent universe of costly information and imperfect cognitive capabilities. The nature, generation and dissemination of economic knowledge are all issues that, following the Austrian insights, must be confronted in any worthwhile theory of economic systems. The treatment of accounting has, however, been somewhat oblique. What, it may be asked, is the relationship between accounting information and economic information in general? What role does accounting play in the process of economic calculation? These question recur throughout the book. Simple one paragraph answers are not on the agenda. They are certainly not to be found in the sort of economic literature cited above. In any case, the more obvious source of answers to these questions would seem to be located in the *accounting* rather than the *economics* literature.

4.1   Some antecedents in the accounting literature

In his discussion of the relationship between institutions and information, Thornton (1979) lists the different types of information that various authors have proposed together with their suggested effect on production and exchange (see Table 1.2). In this taxonomy, information is classified in terms of its effect on the two primary economic activities of production and exchange. It does not attempt to define an intrinsic property of information and therefore provides little guidance on the appropriate domain of accounting. It does suggest, however, that accounting information is likely to form a small subset of all economically relevant information.

Table 1.2
Information, production and exchange

Author	Affects exchange only	Affects production & possibly exchange
Hayek (1945)	Particular knowledge	Scientific knowledge
Mises(1949)	Endogenous information	Exogenous information
Hirshleifer (1971)	Foreknowledge	Discovery information
Fama/Laffer (1971)	Trading information	Operational information

Source: Thornton, 1979, p. 214[8]

One characteristic of such a subset is likely to focus on the monetary aspects of accounting information. This perspective has a famous pedigree. Weber and Mises have both emphasised the centrality of *monetary* calculation in accounting. Thus Weber (1947) states that '(A)ccounting in terms of money, and not its actual use is ... the specific means of rational, economic provision' (p. 17). Similarly, Mises (1949) states that '(M)onetary calculation is the guiding star of action under the social system of division of labour' (p. 230).

Both these authors are cited by Chambers (1966) who is uncompromising on the monetary/financial characteristic of accounting. On the other hand, he does not minimise the role of other types of information or instruments of control. He points out that:

> A business firm, likewise, is a complex system, supervised by the aid of a number of instruments. It has a number of distinctive properties - financial, legal, economic, psychological, social - each of which require to be kept under observation. The accounting system is the instrument by which financial properties are observed ... A person conducting a business may, likewise, rely on his own observations as well as on his instruments (p. 127).

The problem with this approach is that it begs the question as to the meaning and relevance of 'financial properties'. For example, it leaves the issue of the *economic relevance* of the firm's financial properties wide open. As we shall see in chapter eight, the call for 'non-financial' accounting stems from the belief that a firm's financial properties may actually have limited economic relevance. The narrowness of this perspective is also highlighted by the management control paradigm which as we shall see, argues that *financial control* is just one of a number of possible instruments of control.

4.2   A research agenda, rather than accounting, defined

The search for the appropriate domain of accounting is not a topic which can be quickly dismissed. Indeed, it is actually part of the research agenda of this book. From a *positivist* point of view some explanation of the actual domain of accounting may be offered both in terms of the British economy and on a comparative basis. From a normative perspective, some tentative proposals may be sought on what the domain of accounting should be to achieve certain economic objectives.

5.   Some concluding remarks

One inference of the attempts to either assume uncertainty away or adapt to it in a passive, stochastic model is that the mainstream economics approach seems to work within the framework of an implicit question: 'Given that we have markets, how do agents cope with uncertainty?' A more fundamental approach would start with the question: 'How do agents cope with uncertainty in economic life'. This later approach is close to the Austrian viewpoint with which the chapter began.

In subsequent chapters an answer will be sought to the latter question. The approach will be based on a comparative institutional methodology which examines and compares the interplay between markets and hierarchies, measurement and governance branches. A conscious effort will be made to explore the possible insights offered by the organisation/management control literature for understanding the operation of the economy as a whole. There are many examples of 'economic imperialism' where market logic is applied to analyse non-market institutions - much rarer are theories which apply institutionalist methodologies to broad economic issues.

Notes

1. The term 'Neo-Austrian' is sometimes used to describe the work of a large number of modern 'institutionalists'. At other times it is applied to the more contemporary work of writers such as Hayek. My own application of the term is not related to particular writers but to the modern influence of the basic Austrian premises concerning the centrality of uncertainty and ignorance.

2. It is becoming increasingly difficult to remember how prestigious Keynesian thinking was, not just when Lachmann was writing, but into the early 1970's. Keynesian views on expectations formation now seem as unfashionable as Austrian ideas once were.

3. The importance of institutional factors in the market for control is an important feature of the theory developed in chapter four. It seems quite plausible to have different theories of the stock market for different situations.

4. The 'Path dependency' problem is an important feature of the selection model introduced in chapter four.

5. See especially chapter five.

6. See chapter three for an elaboration of this comparison

7. Williamson has been prolific and addressed different audiences. He has naturally tended to tailor his views according to his audience. Consequently, TCE is open to differing interpretations. This is not a problem as long as the particular interpretation is made explicit.

8. Table reproduced from Thornton, D. Information and Institutions in the Capital Market. *Accounting, Organizations and Society*, volume 4, no 3, pp. 211-237, (1979) with permission from Pergamon Press Ltd, Headington Hill Hall, Oxford OX3 OBW.

2 The theory of the firm and accounting I: The industrial economics paradigm

In the previous chapter the focus was on the treatment of uncertainty in economic theory. A 'family tree' was presented which showed some of the links between various schools of economic thought. It was not intended to provide a comprehensive view of all the branches of economic thinking. A particular omission was the body of literature commonly known as *Industrial Economics*. This may be somewhat surprising since the culmination of the argument was that important institutions such as the firm could be rationalised as a response to uncertainty. This is a somewhat different perspective from that of many Industrial Economists. For example, Hay and Morris (1979) suggest that:

> Most economists would regard industrial economics as being primarily an elaboration of, and development from, one major element in the mainstream of economic thought - the Theory of the Firm. This comprises the analysis of different market structures, and their implications for economic welfare (p. 3).

There are two aspects of this statement which have already begun to be questioned in this book. Firstly, many economists might be surprised to be told that the 'theory of the Firm' has been a major element in economic thought. Secondly, those same economists may argue that an analysis of different market structures is not what *they* understand by the 'theory of the Firm'. They would probably accept, on the other hand, that the last sentence represents a satisfactory definition of a large chunk of 'traditional' industrial economics. In this chapter, I propose to distinguish between what I have called 'traditional' industrial economics and the newer, institutionalist approaches. While the latter has become the accepted paradigm for studying accounting/economics interfaces, the more traditional approach does draw upon accounting, particularly as a source of data. As will be seen, the *measurement* and *reporting* of business profits play significant roles in the debate between the old and new paradigms in industrial economics.

1.   Paradigms in industrial economics

1.1   *A multitude of models?*

The above criticism of Hay and Morris' definition is not intended as a sleight on their book. Indeed, they have written a sophisticated and critically aware book which goes for beyond the usual remit of a conventional text. Their own 'family tree' not only traces the antecedents of industrial economics back to Adam Smith but also highlights the tensions between an *empirical* tradition and a *deductive* tradition which even now has not been satisfactorily resolved. Hay and Morris propose an original synthesis of the subject matter of industrial economics after identifying three distinct but related models - the *market model*, the *financial model* and the *expenditure model*. The market model incorporates the traditional analysis of market structure which will be reviewed later. The expenditure model looks at issues of investment while the finance model looks at modern finance theory. The use of the word 'related' perhaps requires some qualification since, as Hay and Morris point out, the literature has rarely made the sort of connections between the models that they begin to develop in their book.

Because economic theorists rarely attempt to integrate the above approaches, the usefulness of economic theory as an underpinning for accounting theory has been handicapped. Where economic theory *has* become influential in accounting theory, it is often as a derivative of either agency or finance theory. Unfortunately, because many academic accounting researchers (particularly, but not solely, in the UK) find the policy implications of these paradigms uncongenial, economics based theories have tended to be tarred with similar methodological and ideological brushes (Puxty, 1985). Frequently, accounting researchers have ascribed an uncritical, even panglossian, bias to economics based theories (Tinker, 1988). However, the perceived bias in economics is by no means inevitable for, as will be seen below, critical perspectives on modern corporate capitalims and its institutions may be based on long and respectable traditions in economic thinking. Furthermore, as will be argued in subsequent chapters, even the so-called 'new institutional economics' need not inevitably serve as a theoretical apology for the status quo.

1.2 What is industrial economics?

The proposed answers to the above question are not intended to be definitive or even balanced. Attention is deliberately focussed on particular aspects of the industrial economics tradition which are of significance in this book. Thus any criticisms of industrial economics must be interpreted in terms of the purpose of the book rather than in terms of the conventional function of this branch of economics. With these qualifications in mind, it is suggested that industrial economics has the following characteristics:

a. Markets are generally assumed to have an element of monopoly - imperfect competition/oligopoly/monopolistic competition are key theories. In contrast to the previous chapter, rationalisations of firms (horizontal and vertical integration) tend to be based on monopoly/leverage type arguments often buttressed by quasi-engineering notions such as economies of scale, capital intensity and so on.

b. Uncertainty/information problems are rarely analysed. They are certainly not regarded as being central to the existence of the firm.

c. Economic data exist with which theories of market structure can be tested. In other words, while the data may have limitations they are not regarded as being philosophically unsound as they would be according to the 'subjectivist' viewpoint.

d. The firm is frequently treated as something of a 'black box' even in some of the 'managerialist' approaches.

e. There is an emphais on *product markets* (industries). Other distinct branches of economics such as labour economics or financial economics deal with factors of production. This generalisation is less true of managerialist theories.

f. Economic actors are rational maximisers in the traditional sense. They may not, however, be profit maximisers. Market power in the product market and divorce of ownership and control may mean that utility maximising managers do not choose to maximise profits.

In the previous chapter we introduced a 'family tree'. We can now add on the Industrial Economics paradigm.

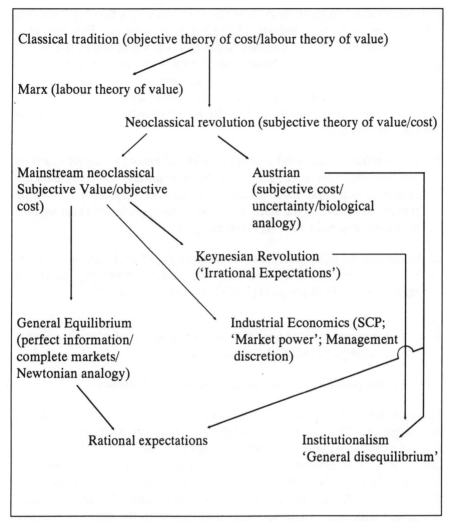

Figure 2.1 **Responses to uncertainty in economic thought and the place of Industrial Economics**

In terms of the theoretical schools introduced earlier, Industrial Economics is both more empirical than general equilibrium and more partial. It follows a Marshallian rather than a Walrasian tradition. It is heavily based on the notion of imperfect markets in the sense of *monopoly power*. In terms of this book, its weakness is its unsatisfactory treatment of issues such as uncertainty and incomplete markets. Yet, I shall shortly argue that it is precisely these areas that impinge on the data used to test the empirical orientated theories of traditional Industrial Economics. It is also this ommission that has led to the development of a 'new industrial/institutional economics'. Paradoxically, critics of this new school frequently argue that it neglects/denies the role of market power. Later in the book, I shall explore some common ground, working on the presumption that the apparent incompatibility of the paradigms is both unnecessary and debilitating for economics as a whole.

The consequences of the above characterisation of industrial economics for this book are twofold:

1. The interface of industrial economics with accounting is largely based on the dependence on accounting data. In most discussions these data are treated as being generated exogenously and the comments tend to be heavily normative in the sense of 'Is accounting profit the same as, or a reasonable approximation to, economic profit?'

2. Some managerialist theories treat the reporting of profit as endogenous. Thus managerialism is a useful link with 'positive accounting' as well as agency theory. Both points (1) and (2) are explored below.

2. The measurement of profit: a case study in the interface between accounting and industrial economics

2.1 The importance of measurement in industrial economics

Empirical research in industrial economics relies extensively upon the use of accounting data. The data have been collected and reported for many different types of users among whom research economists would probably have a rather low priority. It is understandable, therefore, that the information does not always come in the form nor is based on concepts that help economists test their theories. Adjustments have to be made to the data and results need to be interpreted with care. To some researchers, however, the situation is rather worse than inconvenient. It is not that the data are incomplete, in the wrong form or unreliable in a *random* manner. It is rather that they are systematically misleading. Or, in other words, it is inherent in the approaches adopted by practising accountants in organisations such as large corporations that the information will always be a poor measurement of economic phenomena of interest to industrial economists.

Industrial economics represents an attempt to reconcile empirical relevance with theoretical rigour. Indeed, central theoretical concepts such as the relationship between concentration and market power, and barriers to entry and market power depend more on *empirical correlations* than on *a priori* reasoning. For example, evidence of correlation between concentration and profitability or advertising intensity and profitability may be used to sustain the standard structure-conduct-performance (SCP) paradigm. If these correlations are weakened by arguing that advertising expenditure should be capitalised rather than expensed then alternative paradigms become more plausible. Ironically, reported profits are also criticised by some researchers as being underestimates of true profitability and thus an underestimate of the 'real' level of market power.

2.2   Accounting from an industrial economics perspective

This section of the chapter reviews the criticisms of standard accounting practice emanating from the industrial economics literature. This, in itself, is a useful exercise since the focus on accounting practice and principles is rarely a central feature of of this literature. Accounting issues are almost treated as 'footnotes' punctuating the more grandiose endeavour of examining monopoly power. It is hardly suprising, therefore, that the writers neither fully develop their criticisms nor ask the supplementary question of 'Why do accountants do what they do'? I will argue that the treatment of accounting is deficient in both normative and positive terms. Furthermore, I submit that such cavalier treatment of economic information is indicative of a more general imbalance of approach which has already been alluded to in the previous chapter and which will be addressed in future chapters.

This section does not aim to provide an exhaustive survey of *all* the criticisms by industrial economists over the years. Rather it is intended to select those problems which bear most directly on the central controversies in the literature. Thus we have examples of writers who argue that the testing of theories of the market power in concentrated industries is handicapped by 'measurement errors' in the published profit and loss and balance sheet data. Other examples illustrate the sensitivity of the relationship between advertising and profitability to accounting conventions on advertising expenditures. Less controversial, perhaps, to industrial economists is the accounting treatment of *research and development expenditure* which may also form part of the market power model.[1] Since accounting issues are generally treated as being exogenous to the market power model, the problem is presented as one of *adjustment* and *interpretation* of data.

3. Market power and reported profit

3.1 The market power paradigm - origins and criticisms

The seminal work on market power was done by Bain in the 1950's and supported by a number of studies which established a correlation between market structures and profitability. As Phillips (1976) puts it:

> While there has not been an absence of disputation about the results, it seems fair to say that at present the 'conventional wisdom' gained from the studies is that a positive relationship exists between industrial concentration and profits, particularly when concentration exceeds some critical limit and when there are substantial barriers to enter the industry (p. 241).

One consistent and prominent dissenter with this conventional wisdom is Harold Demsetz. Demsetz (1974) put forward a number of objections to the empirical studies representing the market structure doctrine. In the context of this chapter, however, the most significant is his criticism of the accounting data on which the empirical work was based. Demsetz argued that accounting profit can be 'too high' because accountants do not attach proper values to assets. He states:

> That any meaning can be given to persistent correlations between profit and concentration is attributable to the fact that accounting measures are necessarily poor approximations to the theoretical concepts they represent. The most important imperfection is their weakness in attaching appropriate values to those assets that are likely to be associated with the preservation of monopoly or the attainment of superior efficiency. If proper economic values were given on those assets, then all firms, whether monopolies or competitive, could be expected to yield the same rate of return. Thus, the trucking industry obtains a grandfather's clause to block entry. This increases the value of the licenses to operate, but accountants are unlikely to value these licenses at anything like their market value; if they were so valued, the rate of return recorded by trucking firms would be no different than that recorded by free entry industries. A correct evaluation of asssets would capitalize monopoly profits into the value of the assets which shield the firms from competition. Similarly, an explicit or implicit agreement to collude, if successful, is an undervalued asset to companies. Hence it is possible to look at accounting returns and form some guess as to the degree of monopoly that is present (p. 175).

Demsetz's central aim is not to criticise accountants but to question the dominant (as it was then) structure-conduct-performance paradigm. Demsetz reverses the usual direction of causation arguing that firms are large because they are efficient and that is why they have high profit rates. The real difficulty is that 'higher profit rates can arise either for reasons of monopoly or from superior efficiency, because accountants cannot appropriately value the assets or the decisions that may give rise to the profits' (p. 176). As will be shown below, such statements beg a whole series of questions about the definition of profit and ignore decades of agonised debate in the accounting literature.

Demsetz's own example of the rotary engine can, paradoxically, and with the benefit of hindsight, illustrate the difficulties and dangers of anticipating profits (or raising asset values). Demsetz continues:

> Unfortunately, it is not only sources of monopoly that are undervalued by accountants but also sources of efficiency. For example, General Motors has made a decision to push ahead with a rotary-engine car. No element of monopoly is present in that decision, since Ford and Chrysler also could have adopted the same course of action. But they did not. Let us suppose that GM's decision turns out to be correct, and that it gains both profit and market share, which it holds for many years because of the difficulty of quickly imitating that decision, the uncertainty among all firms as to whether the rotary engine will continue to be successful, and the tendency of consumers in this industry to rate experience highly. Accounting procedures are essentially backward looking, but the uncertain value of such a decision rests in the future. Hence, for many years GM may record high profits and high market share even though monopoly is absent (p. 175).

Demsetz's attack on the SCP paradigm has been supported by other Chicago colleagues who have also criticised the results of empirical work based on 'untreated' accounting data. Their attack on the SCP paradigm has focused on the relationship between barriers to entry and profitability. Interestingly, the spirit of these criticisms of conventional accounting has begun to be picked up by accountants involved in the debate on the correct treatment of advertising and brands both in terms of *ex post* reporting (brand accounting) and *ex ante* decision making (strategic financial management).[2]

4. Barriers to entry and profitability

4.1 Advertising and profitability rates

The exercise of market power can only be enjoyed by firms if effective long-run barriers to entry can be erected and maintained. High levels of advertising expenditure are often identified as being part of a strategy (conscious or not) on the part of existing producers to discourage new entrants into the industry. Since the theoretical basis for this viewpoint is relatively weak, the value of empirical evidence becomes that much more crucial. Comanor and Wilson (1967) found a strong positive correlation between industry profit rates and levels of advertising intensity. These writers have maintained a steadfast defence of the 'barrier-to-entry' view of advertising despite determined attacks (see Comanor and Wilson, 1979). For example, Bloch (1974) maintains that the positive relationship can only be sustained as long as advertising is treated as a current expense and not as a capital asset. He found that when advertising expenditure is capitalised, the resulting 'corrected' profit rates do not sustain Comanor and Wilson's strong relationship. According to Bloch:

> "True profit" rate is defined for our purposes as the rate which would prevail if advertising expenditures were treated as an investment and capitalised over their full economic lives. Understatement of reported net worth causes the measured profit rate to be above the true profit rate (p. 267).

Comanor and Wilson's response (1979) is to dispute Bloch's estimate of depreciation as being too low and also to argue that a portion of advertising expenditure is 'cancelled out' by the expenditure of existing companies. They argue that:

> ... even in principle, not all advertising should be amortized. A considerable proportion is defensive advertising designed to protect given market positions. Such advertising, which is largely self cancelling for the industry as a whole, is analogous to maintenance costs for capital equipment and should be expensed (p. 463).

There is virtually no attempt to explain why advertising is expensed rather than capitalised either in terms of a positive theory of accounting practice or as a rationalisation in terms of accounting principles. Clearly, a firm with a positive net investment in advertising is deferring profits and consequently a portion of its tax liability. Weiss (1969) suggests that tax reform is the appropriate arena for discussing the accounting treatment of advertising. Certainly, the usual convention gives managements greater discretion for either 'smoothing out profits' or producing sudden short-term improvements. Indeed, this might suggest that the direction of causation between profits and advertising is reversed. Periods of high profit producing high levels of advertising expenditures while periods of low profit result in cuts in advertising. In other words, the cost of advertising can be quickly turned on or off while the benefits in terms of increased sales are spread more evenly through time. Unlike other costs such as labour, advertising is usually provided through external agencies and media thus quick and dramatic cuts do not entail unpleasant intra-organisational blood baths. This further enhances the 'discretionary' value of advertising expenditure since it is only in the long term that the benefits of past advertising significantly declines.

4.2   Research and development (R & D) and profitability rates

As mentioned earlier, the role of research and development in the structure-conduct-performance paradigm is far less controversial than advertising. Whether or not R & D constitutes a barrier-to entry, there seems an implicit agreement that such expenditure is far more unambiguously socially acceptable than advertising expenditure. Indeed, the usual complaint directed at British companies is that they spend 'too little' on R & D when compared with foreign competitors.

Grabowski and Mueller (1978) suggest that rates of return should be adjusted by capitalising R & D as well as advertising. This approach finds some support in the accounting literature. For example, SSAP 13 suggested a scheme for breaking down R & D activity into *pure* and *applied* research and development expenditure. It suggested that the general rule should be to write off such expenditure in the current year except for that part of development expenditure where the revenues could be identified with reasonable certainty. Taylor and Underdown (1985), in commentating on the twist and turns in this area state that:

> This episode highlights the problems of enforcing an accounting standard when influential parties are affected by the standard ... It is interesting to note that each document produced by the ASC was more flexible than its predecessor (p. 264).

It probably also highlights the huge uncertainties which, by the nature of the beast, are invariably attached to research and development programmes. As we have already seen, 'traditional' industrial economics tends to find the issue of uncertainty and the measurement of profit of only marginal interest. It has

41

sometimes been noted that in a world of perfect knowledge there would be no need for accountants. Some might add there would be no need for economists either! Perhaps more seriously some would argue that in a world of perfect knowledge there would be no profit! Or, if accountant's correctly anticipated profit in their measurements, then there would be no profit! As we shall see in the next section, just as it is argued that the existence of profit is due to uncertainty so the accounting concept of profit is based on *measurement under uncertainty*.

5. The definition and measurement of profit: some normative aspects

As can be seen, the industrial economics literature bandies about various implicit and explicit definitions of profit and pronounces the reported figures as being somehow 'incorrect'. Although the traditional normative literature is now derided by the *Positive Accounting* researchers, many contemporary economists would benefit from a perusal of the classics on the measurement of income and profit.

5.1 Hick's definition of profit

Although the literature is vast, there is one widely accepted definition of profit. It is generally based on the Hicksian notion of income being 'the maximum value which the company can distribute during the year and still expect to be as well off at the end of the year as it was at the beginning' (Hicks, 1946, p. 172). Hick's definition spawned a rich debate which over the years which has involved some eminent economists as well as academic accountants (see e.g. Parker and Harcourt, 1969, and for a survey, Beaver, 1981).

Hick's definition should remind the economist that the usual textbook definition of Profit as simply 'Total Revenue less Total cost' assumes away all the measurement problems agonised over in the accounting literature. One advantage of Hick's definition is that it captures the stock-flow aspect of income measurement which must be of interest once the analysis ceases to be a single period/static one.

5.2 Other viewpoints: a multiplicity of accountings

Beaver (1981) traces the early literature which attempted to relate reporting practice to economic models of income measurement. He suggests that in the early days of financial reporting, the stewardship function was uppermost. This function is, in itself, a matter for debate. For example, many academic economists are entirely ignorant of the 'keeping the shop tidy' aspect of financial accounting. More generally, they do not appreciate the multiplicity of purposes which the accounting system is supposed to meet. Academic accountants are more aware of this multiplicity but cannot agree on how to cope with it (Birnberg, 1980).

Beaver suggests that the adoption of accrual/matching systems of accounting reflected attempts to relate accounting methods to an ideal 'economic income'. He defines this as 'the change in the present value of the future cash flows, after proper adjustments for deposits (e.g. additional common stock issues) or withdrawals (e.g. dividends)' (p. 4). He cites a number of writers who have linked good stewardship with attempts to measure net economic income such as Paton (1922), Canning (1929), Alexander (1950), Edwards and Bell (1961), Chambers (1966), and Sterling (1970).

More recently writers such as Ijiri (1978) have criticised the economic income approach arguing that economic income does not work when there is uncertainty and incomplete markets. Furthermore, it does not take into account different informational requirements of different interest groups. Ijiri argues for a cash flow orientation on the basis that it needs fewer assumptions, is less misleading, and provides a clear link between past cash flows and future cash flows.

5.3   Uncertainty and incomplete markets revisited

The indivisibility of this enquiry should now be evident - *any comparison between the concepts of accounting income and economic income eventually leads back to the issues of uncertainty that were introduced in the previous chapter!* Beaver (1981) puts it like this:

> In the perfect and complete markets and certainty setting, the concept of economic earnings is well defined ... in this setting, economic earnings fall out of the analysis as a by product of the valuation process. Earnings and valuation are two sides of the same coin. This is readily apparent in the permanent earnings property of economic earnings, where earnings are computed as the present value (or market value) times the interest rate. Value and earnings are linked via the interest rate. One is a stock concept, the other is a flow, and the interest rate is used to make the transition from one to the other. Both are scalars representing a vector of intertemporal future cash flows. The assumptions about the markets ensure that nothing is lost in representing a vector of cash flows in terms of a single number ...
> ... In this setting the notion of earnings is a valuation concept ... no

knowledge of financial accounting is required ... an earnings concept is redundant (p 84-85).

Subsequent analysis suggests that the real problem is not *uncertainty* but *incomplete* markets. If there is uncertainty but complete markets then '(V)aluation under uncertainty is a simple extension of a similar expression under certainty and merely requires an additional indexing of claims to reflect the states as well as the time periods' (p. 88). This argument may be related to the CCM model outlined in chapter one. As before, we cannot rely on complete markets to resolve the valuation problem any more than we can rely on a pure market solution to the allocation of resources under uncertainty!

Historic cost accounting is thereby both explained and rehabilitated. In incomplete markets, 'the role of accounting data, such as earnings, is an informational one in which earnings are used as an input into the valuation process rather as some output derived as a byproduct of the valuation process' (Beaver, 1981, p. 103).

5.4   Paradigmatic inconsistencies?

The above discussion reveals an inconsistency between the traditional industrial economics paradigm which focuses on resource constraints and simple models of preferences and an accounting paradigm which confronts issues of uncertainty and incomplete markets. Yet, the data inputs of the SCP paradigm require a reconciliation of the two paradigms - a clear example of the 'uncongenial twins' syndrome![3]

In conclusion, there seem to be two issues which are inadequately covered in the economic model of income measurement:

    a.   Uncertainty and incomplete markets.

    b.   The multiplicity of objectives of accounting.

As we have already seen, recent developments in economic theory have to some extent attempted to come to terms with problem a. One of the many implications of the 'rational expectations' revolution in financial economics is that the 'valuation model' described by Beaver has been reasserted. Arrow spotted this aspect of rational expectations in his observation that '(E)conomic decisions are seen as mostly concerned with decisions on holdings of assets rather than on choices of flows'. (Arrow, 1978, p. 157) In other words, the earnings approach is redundant given an efficient capital market. If earnings have little informational content then the method of calculation and even the regulation of the accounting process are, in terms of economic efficiency at least, unimportant. This is the view of the self styled 'Positive Accounting school' and the related 'Agency' theory of the firm discussed in the next chapter.

Before this is considered we will look at an early and neglected approach which has both anticipated some of the ideas of the Positive Accounting researchers and is also acknowledged to be an intellectual antecedent of agency theory. The approach is managerialism. For largely historical reasons, it is traditionally handled as a part of the Industrial economics paradigm.

6.   Managerialism and the reporting of profit

Managerialist pioneers such as Baumol (1959), Williamson (1964) and Marris (1964) have given birth to a substantial literature. Unlike agency and transaction costs their approaches have become widely disseminated throughout the economics profession and have long been standard fare in undergraduate economics courses. This may be because the conventional analytical tools only require slight adjustment in order to make comparisons with conventional profit maximising outputs and prices in a partial equilibrium framework. Alternatively, it may simply reflect the usual timelag between developments in the literature and their incorporation in textbooks and courses.

6.1   Key aspects of managerialist theory

In terms of looking at the role of accounting in a managerialist world there are three issues. The first issue is the main focus of analysis in this chapter. The other two issues are looked in much greater detail in later chapters.

a. Because of market power in the product market management has discretion over a wide range of policies including the reporting of profit (Williamson, 1964). This introduces the possibility of developing a simple positive theory which anticipates the more recent agency based models.

b. Management has discretion but not only because of market power in the product market. Because of a divorce of ownership and control (Berle and Means, 1932) it need not adopt the profit maximising objective presumed in traditional theory. While decision makers within the firm may not have the direct interest in profit assumed by the simple profit maximisation model, they cannot totally ignore pressures from the market for control. In other words, the capital market takes on a prominence missing in the S-C-P paradigm. This means that, firstly, financial issues correspondingly become more important. Secondly, the market for control and the theory of the takeover invites special attention.

c. The 'Black box' model of the firm is harder to sustain. In other words, issues concerning the allocation of resources within the firm begin to arise within an economics paradigm. For example, in a development of managerialist thinking, the divisionalised corporation was presented as an organisational device which not only reduced managerial discretion and re-established the profit objective but could be seen as an internal capital market that outperformed the external capital market (Williamson, 1970). In accounting terms, the areas of decentralisation and transfer pricing are an important part of the management accounting/control literature.

In this chapter I shall mainly be concerned with the first issue-managerialism and the reporting of profit. The focus on managerialism is not meant to imply that managerialism or any particular version of it has become the generally accepted view on modelling the objectives of the firm. As Hay and Morris (1979) point out in a complex review of the literature, there are theoretical and empirical problems with both the supposed separation of ownership and control and the specification of models based on non-profit objectives. Some of these criticisms have been raised by Agency theorists and thus will be looked at in the next chapter.

6.2 *Managerial discretion and the reporting of profit*

The difference between *maximum profit, actual profit* and *reported profit* is a central feature of Williamson's managerial utility function. *Maximum* profits are reduced by 'excess' expenditure on staff. *Actual* profits are reduced by management slack to result in *reported* profits. The latter may be reduced by discretionary investment expenditure. The resulting published accounts which may then be used as data in tests of SCP relationships have the effect of underestimating monopoly power. For example, Cowling (1982) argues that managerialism may not reduce the share of profits. It may, however, lower the level of *reported* profits by producing at a higher level than profit maximising output. He argues that managerialism tends to push up the share of profits by choosing higher levels of overhead labour, some of whom will be involved in the sales effort (p. 54).

It is not suggested that the apparent contradiction between the Cowling view (published profit figures underestimate true profitability) and the Demsetz view (published profits tend to exaggerate profitability rates) are due to intellectual confusion either among economists or accountants. The Demsetz problem is one based on inevitable uncertainties in measuring business income and the conventions adopted as a result of this uncertainty. It may, in fact, be easy to reconcile both views in a managerialist world. If accounting convention leads to an 'overestimate' of profitability then managements should welcome the additional opportunities for discretionary expenditures and, as suggested above, the possibilities arising for income smoothing and 'window dressing'.

Other managerialist theories certainly support conservative asset valuation techniques. For example, in Marris' well known model (Marris, 1964) one of the key financial ratios is the Valuation ratio defined as:

$$\frac{\text{stock market value of the firm}}{\text{book value of the firm}}$$

Since according to the theory, exisiting management are threatened by takeover when this ratio falls below the ratio of a potential predator, there seems little incentive to raise the denominator by writing up the assets. The congruence of interest between shareholders and management is also illustrated when accounting conventions causes a third party such as the government to benefit at their expense. Thus in the 'stock appreciation crisis' of the mid-1970's, the inability of conventional accounting to cope with high rates of inflation led to a rise not just in paper profits but also in company taxation which was only assuaged by the introduction of a pretty *ad hoc* system of stock relief.

The efficiency of accounting manipulation depends to some extent on the informational efficiency of the stock market. Managerialism, at least in its earliest manifestations, is silent on this matter but seems to be implicitly based on at best a very weak version of efficiency. As we shall see in the next chapter, agency theory is explicitly based on rational expectations and at least a semi-strong form of efficiency. If accounting rules fail to prevent 'management from eating their factories' then according to Jensen and Meckling (1979), the managers will be penalised by a fall in their stock prices (p. 495).

6.3   Divisionalisation and the reporting of profit

Before considering such bold claims, it should be noted that managerialism influenced some of the early works on the 'economics of internal organisation'. As mentioned above, Williamson proposed that internal re-organisation of the firm from a functionally based form to a divisionalised or M-form serves to reduce manageral discretion. With the head office operating an internal capital market and with a presumed informational advantage over the external capital market, Williamson suggested that the profit goal would be restored to at least some of its former glory. This does not mean that *true* profit will be the same as *reported* profit. For example, Cowling (1982) argues that the M-form company may reduce managerial discretion at the level of the operating division only to absorb it at the head office. This is because it is not as clear how the M-form helps outside shareholders to monitor senior managements given that 'an extra million pounds diverted to salaries or internal consumption ... will be more beneficial to those comprising the head office than would an extra million pounds reported as profits ...' (p. 87). Some part of reported profits have to be distributed to outside shareholders and other 'outsiders' such as the taxman. Against this, it could be argued that it is easier for predators to observe head office extravagance rather than divisional slack thus improving the efficiency of the market for control.

Even Cowling's views may actually flatter the efficiency of the M-form. As I will argue later, especially in chapters six and nine, there is mounting criticism of the M-form. Much of this criticism comes from accounting researchers who are far more aware of the internal information problems of the divisionalised firm. These are issues that most economists have only recently begun to address. The exception is, of course, the Austrians. As I argued in the last chapter, their criticisms of *planning* are almost as applicable to the giant firm as they are to the planned economy.

7.   Contestable markets theory

As stated earlier, the characterisation of industrial economics in this chapter must be viewed in the context of the overall book. Thus the theories surveyed are those which highlight the interface between economics and accounting rather than those which represent the 'state of the art' in either economics or accounting. I have for that reason said nothing so far about an important new development industrial economics, namely 'Contestable Markets' theory. So far, developments in this theory has been largely based on deductive rather than empirical methodologies. There is, however, every reason to expect this new theory to become incorporated into empirical industrial economics as well as shedding light on some accounting issues (Bromwich, 1990; Manes, et al., 1985).

The new literature emphasises the economies of scope and the special economics of the multiproduct firm. It also relates costs to barriers to entry. For example, Baumol, et al. (1982) argue that it is *sunk costs* and not economies of scale which constitute the entry barrier that confers monopoly power. In their view, the essence of competition is not the structure of markets, as in the SCP paradigm, but the 'degree of contestability'. Thus the focus is far more on entry barriers than it is in conventional theory where existing structure is paramount. They argue that 'virtually the entire literature on entry deterrence and entry barriers has implicitly assumed the presence of substantial sunk costs in its analysis' (p. 292).

In terms of the 'family tree' shown in figure 2.1, contestable markets theory is very much in the mainstream neoclassical tradition emphasising high levels of individual rationality and a commitment to equilibrium modelling. It has also, however, been seen as a convenient adjunct to new institutionalist theories. For example, Williamson states that transactions cost economics assumes contestable markets.[4] It is clearly on this basis that he and other proponents of the 'efficiency' school of institutionalism minimise the 'monopoly' explanations of the firm. Thus contestable market theory is exploited to support, but is not integrated into, theoretical structures which, as will be seen, are based on quite different assumptions of cognition and institutional adaptation.

8.   Concluding remarks

Given that an important feature of industrial economics is its commitment to empirical work and given also a theoretical basis in mainstream neoclassical theory, the main impact of accounting has been as a source of data. The measurement of profit - a central aspect of accounting theory - is an issue that has impacted on the interpretation of much empirical work in industrial economics. The reasons for the methods of measurement are rarely discussed by industrial economists. The generation of the data is treated as being exogenous to the theory. Clearly, in this theory, accounting and economics are *not* seen as being 'co-determinous' concepts.

This point is less true of 'Managerialist' theory. Indeed, Managerialist theory represents a vital link in the development of this book. In particular, it introduces a link between aspects of internal organisation and internal accounting (management accounting) with aspects of external market allocation and reporting (financial accounting). This link will be further developed in the next chapter.

Notes

1. It is less controversial in a policy sense because advertising expediture is more likely to be criticised than R&D expenditure which is generally seen as being 'a good thing'.

2. This is analysed further in chapter eight.

3. This term was coined by Boulding (1962).

4. This is literally treated as a footnote in Williamson (1985).

3 The theory of the firm and accounting II: The contractual approach

This chapter looks at the so-called contractual/contractarian approaches to the theory of the firm. It is primarily concerned with agency theory (AT, henceforth) and transaction cost economics (TCE,henceforth). The contractual approach is defined and explained by Williamson (1988) in the following manner:

> Both TCE and AT take exception with the neoclassical theory of the firm whereby the firm is regarded as a production function to which a profit-maximisation objective has been ascribed. Rather, TCE regards the firm as a governance structure and AT considers it a nexus of contracts. A more microanalytical study of contracts has resulted (p. 569).

Contractual approaches reject the so-called 'engineering' model of the firm which seems to emerge from the industrial economics literature. The production function is not technologically determined. Indeed, contractual perspectives see it as being imperfectly specified due to informational asymmetries, bounded rationality, opportunism and other lacunae of the contractual world which will be explored in this chapter.

As with earlier chapters, the concern is not with a comprehensive review of the entire literature. Although this is a relatively new literature there are already a number of surveys and interpretations which have undertaken this task. They will be referred to when appropriate in the text. Indeed, since the whole literature is still at an early stage of development, the seminal contributors, themselves, are a major source of definition and interpretation (see for example, Williamson, 1988; Jensen, 1983).

The aim, as before, is to focus particularly on the implications for accounting. This is a much easier task than in the previous chapter since the institution of accounting is generally seen as being *endogenous* to the institutional framework of contractarian economics. Or, to repeat Ball's observation, accounting and the firm are 'co-determinous' institutions (Ball, 1989).

Although a number of survey articles have appeared on agency theory (see e.g. Arrow, 1985; Baiman, 1990), TCE has not been accorded the same degree of respect. In fact, a survey article on TCE and accounting would probably be a fairly brief paper. I submit that accounting researchers have generally failed to make full use of the TCE framework preferring instead to use versions of agency theory. I will further argue that this theoretical bias has had regrettable consequences leading to inappropriate models of accounting that have given contractarian approaches an unjustifiably poor reputation in the eyes of many accounting researchers (Puxty, 1985). I will argue that at least some of the explanation for the lack of impact of TCE on accounting can be attributed to a misleadingly legalistic terminology and a desire to remain 'respectable' in the eyes of a predominantly neoclassically trained economics profession.

These viewpoints may partly be supported through critical analysis of existing literature and applications. It is not enough, however, just to criticise - superior theoretical alternatives must be proposed. These alternatives can only be introduced in this chapter.[1] Their further development is the subject matter of the remaining chapters of the book.

The chapter has five main sections. Section one considers some of the controversies generated by the new approaches. Section two compares and contrasts Transaction Cost Economics (TCE) with Agency Theory (AT). Section three looks at the relative merits of the two approaches with respect to accounting research while section four looks at the organisational failures framework (OFF) as a prelude to the management control paradigm introduced in chapter five. Section five considers the even more recent literature comparing the firm to a 'treaty'.

1. Paradigm wars

The literature on contractual theories of the firm is characterised by an unusually high level of debate and controversy. Antle (1989) calls these 'paradigm wars.' He argues that '(A)dvocacy and paradigm wars displace productive scholarly efforts' (p. 109). This is not always the case - not only can these debates raise substantive theoretical issues but they can also create interest and provide stimulus to scholarly work. It is true, unfortunately, that not all the advocacy has been particularly honest. Value judgements and ideology have been buried under a veneer of supposedly earnest research while arguments about methodology have really disguised disagreements about the choice of problem under investigation. As Boland so convincingly argues, many methodological debates are really proxies for fundamental disagreements concerning the research agenda (Boland, 1982).

1.1   Paradigm wars in the economics literature

a. *The monopoly v efficiency model of the firm.* A flavour of this debate was touched on in the previous two chapters. In the first chapter the rationale for the firm was presented as an institutional response to uncertainty. This could be contrasted with the 'traditional' industrial economics model where the firm is more a product of quasi-technological issues such as economies of scale/scope. These latter arguments are usually allied with a market power explanation of horizontal and vertical integration. The ideological battle lines are quite clearly drawn with transaction cost economics (TCE) seemingly inevitably located on the laissez-faire end of the policy spectrum.

 Much research of a high quality has been stimulated by this debate. Unfortunately, the policy debate has hindered the acceptance of the less ideologically loaded aspects of TCE. In other words, given the well known policy views of many of the leading advocates of the paradigm (led of course by Williamson, himself), it is difficult to show that the approach can also be used to advocate quite different policies. Another problem engendered by the debate is that there has been a degree of obscurantism concerning the meaning of cost minimisation in a TCE setting. In some instances the difference between 'X-efficiency' and Pareto efficiency is not made explicit. Much of the mainstream literature could benefit from a study of the Multinational Enterprise (MNE) literature which has tended to be more eclectic in its use of both market power and TCE models (see, for example, Casson, 1987).

b. *Natural selection/survivor theory.* This last mentioned literature is concerned with the origin of a particular organisational form - the MNE. The more general research agenda of both TCE and AT is concerned with theories of organisation and organisational change (Jensen, 1983).

 In these discussions, the advocates of contractual approaches are generally quite explicit that their theories are based on a version of 'natural selection' theory. In this context, the whole welfare issue becomes much less clear as Williamson and, to a lesser extent Jensen, are happy to admit. These issues will be discussed at some length in chapter four. It is worth pointing out, however, that in a survivalist paradigm the best we can hope for are tentative/comparative type welfare propositions. This may seem obvious but it has not stopped writers such as Antle rejecting TCE partly because of its welfare indeterminancy.[2]

c. *Power v efficiency in organisations.* TCE has a well articulated theory of hierarchy as well as an interpretation of institutional change. This has generated a number of interesting debates around questions such as 'What do bosses do? (Marglin, 1974) and 'Why does capital hire labour?'(Putterman, 1986). To Williamson's credit, he has confronted his radical critics resulting in a debate which in my view illustrates the potential fruitfulness of 'paradigm wars'. These questions will be looked at in some detail in later chapters, especially chapters five and six, where issues of control and hierarchy are given a more explicit treatment.

AT has avoided much of this particular debate simply by minimising the role of authority and hierarchy. The firm is a 'legal fiction' (Jensen and Meckling, 1976) while the economy is modelled, not in terms of market and hierarchy, but as a web of interlocking contracts. Advocates of the 'principal-agent' approach often extol its neutrality. They point out that it frequently does not matter analytically *which* party is assumed to be the agent and *which* the principal. Critics of the approach find this neutrality is actually a major weakness.

1.2 Paradigm wars in the accounting literature

Antle's concern *vis a vis* the destructiveness of paradigm wars is probably more applicable in the field of research with which he is concerned - the application of AT to accounting issues. Some of the problem is that time and journal space has been wasted because many of the *general* arguments have already been aired in the general social science literature and have little to do directly with accounting research (see, for example, Tinker, 1988). There are, however, specific aspects of applying contractual theories to accounting research which have legitimately added to the heat already generated in the wider literature. The following examples illustrate this point.

a. *Models of man.* As already discussed in the introduction to this book, research in accounting is increasingly eclectic in terms of discipline orientation and problem choice. To many researchers, AT equals economic hegemony. In particular, what would be regarded as unexceptional assumptions about human behaviour to an economist would be regarded as being absurdly reductionist to other social scientists (Puxty, 1985).

b. *Methodological objections.* AT is associated with the new aggressive, self-styled 'School of Positive Accounting' based at the University of Rochester (Watts and Zimmerman (WZ), 1979, 1986). Once again, a methodological approach which is more or less taken for granted by many economists (possibly to their discredit!) requires a much more critical reception from researchers who have reservations both about the methodological approach as well as the extravagant claims of explanatory power made by WZ in particular. The bad feeling generated by the Rochester school may be gauged from this comment by Christensen (1983):

> The Rochester School ought to put its own program in order before it asks others to take that program seriously. A useful first step would be for them to stick with one set of phenomena until they have understood it well and satisfactorily explained it, rather than leaping to a different phenomenal domain in each new article in an effort to establish squatters' rights (p. 20).

Christensen then approvingly quotes Lakatos (1978) on the role of waste paper baskets in research:

> "Wastepaper-baskets" were containers used in the seventeenth century for the disposal of some first versions of manuscripts which self criticism - or private criticism of learned friends - ruled out on the first reading. In our age most people have no time to read manuscripts, and the function of wastepaper-baskets has now been taken over by scientific journals (Christensen, 1983, p. 20-21).

c. *Policy/ideological objections.* Although, as argued above, this is also a matter of debate in the economics literature, it is particularly bitter in the accounting literature where the link between accounting research and the role of standard setting seemed so obviously intertwined. A 'School' which is so critical of conventional accounting research and standard setting is bound to arouse considerable hostility. Apart from the obvious ideological disagreements, much of the debate is underpinned by an undertone of professional jealousy which is hardly surprising given the assertiveness of the main protaganists.

One of Puxty's criticism of AT is that it has made little impact on mainstream economics. He argues that:

... if the theory is good and economists wrongly ignore it, they will suffer in the labour market, notice this, and act accordingly to research within the agency framework. This has not happened. Alternatively, the theory is poor and economists are right to reject it. Either way it raises doubts about the theory (1985, p. 15-16).

Clarke and McGuiness (1987) make a similar observation about the lack of impact of both AT and TCE on the teaching of economics at an undergraduate level. They suggest that it is both too technical and at too formative a stage. There may be other reasons. Firstly, the much maligned 'black box' model is still serviceable and justifiably popular for many purposes. Secondly, whatever the apparent promise of the AT paradigm, there is a difficulty in integrating it with the still dominant general equilibrium model.

Many of the critics of AT and TCE lump the two paradigms together as though they are substantively similar. In some respects the differences are little more than ones of terminology. There are, however, important differences which, as will be discussed in the next section, are especially central to their use in accounting research.

2. Agency theory and transaction cost economics: commonalities and contrasts

2.1 The triumphalism of the agency theorists

Apart from Clarke and McGuinness (1987) other surveys and interpretations are beginning to emerge which compare and contrast AT and TCE with each other as well as with the more 'traditional' theories (Putterman, 1986; Ricketts, 1987; Thompson and Wright, 1989). The journal literature is sparser in this regard as Williamson himself has noted (Williamson, 1988). Much of the following comparison is based on Williamson's version of both AT and TCE. AT theorists have made little contribution to this comparison. The tendency is to treat TCE in a fairly dismissive manner. This position seems well summarised by Ross (1987) who asserts:

Many of our theories are now indistinguishable from those of the transactional approach to the theory of the firm. Agency theory, be it informal and in the verbal tradition or the formal neoclassical models of the agency and moral hazard literature, is now the central approach to the theory of managerial behaviour (p. 33).

This quotation probably represents the views of many AT researchers. For example, in conversation with me, Antle was less complimentary of the contribution of TCE and expressed almost identical sentiments to Ross and Baiman. The impression projected is that there is an almost overwhelming similarity between the two approaches and that, in any case, TCE may be regarded as a subsidiary of agency theory.

2.2   Williamson's comparison of AT and TCE

As the seminal contributor to the TCE literature, Williamson unsurprisingly rejects any notions of subservience. He accepts the emerging distinction between the two forms of agency theory - formal and informal, or 'principal and agent' and 'positive agency'. He also distinguishes two branches of TCE - a measurement and governance branch. He accepts that the two are related but has explicitly concentrated his own efforts on the latter branch. His quasi-legal terminology seems to invite linkages with law rather than accountancy. Yet, paradoxically, the logic of TCE finds the solution for transactional difficulties in non-legal remedies!

While the emphasis on legal terminology and concepts may be explicable in terms of Williamson's tastes and professional obligations, the imbalance of development of TCE may have weakened both its claims for distinctiveness and its appeal to accounting researchers. Although AT's treatment of measurement issues is far more *ad hoc* than in TCE, it is still regarded by those sympathetic to contractual approaches as a central paradigm in accounting research. Yet, as will be seen, the insights on organisational control proposed by Ouchi and others (see section 4) are based on the markets and hierarchies/TCE tradition rather than agency. These developments not only increase the distinctiveness of TCE but also, at least potentially, make it far more acceptable to a large body of management control researchers who are repelled by the more uncompromisingly neoclassical approaches.

In terms of theoretical antecedents, Williamson argues that AT and TCE have different origins. AT has grown out of the management discretion tradition started by Berle and Means (1932). On the other hand, TCE grew out of the seminal paper on transactions costs of Coase (1937). Modifying the views expressed in his 1985 book in more recent work, Williamson has changed his position on behavioural assumptions. He argues that AT and TCE use a similar concept of bounded rationality although AT theorists are coy about actually using this term with its association with satificising or even irrationality. He makes a similar point concerning 'opportunism' (TCE) and 'moral hazard' (AT) suggesting that the differences are terminological rather than substantive.   Williamson argues that both AT and TCE look at the problem of incomplete contracts although 'AT examines contract predominantly from an *ex ante* incentive alignment point of view while TCE is more concerned with crafting *ex post* governance structures within which integrity of contract is decided' (1988, p. 571). Many writers (including this one!) would dispute the above reconciliation not least because it fails to do justice to the strengths and weaknesses of what should be regarded as distinctive approaches.

To Williamson, the crucial distinction lies in the realm of the unit of analysis. In TCE the unit of analysis is the *transaction* which 'leads naturally to an examination of the principal dimensions with respect to which transactions differ ... the most important is the condition of asset specificity' (p. 571). It is on this unit of analysis that the whole market versus hierarchy paradigm is erected. AT, seeing the individual agent as the unit of analysis, has no equivalent structure. There is, in fact, no analytical difference between the market and the firm in an agency world of contracts (Puxty, 1985; Baiman, 1990).

Williamson notes another significant difference in his comparison of agency and transaction cost paradigms. The assumption in agency is of a strong form of market efficiency implying that 'the [entrepreneur] will bear the entire wealth effects of these expected costs so long as the equity market anticipates these effects' (Jensen and Meckling, 1976, p. 314). In contrast, Williamson talks about the *ex post* costs of TCE ('maladaptation costs') arguing that '(r)educing these costs through judicious choice of governance structure (market, hierarchy, or hybrid), rather than merely realigning incentives and pricing them out, is the distinctive TCE orientation' (p. 573). This is also the entrée for the 'measurement branch' which is part of the 'detail' for settling '*ex post* contractual relations' together with matters of internal organisation such as hierarchical decomposition.

As already mentioned, AT and TCE are *both* based on natural selection analogies. This area will be extensively discussed in the next chapter where it will be argued that *none* of the contractual theories have analysed the natural selection process very thoroughly. Williamson seems more willing to admit this omission than the AT theorists whose assumptions about the efficiency of selection mechanisms are, in equal proportions, both perfunctory and heroic. To his credit, Williamson is far less confident about the efficacy of the selection process. He quotes Simon (1983), who defines *weak form selection* as being that 'in a relative sense, the fitter survive, but there is no reason to suppose that they are fittest in any absolute sense' (p. 69).

Williamson discusses the impact of the 'Fundamental Transformation' arising from asset specificity which has no equivalent in AT. Particularly instructive is Williamson's view that 'the high powered incentives found to be

58

effective in market organisation give rise to dysfunctional consequences if introduced into the firm' (p. 575). This is a theme we have already come across and which will be repeated throughout the book. For example, since I argued in chapter one that the firm could be viewed as a non-market response to uncertainty then it would seem to be illogical to then administer it on the same basis as the market. Such a proposal would seem trite if it were not for the theoretical frameworks and decision rules which have been proposed and implemented in recent years in both public and private sector organisations in the UK As will be seen, the flaw in most of the rules is the underlying assumption that market-type decision processes may usefully be simulated within firms. Indeed, *if* market-type decision rules and incentive systems are appropriate, why are the activities organised within firms in the first place?

2.3   Other comparisons of AT and TCE

As Williamson admits, he is far from being a disinterested party in any exercise in comparison and evaluation. Yet, in my judgement, Williamson has been over-generous to AT, allowing it to claim both the prizes of rigour *and* richness. Antle may be a leading proponent of AT but he rightly stresses in his comparison of the two approaches that 'each perspective is incomplete, and for each advantage offered by a method, there is an associated disadvantage' (Antle, 1989, p. 106).

Antle argues that the strength of agency theory rests on its relative rigour which must, of necessity, be based on a simplified model of human nature. As he puts it:

> Like all models, agency theory imposes its own bounds. The most striking one is probably its model of human behaviour. For example, we assume the principal and agent behave as if they maximise expected utility. Their utilities are modelled as being functions of very few variables, and after the principal and agent strike a contract, all their actions represent a playing out of a score written in the contract. The principal-agent model is a "completely orchestrated" behaviour model, in which the actors are puppets on contractual strings (p. 105).

In more general terms, the comparison may be seen in terms of trade-offs and comparative advantages rather than in terms of absolute superiority. Thus, for example, if, as Jensen (1983) argues, that in the so-called 'positive theory of agency', contracts might be incomplete, then, according to Antle, AT would be throwing away the main comparative advantage of its approach! Complete, if complex, self-policing contracts are conducive to rigorous formal analysis. Incomplete and adaptive non-contractual mechanisms are less determinate and less amenable to formal analysis. This is the strength of the TCE paradigm and is also the sort of world which the accounting researcher finds easier to recognise.

The summary of contrasts and similarities illustrated in table 3.1 agrees with Antle's sharper distinction rather than with the Williamson's or Jensen's compromises.

Table 3.1
A summary of key characteristics of transaction cost and agency theories

	Behavioural Assumptions	Unit of Analysis	Monopoly v Efficiency	Treatment of Uncertainty
Transaction Cost Theory	Bounded Rationality/ Opportunism	Transaction	Efficiency survivor theory	Information Impactedness Adaptive behaviour
Agency Theory	Unbounded rationality/ Moral Hazard	Individual Agent	Efficiency survivor theory	Asymmetric Information Rational Expectations

2.4   AT and TCE in the family tree of economic thought

AT and TCE are thus viewed in this book as having some similarities but ultimately representing divergent traditions. These divergences will emerge throughout the book in terms of contrasts such as *passive* versus *active* responses to uncertainty, *equilibrium* v *disequilibrium* models, strong '*natural selection*' v *malfunction in selection process*, *tractability* v '*richness*' and so on.

It is not just a matter of terminology or semantics. It is not even a matter of strong fences making good neighbours. As we shall see, the differences between AT and TCE are significant when they are applied to modelling the economy and attempting to draw some policy implications. The penchant for rigour and the caution of the rational expectations position all pull economic theory back to a version of general equilibrium. Indeed, given the dominance of the latter throughout the economics profession it is perhaps less surprising that AT may be presented as the favoured paradigm. In this book, however, general equilibrium is a limiting case at the margins rather than at the centre of the research programme. The divergence of traditions is emphasised in the updated flow diagram below (figure 3.1)

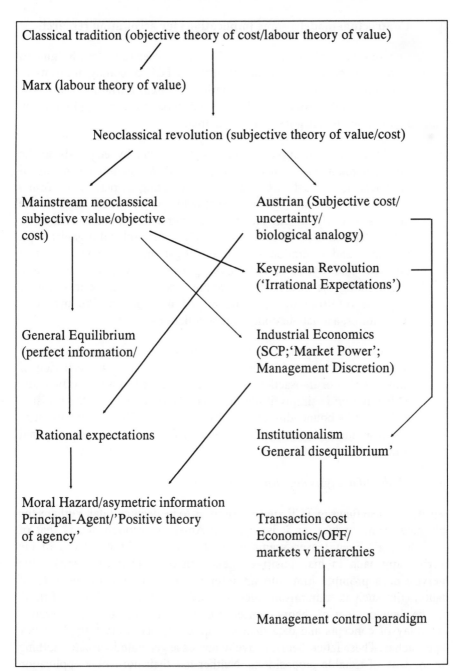

Figure 3.1 Responses to uncertainty in economic thought

3. Contractual models: some implications for accounting research

Antle's paper is valuable on two counts. Firstly, it sweeps away the fudging of distinctions between positive agency theory and TCE. Secondly, it discusses both paradigms in the context of accounting research. Earlier, we saw how Antle saw AT as an approach which achieved rigour by imposing bounds on individual rationality. He goes on to argue that:

> A transaction cost approach relaxes this bound by emphasising the bounded rationality of decisionmakers and the incomplete nature of contracts. It would focus on financial reporting as part of the firm's governance structure. Governance structure is the phrase used for the devices that arise to fill in, *ex post*, contracts that are known to be incomplete, *ex ante*. These devices include hierarchical organisations, grievance and arbitration procedures, litigation, markets for corporate control, and dynamic rule-making bodies such as the FASB. Highlighting the governance structure leads us to think in terms of implicit relationships and points of disruption, like mergers, divestitures, and labour contract renegotiations.
>
> However, since nothing is free, the transaction cost approach must impose its own set of bounds. A key one is the vague criterion of minimisation of transaction costs that is imposed to assess efficiency. This criterion is simply ill-defined. To elaborate, what is the decision criterion of a boundedly rational decisionmaker? How are we to judge whether he is better off or worse off with a new institutional arrangement? (p. 105).

3.1 Modes of analysis and discourse

To Antle these flaws in TCE are so serious as to be deemed fatal. Perhaps the ultimate crime to him, as it is to many American economists, is that of 'bullshitting'. Even Jensen seems unusually nervous about the use of the verbal approach in his "positive agency theory." (Jensen, 1983). This nervousness prompts him into an interesting discussion of the role of tautologies such as "minimising agency costs" or "the survival of the fittest" in the development of theory. Jensen argues for a more tentative/iterative interplay of concepts and data than is implied by the more formal agency approaches. These latter theories have in any case generated virtually nothing in the way of testable propositions. Neither has their normative application produced significant technical advance in management practice. As Jensen points out, the real successes of formal management science have been in operational research and, even here, the scope of the techniques developed has been limited to highly structured 'engineering' type problems. More general issues of wider management control and the boundaries of the firm take the analysis into an altogether fuzzier reality where fuzzier modes of analysis are inevitable.

The choice between paradigms does not involve straightforward comparisons between theories based on simple minded criteria such as numerically measurable predictive power. The issue is a more general one of choosing a 'way of thinking' about accounting and management problems. The precedent for choosing theory on this basis was set by Keynes who advocated economics as a 'way of looking at the world' rather than as a rigid box of theoretical techniques/prescriptions.

The choice of a 'mode of thinking' is not trivial even if it is a matter of choosing between two such apparently similar paradigms as AT and TCE. As we have already seen, the application of AT to accounting may not have produced detailed recommendations on matters of accounting convention or system design but it has added to the debate on more general issues of the role of accounting in the firm and in society. If the TCE 'way of thinking' had been more influential in these debates then the 'paradigm wars' described earlier might have been less acrimonious. As an example of the effect of different modes of thought at a more applied level, we might consider the contemporary task of developing new management control and information systems in British Universities. It does not take much imagination to realise that a management control system designed by an AT-influenced consultant would be different from a system designed by a TCE-influenced consultant - particularly one familiar with the works of Ouchi and others![3]

The TCE approach is actually far less challenging to traditions in accounting theory and practice. It is far less dismissive of institutions and conventions whether in external reporting or in internal management issues. For example, the traditional division of accounting into financial and management accounting has little meaning in agency theory where the distinction between the firm and the market has been dissolved into a general contracting scheme. This is quite distinct from the paradigmatic issue of TCE which is one of drawing the boundaries between governance structures or between 'markets and hierarchies'.

As we shall see in the next section, TCE explicitly accepts the need for a 'measurement branch' as part of the general transaction costs minimising process. The underlying spirit of AT is that accounting measures and conventions are unimportant. This reflects the assumption of rational expectations especially the Efficient Markets Hypothesis (EMH). Although nothing has been published on this matter, it might be safely assumed that TC economists would agree with Ross' opinion on the EMH that it should be regarded as an important intuition of great utility in *finance* theory rather than an automatic assumption to be applied to *all markets* as it is in Agency Theory (see Ross, 1987, Seal, 1990).

TCE is easier to relate to *contingency theory* which is probably the dominant theoretical framework in both organisational theory and management accounting. Some accounting theorists are quite explicit in placing both AT and TCE in a contingency theoretical framework. For example, Tiessen and Waterhouse (1983) argue that AT works best where technologies are routine and environments are predictable since it is these circumstances that a formal approach is more appropriate. In general, however, they accept the Williamsonian viewpoint that 'hierarchical organisations are not susceptible to analysis from a contracting point of view because hierarchies are created to mediate exchange where complete contracts cannot be written or enforced.' (p. 257). Given the centrality of this insight it seems incredible that AT has been the dominant paradigm rather than TCE!

Some of the above problems are beginning to be addressed by agency theorists. In particular, the 'Rochester school' are bothered by two weaknesses in the highly formal Principal-Agent literature. One, as already mentioned, is the difficulty of actually empirically identifying the Principal (Baiman, 1990). The second difficulty is understanding the role of an institution like accounting in a world of full contracting. The first problem has emerged in the analysis of a management compensation contracts where it is hard to decide at what level in the firm the principal's interest is located. The second problem has been addressed by Ball (1989) who argues that accounting fulfills a vital role in contract completion.

4. The organisational failures framework and accounting research

Those few accounting researchers who have based their work on TCE seem to prefer the earlier 'markets v hierarchies/organisational failures framework (Ouchi, 1977, 1980; Tiessen and Waterhouse, 1983; Spicer and Ballew, 1983; Spicer, 1988; Johnson, 1983; Flamholtz, 1983; Flamholtz, et al., 1985).

The central insights are all there in Williamson's earlier work (1975). The main later advances would seem to be more a matter of tidying up by reducing the number of assumptions. The refinement of the concept of *asset specificity* has been an important part of this process and has really only appeared in the accounting literature in the last work by Spicer (1988). There may actually be a more fundamental reason for drawing on the earlier work in that Williamson's more recent work does tend to emphasise *contractual* rather than *measurement* issues. For example, accounting researchers have found the concept of *information impactedness* of particular relevance for studying management accounting systems. Yet this is a concept which now seems to be regarded as being redundant.

The neglect of the OFF and apparent preference for the agency paradigm is all the more regrettable since, in my view, the former has considerable merit in terms of providing a conceptual framework for accounting research. This theme will be developed throughout the rest of the book as the above omission is remedied. Indeed, it could be argued that if the paradigm is defined in broad enough terms, then it can accommodate quite drastic additions and modifications. Whether developing the paradigm means fundamentally changing it, then it is for others to judge. In any case, the ultimate label that is attached to a theory is of little importance, as long as intellectual debts and antecedents are acknowledged.

4.1 The boundary of firm and market as an ongoing research issue

I submit that one of the great insights of TCE is to make the boundary of the firm an active research issue. This issue is of great importance throughout this book. In the context of this chapter there are two main implications. Firstly, the TCE paradigm implies that resource allocation within the firm is different from resource allocation in the market. Secondly, in contrast to much accounting and organisational theory, it does not take the boundary of the organisation as given. This is not the same as the familiar argument that the firm should be modelled as an 'open' rather than a 'closed' system.[4] In TCE, the firm may not only draw upon external resources, it may also seek solutions by changing its boundaries. For example, if a corporation is having problems with motivating management in a particular division then it may consider some form of sell-off rather than take the boundary of the corporation as given and attempt a solution via changes in personnel and management style. Of course, AT theorists might also propose such a 'solution' but they are unable to model the firm's transactions in the systematic framework provided by the 'markets v hierarchies' paradigm.

Many recent innovations in modern production such as 'Just in Time' and 'Total Quality Management' can only be understood in the context of seeing the process of production as a vertical chain extending backwards towards component and raw material suppliers and forwards towards the final consumer. These systems are heavily contingent on the appropriate contractual relationship 'outside the firm'. The tremendous growth of subcontracting has had an important impact on all aspects of internal management, especially management accounting (see Bromwich and Bhimani, 1989).

4.2 The economics of hierarchy and hierachical decomposition

The TCE framework is able to analyse an area of great importance in management accounting - the management control of decentralisation and, in particular, the use of divisionalisation. This area - the so-called 'decomposition of hierarchy' - may be seen as a continuous thread in Williamson's thinking from Managerialism to the M-form organisation to the 'markets and hierarchies' paradigm. This continuity is summarised neatly by McGuinness (1987) as follows:

> That transaction specific assets are organised by management rather than markets, is explained by savings on the resources used to decide how to adjust to changes unanticipated at the start of the contract. Given that resources are managed, hierarchy is explained by gains from allowing people to specialise according to their comparative advantage; in particular, those with a comparative advantage in deciding how to co-ordinate the diverse resources used in the firm and how to adjust this co-ordination in response to unforeseen changes, are assigned specialist managerial roles. Finally, the decomposition of managerial hierarchies allows some managers to specialise in strategic decision-making and for this task to be performed by people who not only possess a relevant comparative advantage but also whose corporate loyalties are not compromised by undue devotion to narrow functional goals ... In addition, allocative efficiency may be improved if the shift to an M-form of internal organisation leads to behaviour that is more profit-orientated (p. 57).

The actual outcome may not be as neat as the paradigm proposes. It is, however, a useful basis for both theory building and criticism.

5.   The Organisational Failures Framework (OFF): markets, hierarchies and clans

An ambitious conceptual framework such as the one described by McGuiness leaves plenty of scope both for 'box filling' and for different articulations of the basic theme. One important example of the latter process is provided by Ouchi whose link with TCE is most vividly illustrated in two papers (Ouchi, 1977; 1980). Since Ouchi analyses the issue of organisational control, many of his concerns will be looked at in the next two chapters. Indeed, in the context of a management control literature, many of his ideas may seem familiar and some of his criticisms concerning the lack of study of control issues misplaced.

He does, however, provide an economical presentation of some of the key issues to be looked at in subsequent chapters and his general approach is relatively easy to integrate into a broader framework of management control and organisational change.[5]

5.1   Behaviour control and output control

Ouchi (1977) argues that:

> In controlling the work of people and of technologies, there are only two phenomena which can be observed, monitored and counted: behaviour and the outputs which result from behaviour. Thus, control systems can be regarded as being based essentially on the monitoring and evaluation of one or the other, and these will be referred to as being *behaviour control* and *output control* - remembering that even in the case of output control, real control comes about only through changing the worker's behaviour, although the means is by selectively rewarding certain of his outputs (p. 97).

He then investigates the circumstances under which each form of control will be used. Behaviour control requires a 'knowledge of means-ends relationships'. On the other hand, output control does not require a knowledge of the transformation process but it does require 'reliable' and 'valid' measures of the desired outputs.

Ouchi relates his approach to conventional contingency theory by suggesting that;

> In short, the exercise of control relies on monitoring either behaviour or output. Which one forms the basis of control depends upon the accuracy with which each can be measured. The technological or task characteristics of work will play an important role in this determination (p.100).

In his 1980 paper, Ouchi is more overtly influenced by the markets and hierarchies paradigm. He bases his theory on the choice between market, hierarchy and a new organisational concept which he calls the *Clan* - a form which has particular advantages when monitoring problems are acute. Although he uses a transaction cost approach, he adds new aspects to the framework: *goal incongruence* and *performance ambiguity*. He argues that;

> Different combinations of these causes distinguish three basic mechanisms of mediation or control: markets, which are efficient when

performance ambiguity is low and goal incongruence is high; bureaucracies, which are efficient when both goal incongruence and performance ambiguity are high; and clans, which are efficient when goal incongruence is low and performance ambiguity is high (p. 129).

As table 3.2 indicates, while the clan needs relatively little in the way of conventional management control information, the 'normative requirements' are extremely onerous.

Table 3.2
An Organisational Failures Framework

Mode of Control	Normative requirements	Informational requirements
Market	Reciprocity	Prices
Bureaucracy	Reciprocity Legitimate Authority	Rules
Clan	Reciprocity Legitimate authority Common Values & Beliefs	Traditions

Source: Ouchi, 1980, p. 137) [6]

As Ouchi argues, the clan organisation seems to have significant advantages in certain activities. Part of the agenda in future chapters will be to further articulate what these advantages are, when they are particularly appropriate, and what conditions should pertain in order to establish and maintain such organisational forms. Ouchi's own contribution to these endeavours is relatively strong in the case of the first two aspects but less satisfactory with respect to the last. As he points out, the clan is an advance on the bureaucratic model because it reduces the need for monitoring when performance ambiguity is high. For example, in terms of technological development, the clan plays a crucial role since it is in activities such as research and development where performance ambiguity is likely to be high and formal output controls are not only ineffective but actually dysfunctional. Furthermore, if, as is often argued, technological progress is as much reliant on the ideas of ordinary workers as it is the responsibility of the designated researcher then the innovatory advantages of the clan are further augmented.

5.2 TCE and OFF combined: an isomorphic formulation[7]

One way of modelling both TCE and OFF is to look at them in terms of a contingency approach. Thus concepts such as asset specificity and performance ambiguity may be seen as contingency factors with which the various organisational forms such as market, hierarchy and clan are related. Such a 'transaction cost map of organisation' is presented in figure 3.2.

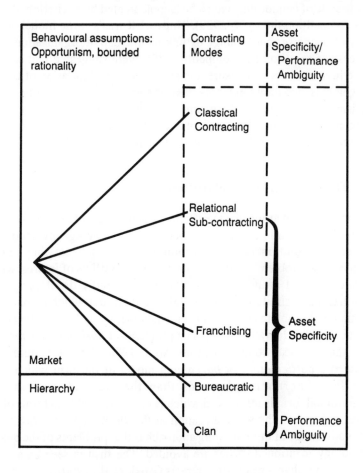

Figure 3.2   A transaction cost map of organisation

5.3   Enter selection processes

The diagram illustrates a number of institutional possibilities with related efficiency properties. As such it could be left as an ideal model showing an appropriate match of institutional and transactional characteristics as suggested by the TCE and OFF literature. Selection theorists talk about an 'isomorphic formulation' (Hannan and Freeman, 1977). They point out that the principle of isomorphism must be 'supplemented by a criterion of selection and a competition theory' (p. 939). Thus, what was a *static* model becomes a theory of *organisational change* by linking the map of organisational form to a process of selection and competition. If it were suggested that selection in competitive markets will ensure that an efficient configuration of contractual arrangements inevitably emerges, then the approach would fully justify the criticism of 'panglossian' theorising as mentioned earlier. The nature of the selection process, therefore, becomes central to the operation of the whole paradigm. This is the subject of the next chapter.

6.   The firm as a 'nexus of treaties'

Some critics might argue that the efficiency superiority of the clan is inevitable but theoretically uninteresting - a special case of the agency problem - the co-operative solution. This viewpoint seems to suggest that interesting organisational problems tend to disappear once conflicts of interest within the firm are assumed away. There is, however, a rapidly developing literature which has many similarities to the OFF paradigm but which emphasises that informational problems can exist even when there may be high levels of goal congruence. This literature focuses on problems of *horizontal communication* rather than vertical communication (Aoki, 1986). This literature has also generated a *participatory* or *bargaining* model of the firm which seems to make fewer normative demands than the clan. In other words, an organisational form is introduced which is more explicable in terms of the self interest rather than the self abnegation of the worker (Aoki, 1984;1990a). A further advantage of this emerging approach is that problems of the quasi-legal terminology mentioned earlier are avoided. The firm is seen as a 'nexus of treaties' rather than a nexus of contracts (Aoki, et al., 1990).

In spirit, many of these developments are basically complementary to the TCE approach. They are pertinent to this book because they further develop the problems of decision making, uncertainty and information which are central issues in a theory of the firm. However, as will be seen in later chapters, there are *some* aspects of the new approach which do not sit easily either with those features of the TCE paradigm which favour the hierarchical organisations and simple forms of decentralisation such as the M-form.

7.   Concluding remarks

This chapter has concentrated on defining and comparing the two main contractual paradigms. It has been argued that both paradigms can be, and have been, related to issues of accounting and management control. It should, however, be stressed that *neither* of these two approaches are likely to offer more than a very broad framework of analysis. Thus they can explain the existence of accounting or suggest possible functions of accounting. They cannot, however, provide detailed decision rules such as may be derived from mainstream neoclassical economics.

Given that they are both 'modes of thought', I submit that TCE provides a superior, if somewhat neglected, framework for analysing accounting and management control issues. If the latter is about measurement then TCE alone sees a need for a measurement branch. It alone provides the sort of bridge between economics and behavioural theory which has been exploited in the organisational failures framework. It alone treats the boundary of the firm as an active research issues and is thus able to model the relationship between financial and management accounting (see chapter eight). This list of relatively strong points should not be interpreted as a unalloyed eulogy of TCE. Indeed, some of the problems and ambiguities of the paradigm will emerge later in the book.

Both contracting paradigms may be seen as being incomplete in their focus on cost minimisation (however defined) as a condition of survival. The apparent neglect of market power in explaining survival strains credibility as well as being analytically unnecessary. Secondly, as Putterman (1988) points out, *neither* approaches have fully articulated the role of ownership in their theories. The 'firm as a commodity' ties it not just to capitalism, but to a specifically Anglo-Saxon version of the genre. These issues as well as the development of the 'measurement branch' and a more detailed analysis of the selection process, are covered in the next two chapters.

Notes

1. See especially section 5.2 onwards.

2. This view on TCE was confirmed in a private conversation with Antle in a recent visit to the LSE.

3. For example, an agency influence consultant might emphasise managerial incentive schemes based on 'efficiency' criteria while a TCE influenced consultant may actually recognise the functionality of promotion based incentive systems.

4. This viewpoint is analysed in the 'Management Control' literature (see chapter five).

5. See especially chapter five for an extended comparison of bureaucracies and clans.

6. Reproduced with permission from 'Markets, Bureaucracies and Clans', by Ouchi, W. published in *Administrative Science Quarterly,* volume 22, (1980) copyright the fellows of Cornell University.

7. Chambers (1966) likens the principle of isomorphism to a map 'in which the relationship between the points of the map correspond with the relationships between the points on the terrain mapped' (p. 126).

4 Natural selection analogies, accounting and organisational change

Since accounting systems are an integral part of most organisational control and reporting practices, an explanation of organisational change should also provide at least some explanation of accounting change. The 'New Institutional Economics' represented by Agency Theory (AT) and Transaction Cost Economics (TCE) purports to provide such a theory. Since these theories are based on natural selection analogies, their application in the accounting area has provoked a number of criticisms such as Panglossian theorising and functionalism. While these criticisms are justified as reactions to the undoubted theoretical vulgarities of crude 'Social Darwinists', it is argued in this chapter that the selection process in AT and TCE has been underresearched and that when the process is made more explicit then the outcomes need not be panglossian or functionalist. It is also argued that accounting and management control systems need not simply respond passively to organisational change but may actively contribute to that change in an essentially 'Lamarckian' version of natural selection.

The chapter is divided into four sections. In the first section there is a general discussion of the promise and pitfalls of evolutionary theories in the social sciences with a criticism of both some of the proponents and opponents of the approach as it is applied in the accounting literature. Section two looks more specifically at economic versions of natural selection. Section three presents a model of institutional change which shows how a distinctly dysfunctional/unpanglossian view of organisational change can be based on evolutionary theory. Section four considers some of the implications of such a theory in view of some current debates in the accounting and management control literature.

1. Darwinism, Lamarckism and Panglossianism

1.1 Do natural selection analogies have particular biases?

Given the political philosophies and attendant policies, it is perhaps not surprising that the application of biological analogies in the sphere of social research requires careful justification. The critics of the use of such paradigms in the accounting literature are generally more concerned with what Tinker (1988) has called 'deregulatory theorising'. His attack on the application of agency and transaction cost economics theories to accounting theory is based on the proposition that they tend to mask the *distributive* role of accounting, partly because they are efficiency based paradigms, and more generally because the use of selection theory can be used to 'naturalise' both human nature and socioeconomic institutions. While he acknowledges in a footnote (p. 179) that what is at issue is the misuse of Darwinian theorising, the suggestion is that such misuse *has* taken place.

Panglossian characteristics tend to occur when the selection process is treated either implicitly or perfunctorily as it frequently is in agency theory. While the TCE literature is also prone to such errors, at least its most prolific and influential contributor has responded directly to his radical critics on the specific issues of panglossianism and functionalism (Williamson, 1987). In general, it does seem that when selection theory is discuss explicitly then the tone becomes more cautious. Even Jensen, for example, suggests that the 'survival of the fittest' should be seen as a tautological device employed in the embryonic phase of theory development (Jensen, 1983). Another supporter of biological analogies in economics, Hirshleifer (1977) put it thus:

> The Social Darwinists, or some of them at least, did confuse descriptive with moral categories so as to attribute excessive beneficence to natural selection on the human level. In the real world, we know, success *may* sometimes be the reward of socially functional behaviour, but also sometimes of valueless or disruptive activities like monopolisation, crime, or most of what is carried on under the heading of politics (p. 6).

Hirshleifer also points out that evolutionary social theories can be radical or conservative depending upon whether the emphasis is on change or on the final state of harmonious adaptation. As I will argue in the next section, selection via a smooth equilibriating process may produce quite different results as compared with those emanating from 'general disequilibrium'.

A further illustration that panglossianism tends to appear where the focus of attention is diverted away from explicit analysis of the selection process is provided by the work of Alchian who is relatively cautious in his seminal paper on natural selection (Alchian, 1950) but then tends to invoke it as an optimising process in his theory of economic organisation (Alchian and Demsetz, 1972). Alchian's 1950 paper also illustrates an important facet of the natural selection debate since it includes two models - one which invokes the pure Darwinian process of random variation and natural selection and the other involving an element of conscious adaptation. In biology, the second process would be termed 'Lamarckian' after the biologist who by arguing that acquired characteristics could be inherited increased the likelihood of a 'progressive' form of evolution.

1.2   A biological perspective

Biologists have long debated the possible biases and limitations of natural selection theory in its 'legitimate sphere' and many of the arguments that occur in the social science literature have direct analogies in the biological literature. For example, Luria, Gould, and Singer (1981) directly pose the question - 'Does Natural Selection Fashion optimal design?'. The answer is negative since 'selection cannot optimise each individual part of an organism' ... 'Optimal design is a balance among the contradictory demands of the parts'. They also point out that:

> If environments were constant and species persisted in them for untold millions of years, this fitful process might lead to optimal design. But environments fluctuate constantly, forcing populations to track an ever-changing ideal, rarely permitting much accumulation toward an optimum (p. 595).

Not all the biological arguments are directly analogous. Biologists generally are quite adamant in stating that *cultural* evolution is *Larmarckian* rather than *Darwinian* which tends to pose the question - 'If Darwinian evolution is not optimal then is Lamarckian?'.

1.3   The Lamarckian model

Lamarckian evolution is clearly the sort of adaptive process implicit in the spread of organisational forms, accounting methods and fashionable business techniques in general. While the speed of change is likely to be much quicker than under random variation, it is not necessarily a progressive movement. As Alchian's examples of imitative behaviour illustrate (conventional markup, price followship, orthodox accounting) the adaptive response is not characterised by a conscious attempt at optimisation! In sections three and four, it is suggested that certain changes in accounting and management methods may actually be damaging the whole system - a far from panglossian conclusion!

2.   Some economic versions of natural selection processes

2.1   Selection theory and economic theory

Natural selection models have generally operated on the fringe rather than at the heart of orthodox economic theory. Thus advocates of evolutionary economics such as Nelson and Winter (NW) (1982) have to devote much of their intellectual endeavour defending the paradigm against neo-classical critics. In NW's view the insights of Alchian (1950) were either never properly understood or deliberately misrepresented. Thus Alchian's natural selection theory is sometimes cited as a justification for maintaining the assumption of profit maximisation when he actually argues that the test of survival is *ex post* positive profit rather than *ex ante* profit maximisation. Nelson and Winter are critical of the general obsession with the issue of the goals of the firm. As they point out:

> ... if the firms in the world can get along without being entirely clear about their goals, so can the firms in a theoretical model. The concern that orthodoxy has lavished on the question of objectives is a reflection of the logical imperatives of its own normative structure - and also of its aspiration to reach broad normative conclusions on the efficacy of market mechanisms. To discard that normative baggage is to greatly expand the available options for dealing with motivational issues in the theory of the firm (p. 57).

NW frequently link organisational phenomena to the biological analogy. Thus organisational 'routines' are equivalent to the biologists' genes. As the word implies, following routines results in relatively stable organisational procedures. Thus although there may be a Lamarckian-type learning process, economic change is due to changes in the *population of firms* rather than changes *within* individual firms. Their model suggests both institutional inertia and a reliance on 'rules of thumb' which naturally applies to firms' accounting practices. As in any adaptive theory, the generation, storage and transmission of information is important. Formal information systems such as those provided by accounting may be seen as part of the organisational routine but not necessarily the most important part of the firm's information processing capability. Following Polanyi's emphasis on tacit knowledge, NW argue that:

... information is actually stored primarily in the memories of the members of the organisation, in which reside all the knowledge, articulate and tacit, that constitutes their individual skills and routines, the generalised language competence and the specific command of the organisational dialect, and above all, the associations that link the incoming messages to the specific performances that they call for (p. 104).

The organisational outcomes of expected by NW are not optimal in the 'best of all possible worlds' sense. As they put it:

The general issue here is this. A historical process of evolutionary change cannot be expected to "test" all possible behavioural implications of a given set of routines, much less test them repeatedly. It is only against the environmental conditions that persist for extended periods (and in this loose sense are "equilibrium" conditions) that routines are thoroughly tested. There is no reason to expect, therefore, that the surviving patterns of behaviour of a historical selection process are well adapted for novel conditions not repeatedly encountered in that process. In fact, there is good reason to expect the opposite, since selection forces may be expected to be "sensible" and to trade off maladaptation under unusual or unencountered conditions to achieve good adaptations to conditions frequently encountered. In a context of progressive change, therefore, one should not expect to observe ideal adaptation to current conditions by the products of evolutionary processes (p. 154).

The economic concept of 'equilibrium' does help distinguish between different evolutionary outcomes. In this context there are two ways of looking at natural selection in markets.

a. The 'Equilibrium' model. This may be perceived as a process of piecemeal adaptation by the organisation to its environment or the gradual change of populations of firms in response to a relatively stable environment.

b. The 'Disequilibrium' model. This conjures up a more violent story of highly unstable environments. The source of instability may be technological change (Schumpeter's 'gales of creative destruction' [1942] or world wide instability (for example, at the end of the 'long boom' in 1973). Alternatively, the instability may be more endemic as a result of a recurring cycle of corporate takeovers, 'bust-up bids' and corporate restructuring.

In the first, 'equilibrium' view, the story is a gentle one of creating economic organisations in a market economy, maintaining, adapting, and expanding them - all contingent on creating an economic surplus. The reverse process of decline is similarly gradual. The process is well described by Salter and Weinhold (1988):

> ... unless a firm can outperform its competitors in generating economic surplus, critical resources will tend to flow away, diminishing the firm's capacity to innovate and expand. The inevitable result is reduced competitive strength and the eventual disintegration of the enterprise as a viable entity (p. 138).

This version of the 'invisible hand' parable with its picture of a gentle movement of economic resources between firms and between markets and firms based on the ability to create economic surplus contrasts with the more violent and less obviously benign mechanisms of the market for control where terms such as 'organisational bust' suggest, at the minimum, a more ambivalent attitude regarding the social pay-off. The market for control projects an altogether more 'tooth and claw' version of market competition where even the use of terms such as 'predator', 'victim', 'raider', 'greenmail', 'white knight' conjure up a more obviously blood thirsty version of natural selection. It is argued in this chapter that a far from optimal adaptation may be expected in response to the disequilibrium forces which characterise the market for control. The emphasis on this source of environmental instability is justified because it may be argued to be endogenous to the market mechanism in *some* national economies such as the UK and the USA but relatively unimportant in others such as Japan and Germany. Other forms of instability such as technological change or 'oil shocks' may be regarded as being common problems faced by firms in all market economies and as being exogenous to the diversity of institutional configurations.

Tinker (1988), in common with many commentators, makes little of any possible distinction between the survivor paradigms of agency theory and transaction cost economics since both are seen as being panglossian theories. Other commentators recognise that the former has a more marked panglossian tendency than the latter. For example, as Putterman (1986) writes:

> ... authors such as Alchian, Demsetz, Fama, Jensen, Meckling, and Klein, ... play down firm-market distinctions, play up the market like qualities of firms and the permeation of market forces into the

operations of firms, and incline to the view that unregulated competitive markets generate economically optimal institutions as allegedly indicated in the preferences of market participants ... At some remove from this position are analysts such as Coase, Simon, and Williamson, who differ from Alchian et al. in drawing a sharper boundary between firm and market ... (p. 22)

... Concern for organisational evolution and awareness that efficient adaptations are not necessarily automatic also separates Williamson from analysts such as Jensen ... (p. 23).

In view of the different outcomes that may be expected from a disequilibrium as opposed to an equilibrium view of selection, it is perhaps not surprising to find that agency theory tends towards equilibrium models while transaction cost theory is more concerned with disequilibrium situations (Antle, 1989). Agency theorists tend also to specify competition and rational expectations in all markets. TCE theory is less explicit. Indeed, Williamson's rebuttal of panglossianism rests partly on his viewpoint that the selection aspects of TCE has been relatively neglected which is rather curious given the vast literature on takeovers and mergers which could be drawn upon.

It is generally true that the takeover literature tends to relate to standard neoclassical analysis rather than institutionalist evolutionary theory. An example of an explicit attempt to test natural selection theories of the firm is provided by Singh (1975). Singh's study is specifically concerned with firms which perish via takeover rather than via liquidation. He concludes from his empirical work that the takeover mechanism is either 'loose and permissive', (or) '... selects on grounds other than profitability, such as growth maximisation' (p. 500). His study suggests both a managerialist motive for takeover and an environment where size is a surer protection against predators than profitability.

As will be discussed in the next two sections, other critics of the market for control seem to argue that it is 'too tough' in that it tends to shorten managerial time horizons and encourage asset stripping and other short-termist forms of behaviour. Whatever the specific criticisms, the general view on the market for control seems to be distinctly 'unpanglossian' (see Cooke, 1986, for a survey of the empirical evidence). Unfortunately, the critics cannot agree on whether the problem is one of managerialism or short-termism! Jensen, in common with other AT theorists, argues that neither the capital market, in general, nor the market for control, in particular, are short-termist. Managers may be short-termist but it is partly the operation of the takeover process that maintains effective checks on this as well as other managerialist abuses (Jensen, 1988).

It is beyond the scope of this chapter to review the huge literature on takeovers and mergers or fully discuss the meaning and cause of short-termism. The aim is merely to indicate that economic models of natural selection are not inevitably panglossian in their theoretical specification and also that there are numerous tests of economic natural selection processes which do not suggest optimal outcomes.

3. Multi-market survival and contradictory practices

One of the methodological difficulties of survivor theory is to specify a criterion for survival that is not tautological. If only the fittest survive what is 'fitness'? Both AT and TCE propose that fitness = efficiency. This, however, begs the question as to the definition of efficiency (Jensen, 1983). A second related problem is the question of whether the demise of a particular firm or even a whole population really matters. For example, it could be argued that if a firm goes into liquidation or is taken over, the assets do not disappear but are simply redeployed under new owners and managers. In other words, the selection process is not analogous to a frog eating a fly! From a conventional, neoclassical point of view, nothing need have changed since the conventional factors of production have simply been 'rearranged'. AT and TCE theorists may argue that the assets will be more efficiently organised and managed by the predator but this may be hard to test. Since survival cannot be its own vindication independent measures of 'success' need to be applied (see chapter nine).

3.1 A natural selection model of the UK economy[1]

In this section of the chapter, a model is presented in which it is shown that organisational change driven by a natural selection process can be used to explain fundamental change in the economic structure of an economy. It is argued that the productive process can be disrupted and distorted by 'organisational bust' and that this can help explain phenomena such as deindustrialisation and changes in the international organisation of production. Furthermore, as an intimate part of both the internal and external monitoring mechanisms of the firm, accounting plays a passive and an active role in the selection process being both subject to change and an agent of change.

The economics literature has generally failed to recognise the importance of organisational structure and control in explaining economic change. As seen in chapter two, the key theoretical construct is the production function which is a technologically determined relationship between inputs and outputs. In the neoclassical paradigm, production is not viewed as a process requiring management but more 'like a recipe for bouillabaisse where all the ingredients are dumped in a pot, (K,L), heated up, f(), and the output, X, is ready' (Leijonhufvud, 1986, p.203).

The model presented here is based on a 'rearrangement' of the new institutionalist approach to production. It uses many central concepts of TCE but proposes that the *direction of causation* is from the selection process to organisational form and from there to economic activity. This compares with the more conventional argument that organisational form is contingent on production imperatives such as economies of scale, technology and asset specificity (Riordan and Williamson, 1985). As with standard TCE, contractual difficulties arise from the interplay between these contingent factors and the behavioural assumptions of bounded rationality and opportunism.

Since the firm is seen as a central part of the *socio-technical system* in which technological processes are embedded, it is necessary to:

i) analyse the likely boundary between the market and the firm and predict the technological implications;

ii) analyse the internal organisation of the firm with particular reference to management control mechanisms;

iii) understand the selection process which leads to changes in boundaries between market and firms and to changes in the population of firms.

It is proposed that all this may be achieved using a consistent and relatively short list of assumptions about human behaviour and environmental uncertainty. These assumptions have been discussed in the previous chapter where it has been shown that they are sufficient to set up a simple model which establishes the basic boundary between 'markets and hierarchies'. It may also be used to discuss other devices for protecting investments in specific assets in addition to the 'unified ownership' of the conventional capitalist firm. The 'markets and hierarchy' distinction is an important one but it is only part of the picture. In a comprehensive theory of contracting, variations in contracting modes other than classical contracting need to be considered along with a variety of hierarchical models including 'hierarchical decomposition' and sub-contracting. The latter may be analysed as a consequence of the assumption of bounded rationality with its implication of incomplete contracting and step-by-step decision-making. In addition, incomplete contracts and the need for *ex post* monitoring both imply a role for what

Williamson terms a 'measurement' branch as well as the more familiar 'governance' branch.

As has been shown in the previous chapter, an isomorphic formulation is suggested matching contractual and organisational characteristics with contingency factors such as asset specificity and performance ambiguity. The resultant mapping has been represented diagrammatically in figure 3.2.

3.2   The selection and adaptation process: the multi-market model

The diagram in figure 3.2 illustrates a number of institutional possibilities with related efficiency properties. As I suggested in the previous chapter, if it were to be contended that natural selection in competition markets will ensure that an efficient configuration of contractual arrangements and control mechanisms inevitably emerges, then the approach would fully justify the criticism of 'panglossian' theorising. A panglossian outcome does *not* emerge because of evident imperfections in the selection mechanism and adaptation process.

In the previous section, one major source of dysfunctional selection was traced to the disequilibrium nature of the process. Other problems in terms of 'inefficient' selection may be generated in other ways. Firms may face a *number* of environments requiring *different* survival traits. Alchian sees firms subject to a competitive struggle where the simple rule of survival is positive profits (Alchian, 1950). However, the selection mechanism may plausibly be far more demanding and complex. For example, the survival of the firm in an economy like the UK's or the USA's usually involves meeting competition in at least *four* markets - the product market, the labour market, the capital market and the market for control. Problems may arise because the contractual/organisational forms that ensure success in one market may not be appropriate for success in other markets. Criteria concerning time horizons, risk and liquidity may well vary between the markets. Some of these differences are illustrated in the four quadrant diagram in figure 4.1.

Labour Market
(sub-contracting)

Control of Labour process
in production may be
'delegated' to sub-contractors.
This may weaken firm's ability
to control quality and produce
new products.

Market for
Control
('Organisational Bust')

Value created for predators
by 'transactions related'
strategies - 'organisational bust'
syndrome - particularly
damaging for 'clan' formation.

FIRMS

Product
Market
Performance indicators:
sales growth, market
share

Success indicators typically
concentrate on Sales growth
and market share where
non-price factors such as
quality and product innovation
are best ensured in clan
type organisation.

Capital
Market

Main survival requirement
is sufficient cash flow to
service debts and meet
dividends. May foreclose
or ration new funds, but
survivability likely to be more
related to 'industrial logic'.

Figure 4.1 A multi-market selection process

There is no great significance in specifying four different markets. Indeed, more markets could be identified if a higher level of disaggregation was adopted. For example, the labour market could be further decomposed into managerial and non-managerial labour markets. However, the minimum requirement is that several markets exist with different and conflicting survival traits being necessary in each one. Instead of the firm developing an efficient matching of contractual arrangements with transactional characteristics as presented in figure 3.2, the selection environment confronts the firm with a variety of conflicting pressures which may require 'contradictory practices'.[2]

From an explanatory perspective, the theory will be tautological unless markets are ranked. Otherwise, almost *any* organisational form could be explained in terms of being efficient in at least one of the markets. In the theory presented here, there is more emphasis on the market for control than in more conventional treatments of structural change and deindustrialisation. In other words, the casual direction is from the market for control to performance in the product market- survival traits appropriate in the market for control are used to explain the preponderance of organisational structures and controls that weaken competitiveness in product market which is reflected *ex post* in terms of long-run structural disequilibrium.

This emphasis on control and ownership will be developed in subsequent chapters. It is worth pointing out at this stage that this emphasis alone distinguishes the model from most contingency theory. 'Conventional' contingency theory generally focuses on 'task' factors as defined in the product market or environmental uncertainty similarly defined in terms of the product market. As will be discussed in chapter nine, issues of ownership are part of the neglected 'political' contingency approach.

3.3   Some empirical derivations from the model

The model seems to explain a variety of stylised facts. In particular, a number of examples of 'conflicting pressures and contradictory practices' may be cited:

a. In an attempt to avoid a well organised labour force in the core industrial areas, a company may increase its dependence on sub-contractors on the periphery. Such 'vertical disintegration' - a common strategy in the 1980's - may increase the flexibility of the firm's production system but make it less efficient from a transaction cost perspective. In other words, the change in the governance structure may turn out to be inappropriate in terms of asset specificity. Unless alternative contractual safeguards can be developed such as 'networking' then there are potential inefficiencies involved in this sort of 'putting-out' process, particularly if technical change is rapid.[3]

b. Value creation in the capital and/or market for control may require quite different strategies as compared with those in the product market. For example, in their analysis of possible strategies that may be pursued by a successful predator, Salter and Weinhold distinguish between 'transaction related' strategies such as refinancing assets and renegotiating "contracts" and 'operation related' strategies such as reconfiguring assets and recombining businesses (Salter and Weinhold, 1988). While the latter may actually contribute to the long-run competitiveness of the firm, the former strategy is essentially a 'one time' pay-off.[4]

c. The premium on liquidity exhibited by the investor in the stock market conflicts with the illiquidity which may result from investment in the sort of highly specific assets required in the product market. This is a familiar criticism with a venerable and distinguished pedigree. For example, as Shubik points out:

> Keynes (1936, Chap.12) likened the attitude of the stock market to a game of snap or musical chairs, noting that what is liquid for the individual is fixed for the community as a whole (Shubik, 1988, p.48).

Firms may therefore underinvest in specific assets even though competition in the product market penalises such a strategy through loss of market share.

d. A more recent phenomenon which has received an extensive airing in the business literature may be traced to an inconsistency between the managerial labour market and the long-run efficiency of the divisionalised corporation. As Kaplan has noted (Kaplan, 1983), the professionalisation of the executive labour market in the US (especially the development of the MBA) has tended to increase the inter-firm mobility of the manager. Consequently, it is easier for the opportunistic divisional manager to make his reputation through short-term 'financial' entrepreneurship rather than by long-term product or process improvement. In transaction cost terms, the human capital of the manager is now more 'general purpose'. This development raises problems for the long run efficiency of the firm's control system which works better when the manager's capital is more 'firm specific' as it was in the early days of divisionalisation.[5]

e. Differences in markets and hence required survival traits may be seen to vary between nation states. This may be used to explain perceived differences in the strategies pursued by multinational companies with different national origins. Using Porter's terminology (Porter, 1986) British multi-national investment has generally been characterised by a 'portfolio' approach rather than a 'globalisation' strategy. This sort of multinational investment may be contrasted with post-war US multinational expansion and the more recent globalisation of Japanese corporations. Indeed, many of the activities established by the latter have attracted the epithet of 'screw-driver' operations because only the simpler operations ('simpler', that is, in transaction cost terms) in the 'value chain' are located in overseas locations. The more complex activities in terms of asset specificity and performance ambiguity such as technological development are located in Japan where the environment is particularly suited to 'clan' formation. Before 1971 this characteristic of the Japanese 'selection environment' could have been attributed to the legal ban on hostile takeovers. Even now a market for control in British or US terms is practically nonexistent since the linkages between the labour market and the capital market in Japan make the hostile takeover bid unlikely to succeed (Odagiri, 1980).

f. Survival traits in the market for control tend to favour decentralised, 'arms-length' systems of corporate control. This implies the use of financial control styles even in product markets where such a style is inappropriate. Firms that use systems of control that clearly apply the principles of 'good financial practice' are more likely to be understood and favoured by the financial community. They may be expected to be given a higher stock market rating than those firms that for operational reasons adopt more organic or more product orientated management styles. Similary, the stock market is likely to be more forgiving of a management style that it approves of. Thus a temporary downturn in profits is more likely to be attributed to uncontrollable external factors rather than management failure. The stock market understands control and incentive systems that penalise capital hoarding or cash withholding even though these systems invariably encourage a cautious attitude toward investment and innovation. The control style also emphasises the salability of business units within the company thus making restructuring easier and clarifying lines of responsibility for the management of these units. The drawbacks are likely to be difficult to observe but must include not only the problem of financial entrepreneurism mentioned about but also a failure to exploit promising technological linkages.[6]

g. Investment decision-making is another area where the closeness of the relationship between owners and managers is likely to affect outcomes. Williamson compares investment decision-making with firms with decision- making by the external market and concludes that the former is likely to be more 'forgiving' and less dominated by 'strict pecuniary benefit' (Williamson, 1985, p.150). Which process is 'best' is clearly debatable since transaction cost economics is essentially based on comparing institutions rather than attempting to specify optimal models as in the orthodox welfare approach.[7]

Biologists usually argue that any particular organism will represent a compromise in terms of the different functions that it has to fulfil in order to survive and reproduce. Thus the stag will impress his rivals by possessing large antlers but may find that excessive size may leave him floundering in the bog.

In the model of the firm proposed in this chapter it is suggested that the imperative of one environment (the market for control) effectively dominates efficient adaptation in other, socially more significant, markets such as the product market. Some of the stylised facts presented above as well as alternative interpretations of conflicting pressures will be looked at again in chapter nine.

4. Some preliminary remarks on the implications for accounting and management control

4.1 Changes in accounting practice are not necessarily 'progressive'

The process of organisational change described above has a number of characteristics which help to explain changes in accounting practices and also suggest a more active role for accounting in the adaptation process. Since it is argued that the organisational changes themselves do not increase economic efficiency except in an extremely partial and transient sense, it cannot be argued that there is an automatic linkage between accounting and efficiency (Burchell, et al, 1980). The process of adaptation is 'Lamarckian' but it is not necessarily 'progressive'. Pressures from the environment (especially the market for control) may hasten accounting changes based on imitation and more formal learning processes. It is not suggested that the actual outcomes result in greater rationality. Indeed, as Alchian has pointed out, the more the environment is characterised by uncertainty the more *ex post* profit is due to luck rather than 'good management' (Alchian, 1950).

4.2 An increase in the importance of financial accounting?

At the very least, it can be deduced that a decline in the use of hierarchies and internal labour markets together with a greater reliance on sub-contracting implies an increased role for financial accounting. Furthermore, if the stock market responds predominantly to financial results then we would expect financial imperatives to permeate the organisation so that management accounting itself becomes more financially orientated (see Kaplan and Johnson, 1987). These ideas are looked at in greater detail in chapter eight.

The theory presented above has a far from sanguine view of the efficiency of the stock-market and cannot be said to have a 'de-regulatory' bias. It is true that proposals for regulation whether of the takeover process or of corporate reporting will be based on efficiency rather than distributional arguments. For example, if, as regulators often seem to believe, and, as is argued by writers such as Kaplan (1983), corporate reports *do* have an indirect impact on resource allocation then it is easier to understand the rationale behind some suggested changes in corporate reporting.

4.3 Variants of decentralisation and corporate governance

Hierarchical decomposition 'de-organisation', deindustrialisation are all part of the process of institutional change that must have implications for accounting techniques and conventions. Thus a model which describes a decline of hierarchical structures in the UK and US predicts that, as hierarchy declines, the measurement mode becomes less important and the contractual/ constitutional mode becomes more important.

A variety of hierarchical forms do still survive 'organisational bust'. For example, in terms of the 'screw-driver' operation, we still have a hierarchical organisation but since we have a stable or 'off the shelf' technology there is low performance ambiguity. There is thus a closer correspondence between the measures used for management accounting and those used for financial reporting and the whole operation is more transparent to the stock-market. The theoretical and empirical characteristics of the 'screw-driver and warehouse' firm are looked at in greater detail in chapter seven.

In spite of the recent phase of corporate unbundling and going private through LBO/MBO's, the diversified M-form of 'decomposed hierarchy' is clearly still important. Both the theory and the institutional data are ambiguous in this respect. For example, takeover booms both create and destroy conglommerates. Indeed, it is difficult to decide what the role of the M-form is in terms of the market for control. Divisionalisation makes both takeovers easier in terms of post-merger integration and also facilitates the control of even larger companies. On the other hand, the semi-decentralised form makes further decentralisation and even break-up that much easier. These issues are looked at in greater detail in chapters six and nine.

The model is based on a peculiarly 'Anglo-Saxon' system of corporate governance. Thus, if the predominant organisational mode in some countries (for example, Japan and West Germany) tends towards a hierarchical relationship within the capital market (the bank-based economy) then the theory would predict that the accounting profession would play a far less important role in these countries than in the UK where a market relationship is more predominant. It does also help to explain the more technical differences in accounting systems. These issues of comparative corporate governance are also discussed further in chapters six and nine.

4.4 A Pro-active role for accounting?

Much of the theory sees accounting reponding passively to organisational restructuring. Yet there is nothing in the model which rules out a more pro-active role. A number of recent articles have stressed the dynamic of accounting controls. For example, Burchell, et al, (1980) explains how accounting can change 'patterns of visibility'. As they put it:

> Measures of efficiency, for instance, can create possibilities for new targets for managerial intervention and new bases for organisational rewards. Similarly, means for the accounting representation of organisational segments can provide the conditions for the reorganisation of the enterprise and the changing locus of power and influence... (p.16-17).

If, however, these measures of efficiency are flawed (as critics such as Kaplan suggest) then the resulting reorganisations may also be flawed! It seems odd that such vigorous critics of development in accounting can be labelled panglossian as Tinker proposes! Perhaps the real problem of some of Kaplan's observations is that he fails to explain how these erroneous measures have arisen. These and other aspects raised by the model will be elaborated on in subsequent chapters.

5.   Concluding remarks

The abundant 'loose-ends' identified above should be seen as a vindication of the institutionalist methodology rather than a problem. As already noted, the survivalist methodology tends to produce *heuristic* rather than *deterministic* theory. It should be seen as providing a broad framework within which more detailed research may be conducted.

The theory explains a major structural imbalance in the economy in a new way, presenting de-industrialisation in *institutionalist* rather than in sectoral terms (Seal, 1990). The theory illustrates that, far from being panglossian, critical analysis may be developed from an appropriate combination of natural selection and institutionalist theory. Survival is a function of *ex post* profit realisation and the capital market does not ask how the profits were generated. Yet, neither does conventional neoclassical economics. Consequently, a critical analysis of the capital market in the UK - almost a cliché in current policy debate - lacks theoretical underpinning outside the Marxist and Institutionalist literature. The irony is supreme. The intellectual system that is most prominent in its defence of *laissez-faire* capitalism has signally failed to provide an analytical mechanism with which to diagnose the ills of the system it is invoked to defend!

There is clearly a need for further work, particularly, in teasing out the implications for accounting and management control. The framework needs filling with more detailed theories and empirical studies. A start on this work is demonstrated in the remaining chapters of the book.

Notes

1. Much of this material is contained in my article in the Cambridge Journal (Seal, 1990).

2. This term was suggested to me by an anonymous referee of the Cambridge Journal of Economics.

3. The example of Amstrad comes to mind. This company has subcontracted virtually all its manufacturing and makes no attempt to maintain long term links (relational contracting). Transaction cost theory would predict that this leads to quality problems and difficulties in introducing new technology. It also makes the company vulnerable to suppliers developing their own marketing operations as the Koreans are beginning to do (see chapters seven and nine).

4. The possibilities of long run success as a predator is strikingly illustrated by Hanson which, as many critics point out, seems to have generated its growth in earnings per share via dealing rather than via organic growth.

5. This aspect is looked at again in chapters five and eight.

6. GEC seems a good example of this. This company and the industry is looked at in more detail in chapter nine.

7. See chapters six and nine.

5 The theory of the firm and management control

The previous chapter presented a model of an economy where the selection process was informed by the (imperfect) operation of market forces while the population of firms and other governance structures took on a somewhat skeletal appearance with the basic contractual outline suggested but with little of the flesh of institutional life. The theory thus far reflects the asymmetry of the markets and hierarchies tradition. Unsurprisingly for an approach pioneered by economists, it is strong on the analysis of the market and relatively weak on the analysis of hierarchy. The theory also reveals another asymmetry common in economic analysis. The emphasis is on *structures* rather than *processes*. As discussed in chapter three, TCE has developed the governance branch to a greater extent than the measurement branch.

A true comparative institutions approach must be more symetrical by looking at the allocative modes offered by the firm and the various forms of relational contracting. In this chapter, I propose to begin a more symmetrical analysis by linking transactions cost theory to the management control literature to create a 'Management Control theory of the Firm'. In terms of the 'contracting map of organisation' (figure 3.2 in chapter three) this theoretical elaboration will require both an investigation into 'hierarchical decomposition' and a far richer taxonomy than the simple 'market, hierarchy and clan' framework.

The focus of these developments will remain the 'theory of the firm' which imposes a deliberate restriction on the scope of the exercise. This limitation is especially important when a new literature such a 'management control' is introduced into the book. It is additionally important when, as will be discussed below, there is some debate concerning the subject matter of a management control paradigm.

Limiting scope does not mean that significant new influences are excluded since, as will be seen, a *process* perspective on economic allocation puts more influence on issues of control, ownership and the labour process - all areas where 'radical' writers have made important contributions. This chapter will concentrate mainly on issues of process control, somewhat unexpectedly revealing that this apparently 'technocratic' approach involves a more explicit analysis of ownership than is usually supplied by contractual theorists. Furthermore, the control approach also highlights the role of the labour process. In the next chapter, the control of labour is compared and contrasted with the control of investment. The ultimate objective is to integrate these two traditions in a new 'holistic' theory of the firm.

I have explained in previous chapters that the TCE/OFF paradigms have many advantages for modelling accounting issues. In particular, the role of accounting is 'constructed' from a theory of the firm. Accounting is similarly located in the management control paradigm in that the research agenda is one of *organisational control*. Accounting, together with other instruments of control, has to justify itself within that agenda.

1. Towards a synthesis of transaction cost economics and management control

1.1 A revised working definition of the 'Theory of the Firm'

Although there has already been much discussion of what is meant by the 'Theory of the firm', an 'update' on a working definition would seem to be appropriate at this stage. The spirit of this endeavour is to stress the *relative* rather than *absolute* superiority of a particular theory. Too much space has already been wasted in the literature over arguments concerning the merits of behavioural versus neoclassical models of the firm. With this caveat in mind, it is suggested that previous theories have been deficient in two areas:

a. Those in the neoclassical tradition have exhibited the well known 'Black box' syndrome. The internal allocation of resources and matters or organisational decision making were grossly neglected/oversimplified because the focus of attention was on market structure and on an equilibrium analysis of output and pricing in an industry.

b. Models of organisational behavioural (including the so-called 'Behavioural theory of the Firm') have relied unduly on *ad hoc* assumptions and been overly microanalytical. This has reduced their generality and applicability to a more macroeconomic perspective.

As has been already been discussed, the new institutional economics responds to both the above criticisms. The Agency solution is to play down the market/firm distinction. The Transaction cost solution is to propose a comparative institutional theory that operates with consistent behavioural assumptions across the market/hierarchy divide yet recognises differences in allocative mechanisms operating in different governance structures. There is, however, the asymetry in development that was noted above- the costs of using the market have been exhaustively analysed while the costs of using hierarchy have been almost totally neglected.

For example, in a pioneering attempt to formalise the basic theory of transaction costs and asset specificity, Riordan and Williamson (1985) present the following diagram (figure 5.1).

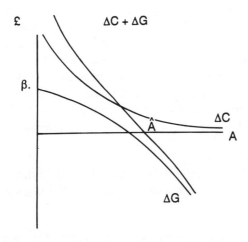

**Figure 5.1 Asset Specificity, transaction and production costs
(from Riordan & Williamson, 1985, p. 368)**

The horizontal axis represents increasing asset specificity (A). The curve (G) shows how the transaction cost difference between firm and market organisation changes with increases in asset specificity. The curve (C) shows how production cost differences respond to increasing asset specificity. As the authors point out, they 'employ a reduced form type of analysis, in that we ascribe rather than derive the basic production and governance cost competencies of firms and markets'(p. 366, Riordan and Williamson, 1985). They later lament the lack of research on bureaucratic costs which may be used

93

in a comparative institutional framework. Since they seem to be looking in what they term the 'sociology literature', it is perhaps not surprising! If they had looked at the management control literature then they might have had greater success.

The proposed way forward is a synthesis of the management control literature and TCE literature. Of course, in the search for commonalities, the sensibilities of the purists in both traditions might be outraged by too many simplifications and compromises. The TCE theorist may baulk at the overt abandonment of neoclassical constraints while the management control researcher may be equally shocked by the spirit of instrumentalism and positivism pervading the whole exercise.

1.2   The management control paradigm

The seminal contribution in this field (at least from an accounting perspective) is generally attributed to Anthony (1965) whose classification of costs and associated activities has provided a focal point of discussion. Indeed, Anthony's perspective on management control (MC, henceforth) has been awarded paradigmatic status by both supporters and critics (see, for example, Lowe and Machin, 1983; Chua, et al, 1989). Treating Anthony's later books (Anthony and Dearden, 1980; Anthony, Dearden and Bedford, 1984) as representing the orthodoxy, Chua, et al, base their critique on a number of counts:

a. The othodox MC paradigm is unduly inward looking- insufficient attention is paid to the relationship between the organisation and its environment.

b. The distinction between planning and control limits the control function to feedback type mechanisms.

c. The hierarchical classification of management activities together with a narrow delineation of the domain of management control should be replaced by a more holistic concept of control.

As Lowe and Chua (Chua, et al., 1989) point out, these criticisms are linked. They also argue that there has been a failure to recognise that 'action to improve control in one area of the organisation will almost certainly have repercussions on other aspects of the organisation' (p. 21). These issues would be explicitly recognised by a more holistic and less hierarchical approach.

The limitation of the hierarchical model means that prediction is the function of top management who are supposed to have sole responsibility for strategic planning. Yet, this rigid delineation will tend to reduce the effectiveness of the middle manager who is responsible for management control. Lowe and Puxty argue that for the middle manager 'a predictive function as to future actions in his environment is essential to his effectiveness as a manager' (p. 21). The traditional model puts an emphasis on the 'feedback function: on corrections of the past.' (p. 21).

These views are quite consistent with the Austrian perspective introduced in earlier chapters which promotes the decentralised nature of economic knowledge and action. Lowe's and Puxty's views on 'voluntarism' and 'rationality' are also consistent with the suvivor model presented in the previous chapter. They are critical of Anthony's discussion of the goals of an organisation, arguing that 'they cannot be considered in isolation from the context in which it exists'(p. 23) While they do not subscribe to a theory of environmental determinism, they do suggest that the 'context will constrain the organisation- it will imbue the organisation through the fact that the members of the organisational coalition are also members of the environment'(p.23). This means that the goals of the organisation cannot be decided 'by' the organisation.

I submit that the discussion in previous chapters has already suggested some responses to the above criticisms. In other words, an explicit use of economic paradigms provides an almost automatic counterbalance to the accounting based tradition of management control. This submission may seem like another example of economic imperialism. The discussion below should dispel such a notion. Indeed, some of the traditional strengths of the management control approach, especially the use of systems theory, fills a significant gap in the usual economics approach. Even the much criticised 'feed-back' mechanism has been neglected with its special role in adaptive decision-making.

With respect to Lowe and Puxty's comment on the *isolation* of the organisation, it should be pointed out that, *so far,* the theoretical analysis has taken a rather 'deterministic' view of managerial goals. For example, the model of the selection process presented in the previous chapter gives managers relatively little discretion concerning organisational goals. Other perspectives which give managers some element of 'strategic choice' will be extensively analysed in chapter nine. Suffice it to say, in the theories presented so far, and emphasised in this chapter, management goals *do* seem to have been determined by the external environment. To put it another way, the emphasis has been on *natural* rather than *rational* selection and on 'open' rather than 'closed systems'.

1.3   Adapting the management control paradigm

In order to effect a synthesis of different paradigms some adaptation of both traditions is necessary. In the light of the above critique, a choice must be made as to how to adapt the management control paradigm and which version of the 'Theory of the firm' to link it with.

Berry in Lowe and Machin (1983) argues that management control research may move in different directions. One direction is concerned with exploring possible alternative definitions of the subject. This approach reflects the eclectic nature of management control and the diversity of disciplines influencing it. As well as the traditional management accounting orientation, research has drawn on sociology, psychology, social psychology, organisational theory (itself, implying different approaches in this area). There is even an increasing interest in the application of political theories, both for studying the organisation internal workings and also in order to understand its environment. This is particularly important when management control is applied to the regulatory challeges generated by the world wide fashion for privatisation. In this manifestation, the emphasis seems to be 'how do we control management?' rather than the more traditional question of 'how do managers control organisations?'.

The disciplinary influence of most concern in this book is obviously an economics one. Many would argue that this means working with a very traditional model of management control where the organisational objective of the firm is something like profit maximisation and the specification of the firm's production function is relatively unproblematic. However, the theory of the firm is not just about achieving this objective. As we have seen, the firm is a vital if relatively underresearched actor in the wider economy. We have also seen that in agency and transaction cost perspectives, the production function is underspecified.

It is indeed true that, as we shall see in the next chapter, these theories have led to a view of the corporation which is remarkably similar to Anthony's hierarchical model. Yet, as we shall also see, the alleged efficiency properties of this model may be criticised from within the institutionalist paradigm.

The main adaptation of the management control paradigm, therefore, is to present it with a problematic derived from economics. In other words, to explore the possibility of developing a management control theory of the firm. In terms of Berry's approach this means assuming an economic definition of the subject and applying to relatively the unfamiliar phenomena and problems which arise in the wider economy beyond the organisation.

The process of choice of an appropriate theory of the firm has been an important part of the discussion in the preceding chapters. To avoid repetition, therefore, the arguments will be presented in a highly abbreviated form with specific reference to the debate in the management control literature alluded to above.

1.4 Adapting the transaction cost economics paradigm: control processes and the wider economy

Much of the adaptation of the theory of the firm has already begun in previous chapters. For example, it has been argued that in the orthodox neoclassical theory of the firm (see chapters 1 and 2) there is an over emphasis on the structure (especially market structure) of which the firm is a part. There is a neglect of process and, in particular, a neglect of the inner workings of firm. Crucially, orthodox theory simply assumes that resources in the firm will be efficiently controlled - costs, whether they be 'managed' or 'engineered', will be minimised. The debate (such as it is) has been limited to looking at the goals of the firm in terms of an appropriate maximand (e.g. profit maximisation v management utility maximisation).

In contrast to orthodox theory, newer approaches to the firm (introduced in chapter three) do not assume technical efficiency - in a world of costly information and limited human cognitive capacities, the new institutional theory recognises the need for the firm to be managed (see Putterman, 1988). In agency theory, the firm is so open as to have no core at all - it is a 'legal fiction'. Although, as was discussed in chapter 3, *two* agency literatures may be identified, both have a strong neoclassical emphasis on the structure (i.e. contractual relationships) of the firm with virtually no comment on process.

Predictably, perhaps, the most appropriate theory of the firm linking the two literatures is provided by transaction cost economics (TCE). The 'TCE firm' has an identifiable 'core' but remains essentially an open system. The extent of the 'core' or, at least, the boundary between the firm and the market is at the heart of the paradigm. The minimisation of costs (engineered and managed) are the motor mechanism of organisational design with organisational boundaries and internal governance structures adapting to minimise transaction costs. It may even be possible to see close parallels between 'managed' costs and 'governance costs'.

As introduced in chapter three, Ouchi (1977; 1980) considers the relative merits of the hierarchical or bureaucratic form.[1] Its advantage over markets is that it can use the employment relation whereby the worker accepts wages in exchange for submitting to the organisation the right to appoint superior officers who can direct work activities day to day. There is no need to deal with the future 'all at once' as might be necessary in the market mode of organisation. Furthermore, the bureaucracy can closely monitor employees' performance and thus minimise instances of opportunism. Unlike markets, bureaucratic organisations can create an atmosphere of trust and thereby develop goal congruence. However, in contrast with clans, bureaucracies are vulnerable when the ambiguity of performance evaluation becomes high (see figure 3.2).

Bureaucratic systems rely upon 'rules'. The problem here is that it is not possible to specify a set of rules which covers every possible contingency. There may, in other words, be a problem of overload. 'Traditions' may be interpreted as implicit rather than explicit rules. They constitute somewhat crude information in terms of performance evaluation. They also tend to take a long time to understand. This is because the aim is to develop a 'philosophy' which enables the individual to deduce an appropriate rule to govern any possible situation. In other words, they are developed through a slow process but one which ultimately produces 'a very elegant and complete form of control' (Ouchi, 1980 p. 139).

The key role in clan-formation is clearly played by the socialisation process. The minimum condition for successful socialisation is stability. Any elements of instability induced by, for example, employment termination is likely to inhibit clan-formation/maintenance. If clan control is weak then the choice is between placing greater emphasis on bureaucracies with their higher transaction costs or switching to activities and technologies which can be organised via markets.

This latter course has already been related to deindustrialisation in the previous chapter. Or, in other words, it provides a new way of understanding of loss of competitiveness and changes in comparative advantage. The theory is unequivocal. *Those economies which have no comparative advantage in clan organisation are forced back to market organisation and the use of low-level/inspecific technologies.*

The OFF seems to meet the criteria outlined earlier - reducing the 'black box' syndrome, remaining economical with assumptions and offering a macroeconomic application. Ouchi has sometimes been accused of plagiarism. While it is true that he could have been a little more scrupulous in acknowledging similar work to his own in the organisational theory literature, he has made a significant contribution by linking the transaction cost model with a wider organisational/management control literature. The originality of Ouchi's ideas may be a subjective matter depending upon the intellectual background of the reader. For example, to an economist, Ouchi's work usefully builds a bridge from contractual theory to behavioural thinking. From the perspective of the management control theorist, many of the ideas above have already been explored in the organisational/management control literature.

As was seen in chapter three, in terms of agency theory, the clan may be represented as the cooperative solution (Baiman, 1990). In other words, the precondition for the archtypal agency problem is absent due to the high level of goal convergence between principals and agents. Another way of characterising the clan is to apply the concepts and language of systems theory. This is a logical development in the book as the research programme moves away from both mechanical equilibrium and homeostatic models towards seeing the economy as a 'complex adaptive system' (Buckley, 1968).

2. The theory of the firm and systems theory

2.1 A 'systems' outlook

The management control literature is redolent with references to cybernetics and systems theory. For many, this may be understood in terms of the practical application of computers to problems of information processing and communication. However, General systems theory has far more fundamental implications which extend beyond technical matters to issues of research methodology and scientific method (Bertalanffy, 1968).

Although writing in a sociological context, Buckley's view of society as a 'complex adaptive system', provides a useful perspective on the OFF model of the firm (Buckley, 1968). Buckley describes equilibrial systems as being 'affected only by external "disturbances" and have *no internal or endogeneous sources of change*; their component elements are *relatively simple and linked directly by energy exchange* (rather than information interchange); and since they are relatively closed they have no feedback or other systematic self-regulating or adaptive capacities'(p. 179, original author's emphasis). He contrasts this with complex adaptive systems which are *'open "internally" as well as externally* in that the interchanges among their components may result in *significant changes in the nature of the components themselves* with important consequences for the system as a whole.' (p. 179, original author's emphasis).

Thus it could be argued that the clan type of firm is concerned with far more than mere homeostatic adaptation since it contains an internally driven dynamic of innovation which actually changes the wider system. As Buckley, describing the complex adaptive system, puts it:

> True feedback control loops make possible not only self-regulation, but self-direction or at least adaptation to a changing environment, such that the system may change or elaborate its structure as a condition of survival or viability (p. 179).

This last point puts a new perspective on the clan as a self-regulating/self directing system. In formal control terms, the ordinary workers are only loosely coupled to a control system. Yet, the organisation is actually more adaptable than a more tightly coupled hierarchical system involving formal controls. As will be discussed later, this superior adaptability is especially significant in dealing with *emergent* problems.

2.2 Feedback or feedforward control?

The traditional emphasis in cybernetics is on negative feedback systems. Such a simple system is illustrated in figure 5.2 This focus has been criticised by writers such as Otley and Berry (1980). Their preferred model is illustrated in figure 5.3 which puts a predictive model of the process to be controlled at the heart of the system.

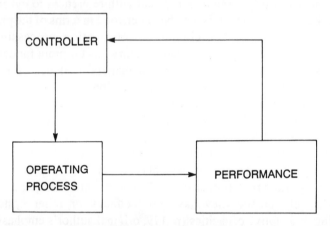

Figure 5.2 Process control: the basic model

Otley argues that such a scheme is superior to the random trial and error process and may be essential 'for the control of human organisations due to the considerable time lags inherent in assessing the effects of a given action' (p. 64, Otley, 1983). He advocates 'feedforward control' arguing that:

> Whereas feedback control awaits the occurrence of an error and then takes action to counteract it, feedforward control anticipates the future occurrence of an error and takes action so as to prevent its actual occurrence (p. 65).

The problem with feedforward control is that the very reason feed back control is used is because a reliable predictive model is unavailable. To put the

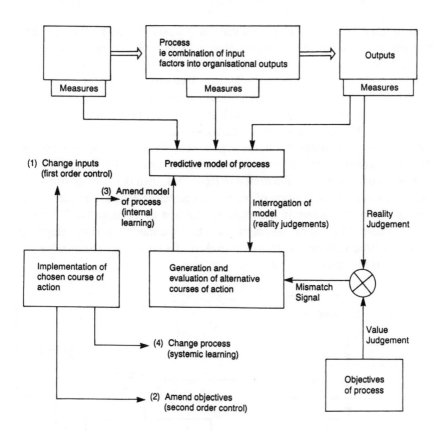

**Figure 5.3 Process control with feedforward
(from Otley and Berry, 1980)[2]**

argument in the context of the theory of the firm, it could be argued that if the future could be reliability predicted then a 'firmlike' decision-making process would be redundant since resources could be allocated through a system of complete contracting. Repeating the point developed in the first chapter, *it is precisely because of uncertainty that the firm and other alternatives to the market have developed!* If all states of the world could be anticipated and planned for, then the agency solution of complete *ex ante* contracts would be the preferred solution together with the return to familiar optimising, equilibrium techniques of analysis.

2.3   Viewing an economy as a 'nested model of control systems'

In this section the OFF is extended to incorporate a model of an entire economy. The perspective on the economy introduced in Chapter four may be recast in terms of a model of nested control systems. While the theory draws on many of the concepts discussed above, its perspective on management control follows the approach outlined by Itami (1975) but adjusted in order to model an economy rather than a single firm. Two aspects of Itami's model are particularly convenient for present purposes, namely:

a.   the importance of feedback in the control process.
b.   a hierarchical view of organisation activity.

With respect to point a., Itami argues that in a dynamic process the difference between planning and corrective action tends to be blurred. Thus if the process of control is as illustrated in figure 5.4, then the "instruction" part of the process is a combination of plans and corrective action. Another useful aspect of Itami's analysis is the explicit adoption of a hierarchical form of control system. This useful assumption enables the model to be developed in terms of 'nested systems' whereby controllers of a system are answerable to a 'superior' as illustrated in figure 5.4.

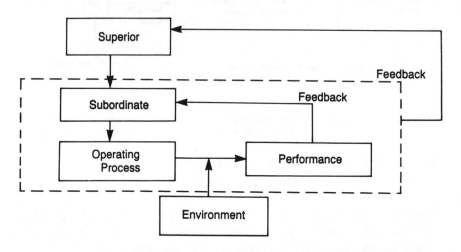

Figure 5.4 **Nested control systems (from Itami, 1975)**

Itami does not discuss the possible criticisms invited by using such terms such as 'hierarchy' or 'superior'. In fact, his approach is relatively easy to relate to the model introduced in the previous chapter. Both the markets and hierarchies literature and its more recent TCE presentation emphasise the general efficiency properties of the *authority relation*. However, this new presentation reverses the tables on the usual markets and hierarchy model. Where traditionally the hierarchy is analysed as an internal market - in this approach, as shown in figure 5.5, the market is seen as a form of hierarchy!

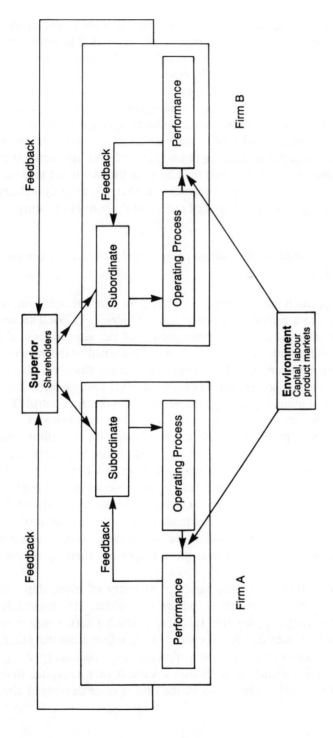

Figure 5.5 The economy as a hierarchy of nested control systems

In figure 5.5 the superior may be seen as the shareholder/owner while the individual control systems may be represented as firms. The environment is, as described in the previous chapter, comprised of different markets - product, labour, capital markets and so on. The diagram illustrates the dominance of the market for control which, it is usually argued, offers shareholders a disciplining mechanism over the firm's managers. The diagram also illustrates the main flow of information. A hierarchical aggregation of information suggests that information is likely to be financial rather than non-financial with control based on *output* monitoring rather than on *behaviour* monitoring.

It is important to emphasise that the aim of this model is not to construct a prescriptive model of a command economy. Rather, it is to analyse the *market* mechanism using the terminology and criteria of the control literature - a quite different endeavour.

2.4 Implications of an information perspective: management control and a theory of ownership.

The above approach models economic activity in terms of *information flows* rather in the more orthodox *resource* terms (Aldrich, 1979). The need for management control is a direct consequence of the assumptions of costly information and bounded rationality. If control is exerted by the owners via the appointment/replacement of subordinates rather than via day-to-day supervision then this power may be exercised either through direct control of voting shares or indirectly through the so-called market for control. To many neoclassical economists, the presentation of the market economy in such stark authority terms is generally avoided. The distaste for modelling issues of management is matched by a similar distaste for explicitly analysing hierarchical relationships. For example, Alchian and Demsetz (1972) even suggest in a renowned passage that the employer has no more power over the employee than the grocer has over a customer. In a neoclassical world, terms such as 'power' and 'authority' are redundant since no one or no institution are deemed to possess such attributes. As we have already seen, there not only is no theory of firms' existence but, more surprising, there is no theory of *ownership*.

Putterman (1988) shows the need for a theory of ownership once the simplicities of the neoclassical world are left behind. He characterises the neoclassical firm as a 'production function to which a maximand-profit - has been assigned', argues that the 'owner' of such a firm possesses the right to select the production programme and appropriate the residual (p. 247). There is no need for this person to actually own a resource such as capital. In the new institutional economics, the theory of the firm is more developed since it is argued that the owner of the firm 'must do more than simply determine a production programme and collect the profits; he must also *manage*' (p. 248, original author's emphasis). As Putterman shows, this new literature explains (in terms of efficiency) why capital hires labour and why the firm must be saleable. Furthermore, the new institutionalist literature implies that 'ownership and control cannot be separated without sacrificing efficiency'(p. 252). Putterman not only demonstrates the fundamental importance of ownership and saleability in the attainment of the alleged efficiency properties of the conventional capitalist firm but also finds a curious coyness in explaining the nature and pivotal role of the shareholder in much of the agency literature. Indeed, Putterman argues that the literature tends to 'obscure a central aspect of the nature of production organisation in the capitalist economy: precisely, the ownability of the entity that undertakes the task of organisation, and the exclusion of factors hired by that entity from control and residual rights' (p. 256, Putterman, 1988). The ideological reason for this coyness hardly needs elaboration!

However, the old debate between the power and efficiency approaches to organisation seems somewhat redundant since the *efficiency* of the firm is seen to rest on the *power* and *authority* of the manager-owner-capitalist! Williamson is sometimes close to acknowledging this viewpoint- most agency theorists do not. Those writers who are associated with the power approach have long recognised the link between power and a knowledge of the organisation of production. This knowledge need not be used benignly for as Marglin (1984) points out:

> ... the essence of the capitalist's contribution is not capital, but organising ability; to secure a reward for this service he must impose an organisational form that makes him essential to the production process on a continuing basis. A rentier class is a class ripe for expropriation (p. 150).

The last sentence may have a less 'radical' interpretation. It will be argued in this book that the control of production via financial controls is essentially the control technique of a rentier class. Or, to put it in terms of the deindustrialisation debate already introduced, an economy that manages its organisations in a rentier fashion is likely to to find that the whole economy and not just the capitalist class pays the price of expropriation! However much radicals may be appalled at the thought, the radical emphasis on control and the labour process has interesting 'technocratic' or efficiency implications which have not been fully developed. The next section illustrates this point by looking at the thinking stimulated by the 'paradigm wars' between Williamson, Marglin and others.

3. The organisation of work: the employment relation, hierarchy and the 'putting-out' debate

3.1 Deindustrialisation modelled as the 'putting-out' debate in reverse

Much of Williamson's analysis in 'Markets and Hierarchies' is specifically concerned with comparisons between internal and external labour markets. In particular, his concern is to explain the special efficiency advantages of the former. In his later works, drawing on the transaction cost approach, he discusses the same issue in terms of human asset specificity. This area has attracted much critical attention, particularly from those who argue that hierarchies are more to do with power than economic efficiency (Marglin, 1974). The so-called 'putting-out' debate is often referred to in this context. Although this is essentially a debate about an historical process, it is of particular relevance in a book which is analysing a contemporary change 'in the opposite direction'. In other words, just as the change of work organisation from putting-out to factories is associated in some way with early industrialisation so the process of work externalisation may be associated with the reverse process of deindustrialisation! This viewpoint may be summarised in the following diagram.

Table 5.1
A transaction costs interpretation of organisational and structural change: a first summary

merchant capitalism	→	industrial capitalism	→	financial capitalism
putting out	→	factory system	→	deindustrialisation
classical contracting	→	hierarchy	→	classical contracting

The first row in the table presents a stylised sequence of events where changes are recorded according to conventional economic systems labels. The second row views events in terms of 'modes of production'. The third row classifies historical change in transactions costs terminology. The usual debate is over whether the above changes can be explained in terms of economic efficiency or in terms of 'power'.

Williamson argues that the system of 'putting-out' was replaced because it was simply more inefficient than the factory system of production. He cites Braverman (1974) who:

> ... goes on to observe that the subcontracting and "putting-out" systems were plagued by problems of irregularity of production, loss of materials in transit and through embezzlement, slowness of manufacture, lack of uniformity and uncertainty of the quality of the product. But most of all, they were limited by their inability to change the processes of production (Williamson, 1985, p. 232).

To illustrate the alternative or, what he terms, the 'radical' viewpoint, Williamson quotes Marglin (1974):

> [T]he agglomeration of workers into factories was natural outgrowth of the putting-out system (a result if you like of its internal contradictions) whose success had little or nothing to do with technological superiority of large scale machinery. The key to the success of the factory, as well as its inspiration, was the substitution of capitalists' for workers' control of the production process; discipline and supervision could and did reduce costs *without* being technologically superior (p. 46, emphasis in original).

It is not intended in this chapter to attempt to resolve or take sides in the above debate. The issue is indirectly relevant because, whatever the rights and wrongs of the early industrialisation process, it is contended that *a theory which explains industrial development can also be used to explain the reverse process*. Indeed, it could be argued that the social, political and economic results of deindustrialisation are far less ambiguous in welfare terms than was the original process of industrialisation. This is clearly evident when so many of the critics of deindustrialisation can also be classified as Williamsonian 'radicals'. Apart from the obvious link with general unemployment in older industrialised countries, the changes in the labour market introduced by the externalisation of work, casualisation and sub-contracting are all criticised by Trades Unions and their political supporters for very clear reasons. In terms of a 'power analysis', deindustrialisation does not imply a return to worker control *à la* Marglin. The capitalists are still in control but they are now 'absentee landlords' rather than 'yeoman farmers' and the workers are transparently both politically and economically weaker!

The more general point emerging from the new putting-out debate is that the control of work is not purely a matter of workers' versus capitalists' sovereignty. Or to put it more boldly, hierarchical models of work may be seen to be inefficient as well as unjust.[3] In particular, it may be argued that they impede both the vertical and horizontal flow of information in an organisation. The first point can be illustrated using the TCE concept of Human asset specificity. The second requires some discussion of slightly different concept of 'organisationally specific assets'.

3.2 Human asset specificity and management control

Just as asset specificity is of crucial importance in the basic analysis of transactions so the specificity of the human asset is of note. Skill alone does not imply human asset specificity. Williamson (1985) puts it as follows:

> ...{S}kills that are acquired in a learning-by-doing fashion and are imperfectly transferable across employers have to be *embedded in a protective governance structure* lest productive values be sacrificed if the employment relation is unwittingly severed (original emphasis, p.243).

As with non-human assets, specificity indicates the necessity of contractual safeguards. Williamson also raises the issue of *separability* of tasks. As discussed earlier, if output cannot be satisfactorily monitored (in this case due to an inability to observe individual productivity) then control must be based on "behaviour control" rather than "output control" *à la* Ouchi (1977). In their celebrated article, Alchian and Demsetz (1972) regarded such a problem as being both necessary and sufficient for the existence of firms. The subsequently recognised element of asset specificity has now to be included in the contractual scheme.

Williamson (1985) lists four possible sets of arrangements:

a. Internal spot market - human assets are separable and nonspecific - 'Workers can move between employers without loss of productivity, and firms can secure replacements without incurring start-up costs.' (p. 245)

b. Primitive team - human assets are nonspecific but individual output hard to measure.

c. Obligational market - individual output easy to measure but human assets are firm specific.[4]

d. Relational team - human assets are specific and there is a significant 'team' aspect.[5]

The implications of human asset specificity may be directly related to the issues raised by Kaplan (1983;1984). Kaplan discusses the difficulties that develop when an internal/external spot market develops in large manufacturing corporations. In other words, he identifies the problems that arise when there is a clash between labour market trends in the executive labour market where mobility between firms and divisions is becoming more and more rapid and the requirements of a long-term strategy of manufacturing development. To some extent, these problems have already been discussed in connection with both divisionalisation and the investment decision. The general problems as we have seen is that the emphasis on 'performance control' is hampered by the ambiguity of the financial indicators. In particular, profit indicators are vulnerable to short-run manipulation. This becomes a serious problem if increased managerial mobility between divisions and especially between companies means that the perpetrators are able to avoid the consequences of their opportunism. Kaplan (1984) seems to be identifying the growth of a 'spot market' in managers when he suggests that;

> ... there may have been a shift in hiring practices during the past 60 years. Formerly, employees, especially those destined to become divisional and senior managers, tended to spend their entire careers with the same firm. This there would be less incentive for them to take actions that would not be in the interests of the firm. As a professional management class developed in the US during the middle part of the 20th century, certainly abetted by the rapid increase of MBAs whose managerial skills were more transferable across different firms, turnover probably increased, thereby reducing the incentives for those managers to avoid actions that would compromise the long-term viability of their current firm (p. 412).

3.3 Organisational specific assets - horizontal information flows, participation and organisation rent

Kaplan's ideas and critics will be looked in more detail in chapter eight. His views can easily be accommodated within a hierarchical perspective on the firm since his main concern is with vertical flows of information. As we shall see, he is a leading advocate of the 'Japanese cure'. Another such advocate, who takes a somewhat different view on what that cure actually consists of, is Aoki (1984;1986;1990a;1990b). He has emphasised the superior *horizontal* flow of information in the Japanese firm. This enables it to respond much more efficiently to 'emergent problems' than is the case with the hierarchical or cell form of firm. Aoki is critical of the traditional hierarchical model of firm. He prefers a new mode of 'intra-organisational co-ordination ... which relies more upon participatory information processing by, and communication among, workers (shops) than does the traditional hierarchical structure, which is characterised by the specialised separation between co-ordination and operating tasks as well as among different operating tasks' (Aoki, 1990a, p. 27).

Aoki argues that participatory information processing generates rents which are both organisationally specific and collective in nature. Aoki's ideas will feature in all the remaining chapters. For the purposes of this chapter, it will be sufficient to note an approach which is compatible with many aspects of TCE but not with its claimed association between an authority based employment relation and economic efficiency.

4. Concluding remarks

The juxtaposition of an economics agenda with General Systems Theory (GST) may at first sight seem overly ambitious - an oil and water operation. However, in some respects the integration of economic theory with GST is less of a problem than it is with other social sciences. For example, there is less need to face up to criticisms of functionalism or authoritarianism- not because they are not possibilities but because conventional economic theory is even more vulnerable to such criticism!

The management control approach may be seen to incorporate some quite contrasting ideological bedfellows. In contrast to traditional neoclassical theory both the new institutionalists and the 'radicals' have revived interest in the role of the labour process in production. The labour process debate need not be seen in stark ideological terms since both radicals and new institutionalist have contributed to a greater understanding of the source of economic surplus. Both are agreed that economic resources need to be managed. Views vary, however, on how and for whose benefit those resources should be controlled. The significance of horizontal information flows as well as vertical information flows has taken the analysis of the firm back to the fundamentals of the nature of economic knowledge. These matters will be pursued further in the next chapter.

Notes

1. This interpretation of TCE clearly emphasises the 'measurement branch'. Williamson suggests that those interested in that branch should consult Ouchi's work rather than his own.

2. Diagram reproduced from 'Control, Organization and Accounting', by Otley, D. and Berry, A. in *Accounting, Organizations and Society,* vol.5, pp. 95-112,(1980) with permission from Pergamon Press Ltd, Headington Hill Hall, Oxford OX3 OBW.

3. It is this sort of debate where a focus on process rather than structure is particularly important. Both the Marglin's model of industrialisation and this book' model of deindustrialisation discuss the role of hierarchy. Yet, Marglin's hierarchy relies on behavioural control while the hierarchical model outlined here is degenerate because of its reliance on output/financial control.

4. Merchant banks provide an example of this type of human asset specificity.

5. The clan is particularly important in this situation.

6 Management control and hierarchical decomposition

In chapter five it was suggested that one way to escape from the 'black box' theory was to view the firm in terms of an open and adaptive system. Two literatures - the management control literature and the TCE literature - were linked with the aim of developing a 'Management Control' theory of the firm. A number of alternative control models were considered. It was argued that a 'Nested Control systems model' could be modified in a way that related internal control processes to external control processes. The level of generality was necessarily high - the content of the boxes discussed were still a relatively short step away from being 'black'!

This chapter continues the development of a richer model of internal allocation - a model which will be progressively elaborated and tested in successive chapters. Once again it draws on both the management control and transaction cost/OFF literature. However, the level of generality is reduced by looking at the economics of internal organisation and, in particular, the concept of 'hierarchical decomposition'. The methodology of comparative institutionalism is critically examined in the context of internal and external markets in capital and labour. Finally, a brief survey of some recent comparative work is conducted which indicates the complex interactions between measurement and control.

The accounting and finance literature presents two basic paradigms - the control of capital investment decision and the control of the labour process. Both are regarded as being necessary functions of management but little theoretical work has been done on the articulation of the tensions between two approaches which have, until recently, been based on quite different theoretical perspectives. This observation, of course, excludes Marxist and radical theorists who have long regarded the firm not just as a domain of tension but as a locus of fundamental contradiction and conflict between capital and labour. A management control model of the firm may be seen as both a path to theoretical reconciliation and as a vehicle for practical accommodation. This latter motive may be regarded by some radicals as being both hopelessly naive and even sinister. It may be the former but it is not the latter. The spirit of the approach is not to deny the existence of conflicting interests as does so much neoclassical theory. It is rather to work on the premise that production under *any* form of ownership or social system will involve a certain level of conflict and inequality.

1.   Hierarchical decomposition

In the previous chapter, the firm was modelled as a simple hierarchy controlled both internally and externally via a feed back process. The model focused principally on vertical linkages. Two important issues were omitted. One concerned the scope of the enterprise - its 'horizontal' dimension. The other was concerned with the *process* of control. For example, what is the nature of the information flowing through the cybernetic model? Is it financial or non-financial? Is the flow continuous or discrete? The TCE paradigm has provided some answers in the so-called 'M-form hypothesis'. This hypothesis serves as a useful basis of discussion. However, I will argue that there are substantial weaknesses in the hypothesis. Some of these weaknesses may be revealed by returning to 'first principles' as outlined in chapter one. Others are revealed by the growing body of research into international comparisons of business organisation and management control.

1.1   The M-form hypothesis

The basic arguments of the M-form hypothesis are well known and will not be repeated in detail (see Williamson, 1970; 1975; 1985; Chandler, 1962; 1977). Most of the main ideas have been absorbed not only into the academic literature but also into management education syllabi and texts. The hypothesis is not without its critics. For example, as he clearly anticipates, some of the debate in economics has been around Williamson's assertion that 'the modern corporation is mainly to be understood as the product of a series of organisational innovations that have the purpose and effect of economising on transactions costs' (1985, p. 273). Or, in other words, organisational form here, as elsewhere in the paradigm, can be explained largely by the *efficiency* rather than the *monopoly* branch of economics.

This important debate is largely beyond the scope of this book. I submit that the M-form hypothesis can be criticised in its own terms - that there are both theoretical and empirical reasons for questioning Williamson's rationalisation of the divisionalised company on efficiency grounds alone! Although I will criticise the M-form both in terms of the measurement branch and the governance branch, as the following discussion indicates, the two branches are particular intimately connected in this area.

The M-form hypothesis rationalises a *structure* precisely because of its *information processing* capabilities. Yet, from an architectural perspective, the organisational chart of the M-form is almost indistinguishable from the H-form (holding company). Williamson argues that the M-form 'adds (1) a strategic planning and resource allocation capability and (2) monitoring and control apparatus' (1985, p. 281). More specifically, he proposes that the M-form has a Head Office which will provide these capabilities.

1.2 Double feedback and hierarchy

In the M-form hypothesis, information processing is 'factored' in two ways. Firstly, there is a distinction drawn between operating and strategic decision-making. Williamson draws on Ashby's double feedback model of adaptation which proposes a primary feedback loop and a secondary feedback loop (1985, p. 282). The former deals with operating decisions while the latter deals with strategic decisions. Secondly, these decision-making functions are factored in a vertical, hierarchical fashion.

The operating part of the organisation uses given rules and is composed of parts which have frequent interaction. It has to adapt to changes of degree rather than of kind. In contrast, the strategic part of the organisation adapts to changes in kind which are assumed to involve a lower degree of frequency both in terms of decision making and organisational interaction.

In assessing the need for changes in kind, the simple double feedback model seems to suggest that the strategic part can monitor the environment as easily as the operating part. This approach conflicts with the insights of the 'Austrians' among others. Thus, while it is easy to draw systems diagrams showing information flows, we need to know whether relevant information can actually be codified and transmitted through the hierarchy. For example, financial information may be routinely collected and easy to transmit but, as we have already discussed, it is not the same as 'economic knowledge'. Of course, if the systems solution was really that straightforward then the performance, or at least the reform of, centrally planned economies might have been more successful!

Of course, the general arguments for decentralisation of decision-making are very convincing. However, it is less obvious that the proposed vertical factoring is appropriate in the context of economic decision-making. For example, it assumes that knowledge of strategic matters resides higher up the organisation. In the M-form hypothesis, the head office is supposed to maintain the entrepreneurial vigour of the corporation and curtail goal displacement. Yet, this 'central planning' role contradicts Hayek's insights on the 'knowledge of time and place' which almost, by definition, is located at the *bottom* rather than the top of the organisation (Hayek, 1945). Furthermore, if we add Aoki's 'emergent information', then this also is primarily perceived at the bottom of the organisation. Aoki argues for a decentralised decision-process which facilitates a *'localised'* response to these problems rather than a laborious attempt to transmit information upwards and instructions downwards as envisaged under the hierarchical mode (Aoki, 1984; 1986; 1990a; 1990b).

1.3   The corporation as an internal capital market

The M-form hypothesis claims that the head office will ensure that 'cash flows are re-allocated among divisions to favour high value uses, and internal incentive and control instruments are exercised in a discriminating way'(Williamson, 1985, p. 281). This perception of the corporation as an 'internal capital market' is a central aspect of the hypothesis. It implies that the form of control is *financial*. It also neatly sets up the management problem in terms of the finance paradigm of investment appraisal. Strategic management is thereby reduced to a question of portfolio selection. As the well known 'Boston consulting matrix '(BCM) model demonstrates, even product-market decisions can be presented in this framework. The BCM has been criticised elsewhere (Porter, 1980). My main concern is to question the relevance of the finance model in a world of positive transactions costs.

2.   Capital budgeting, the present value rule and transaction costs

Earlier in the book it was argued that the failure of economic concepts of income asset valuation to gain acceptance could be explained in terms of the *dual* raison d'etre of the firm *and* accounting. In a world of zero transactions costs, there is no need for either firms or accounting - the only economic information required is provided by prices. Conversely, in a world of positive transactions costs, the simultaneous emergence of both accounting and firms as alternatives to market contracting implies that accounting information and contract completion must both be informed by decision rules and information inputs which are based, not on (imperfectly) simulated market processes and market prices, but on conscious attempts to discover alternative criteria and data bases.

In this chapter a similar explanation is offered in the sphere of investment appraisal/capital budgeting. The widespread acceptance of the orthodox economic model in capital budgeting may, at least superficially, present a contrast with its lack of acceptance in the sphere of income measurement. The superficiality of this acceptance is, however, revealed by contrasting the adoption of the present value rule in accountancy and business *education* with the evidence for its sporadic and half-hearted 'real world' application. These stylised facts have been reported by several surveys and a number of *ad hoc* explanations have been offered (Pike, 1982; 1983; 1985; Pike and Ooi, 1988). The aim of this chapter is to explain the stylised facts in terms of the economic theory of the firm that has been elaborated in thisbook. It is argued that the Present Value rule is only theoretically correct in a totally artificial situation in which there would be no need for a firm, let alone a system of formal capital budgeting. It further queries whether capital budgeting deserves separate treatment from other areas of management control such as marketing or the labour process. In other words, it explores the notion that this separation is an artifact of accounting convention in which investment in tangible assets are recognised as capital budgeting decisions such while investment in intangibles are treated as matters of operational control. It is also critical of an approach where decision rules for the internal appraisal and control of the firm's expenditures are based on the same paradigm as those applied in the appraisal of external financial assets. In the latter case, relatively complete markets exist and the PV rule has some legitimate normative authority. In the former case, incomplete markets and interdependencies between projects decisively weaken the authority of the PV rule.

2.1   The present value rule and the orthodox model of investment appraisal

The dominant paradigm of investment appraisal is the so-called Present Value rule and is based on the pure theory of finance as developed by economists such as Hirschleifer (1958). Versions of this theory are disseminated in texts for accounting and business education in addition to being enshrined in professional syllabi. The techniques have become operationally robust with the incorporation of risk into the cost of capital via the Capital Asset Pricing Model. Yet, in the course of this process of development and dissemination, there has been a tendency to either forget or ignore the view of the world informing it!

This may produce curious results in textbooks where a usually brief description of capital budgeting as a process is followed by a lengthy exposition of an economic valuation model based on neoclassical objectives and methodologies. For example, Levy and Sarnat (1990) suggest that:

A systematic approach to capital budgeting implies:
1. The formulation of long-term goals.
2. The creative search for the identification of new investment opportunities.
3. Classification of projects and recognition of economically and/or statistically dependent (independent) proposals.
4. The estimation and forecasting of current and future cash flows.
5. A suitable administrative framework capable of transferring the required information to the decision level.
6. The controlling of expenditures and careful monitoring of crucial aspects of project execution.

Finally a set of decision rules which can differentiate acceptable from unacceptable alternatives is required (p.26).[1]

The choice of the above quotation is intended to illustrate the contradictions underlying the orthodox approach rather than to pick on Levy and Sarnat as examples of poor textbook practice. Indeed, in contrast to many texts, it is to their credit that they have at least given some recognition to the process/administrative aspects of capital budgeting and thus implicitly revealed the conflicting modes of analysis implied in most expositions of the capital budgeting process. In most texts, the choice of 'a set of decision rules' differentiating 'acceptable' from the 'unacceptable alternatives' is generated from a theoretical world of finance where the internal appraisal of a project is assumed to be analytically identical to the external investment in the capital market and there is no discussion of the process of investment decision making.

2.2   The finance view of the world

The techniques of investment evaluation are well known. Less well known are the often implicit assumptions which, if fully articulated, would substantially reduce the normative authority generally attributed to the 'theoretically correct' rules. Both the familiar and the relatively unfamiliar are included in the following list:

a. The firm is viewed as a bundle of projects - a convenience for investors whereby decisions made about the choice of internal investment are exactly analogous to the choice of external investment in financial assets. However, the assumptions about decision-making are so 'neoclassical' that it is not clear why firms are needed in such a world.

b. The PV rule is based on a pure exchange view of the world. As Ball (1990) has pointed out, all modern financial models address the implications of pure exchange assuming that supply is determined exogenously. As Ball puts it:

> The Present Value model addresses the present price of a given future amount, at a given market rate of interest. It is merely an implication of rational investor behaviour in perfect securities markets and does not address the (supply) issue of how the future amount (i.e. a project cash flow) is determined (p. 16).

Ball goes on to develop this critique in the context of the efficient market hypothesis. It would seem, however, that the criticism is actually just as telling when applied to capital budgeting where stylised calculative routines are based on heroic assumptions concerning the estimation of cash flows (see next two points).

c. The emphasis is on financial information/returns to shareholders. This is a well known assumption discussed at least perfunctorily by nearly all the textbooks. The implication for capital budgeting is that capital allocation decisions should be based entirely on the basis of the financial returns to shareholders. The issues raised by managerialism are well known. Less well known are the implicit assumptions concerning the completeness of markets and the Pareto optimality of the stock market (see Stiglitz, (1981)).

d. Markets are complete. In other words, there are no problems in identifying and measuring future revenues. As Kaplan (1983; 1984) and others have argued, this assumption may be an acceptable assumption for well established technologies but it becomes particularly problematical with rapidly changing technology.

e. The treatment of risk is based on portfolio theory and the Capital Asset Pricing Model with all the well known theoretical and empirical problems. In addition, the approach to uncertainty is passive rather than active (see chapter one).

f. The PV rule is often advocated because it concentrates on cash flows and is thus independent of the conventions of accrual accounting. However, the estimation of cash flows is *not* independent of *management accounting*. Various conventions on issues such as overhead allocation and transfer pricing have been developed but no *general* rules have been established to resolve these issues.

The general point, which is developed at length in the next section, is that internal and external capital markets and the associated decision making processes are different. If they were not, then we are in a world of zero contracting costs in which there is no point in having firms at all!

3. A comparative institutional approach to investment appraisal: internal versus external capital markets

The 'finance model of the firm' cannot be dismissed as being little more than a theoretical artifact. Whether by accident or design, some companies 'fit' the theoretical model quite closely. As will be shown later, these companies do seem to run their divisions via a system of financial controls whereby the difference between internal and external investment is quite explicitly minimised. The theory presented in chapter four even suggests that, in certain environments, such firms have superior survival propensities. Some of the macroeconomic implications have already been hinted at - financial efficiency does not necessarily equate to economic effectiveness.

The M-form hypothesis lends itself all too easily to financial control systems using either variants of the PV rule or cruder accounting measures. If the firm can safely be modelled as an internal capital market then the use of methods based on investment appraisal in markets is hard to criticise. Yet, on this line of reasoning it is easy to see how 'corporate unbundling' has become a logical step in the 1980's! In view of the above criticisms, perhaps a more fundamental and theoretically correct use of the 'finance' paradigm is to use it as a stick with which to 'beat' the diversified firm. A critique has emerged in both practical and theoretical domains which poses the question - "What is the point of the 'centre' if all it can offer is a costly monitoring system which can be had for nothing in the external market?"

The diversified firm is coming under increasing pressure to justify its existence rather than simply demand management techniques and decision-making rules designed to sustain it. It may reasonably defend itself by claiming that the centre adds value by managing technological or product interdependences. In this case, it cannot expect to use a hands off/market based system of control. As the growing literature in international comparisons suggests, large firms do not have to rely on such methods of central coordination. Indeed, this evidence may indicate that the alleged superiority of the M-form corporation is only sustainable in an Anglo-American context. In other words, the success of the organisational form is specific to the economic and cultural environment of these countries. Even that 'success' may be questioned for, as will be argued in chapter nine, the triumph of divisionalised firms such as GEC may be interpreted as a being of dubious value for the electronics industry as a whole.

It would be unfair to Williamson to suggest that he proposes that the firm's internal capital market is exactly analogous to the 'finance' theory of the firm or that 'management by numbers' generated via the PV rule is the basis of the comparative efficiency of the M-form. Indeed, the paradox of his approach is that, having characterised the firm as an internal capital market, he then proceeds to describe a process of investment appraisal which owes much to the existence of an internal labour market! Or, to put it another way, the effectiveness of the M-form depends as much on the control of the labour process as it does on the control of capital investment. This insight, however, emerges only indirectly from Williamson's comparison. A greater emphasis on the *labour control* aspect of the firm is required. For example, one of the characteristics of Aoki's 'J-firm' is the explicit use of the *personnel office* as an instrument of corporate governance (Aoki, 1990b).

3.1   Internal versus external (capital) markets

The markets and hierarchies paradigm may be seen as a two stage argument. Firstly, a case is made for establishing the M-form as being both organisationally superior to other forms such as the unitary or holding company form. An analogy is made with an internal capital market. Secondly, the characteristics of an internal capital market are compared with those of the external market. Corporate governance is thus presented as being primarily a problem of controlling the *investment* process rather than the *labour* process. To be fair to Williamson, this perspective is also reflected in much of the corporate strategy literature where the paradigmatic problem is seen as being concerned with choosing markets and activities - these are perceived as being *strategic* choices - whereas issues of labour control are relegated to the apparently less important operating sphere. It is also reflected in Anthony's approach to management control with its hierarchical classification of costs (Anthony, 1965).

Recent developments in the management literature, stimulated by the obvious success of Japanese management styles which lay a much greater emphasis on a 'hands-on', painstaking approach to operating details, have to some extent begun to redress the imbalance. The TCE approach need not have a 'hands-off' bias - the same general insights concerning asset specificity, bounded rationality and opportunism may be applied to the organisation of work as easily as to the organisation of capital. Indeed, the alleged informational advantages of the internal capital market noted by Williamson can only be explained in terms of the informational properties of the internal labour market!

Although Williamson emphasises an internal capital market view of firm much of his analysis is actually broader and more holistic. For example, he makes favourable comparison between hierarchical investment appraisal and the appraisal capability of the external capital market arguing that, in the former case, not only can the incentive machinery be more finely attuned to corporate management objectives but decisions may be made on the basis of superior information. In particular, Williamson stresses the role of internal audit in allowing distinctions to be made between outcomes based on changed circumstances and those based on managerial decision-making - a distinction which may not always be expected from the external capital market due to lack of information.

In general terms, the firm has *informational* advantages over the market while the market has *motivational* advantages. Williamson (1985) argues that:

> As compared with market organisation, internal organisation displays a differential propensity to manage complexity, to forgive error, and to engage in logrolling (p. 149).

In a section entitled 'Forgiveness', Williamson visualises bureaucracy and markets as alternative 'systems of justice'. He suggests that 'systems of justice vary systematically with organization'(1985, p. 150). For example, at one extreme, Williamson argues that the family will have 'deep knowledge of transactions, employ long time horizons, and be relatively forgiving' (1985, p. 150). At the other extreme, markets have 'less knowledge of idiosyncratic circumstances, employ shorter time horizons, and are relatively severe...'(1985, p. 150).

However, he qualifies this information processing superiority by suggesting that since bureaucracies are more 'forgiving' than markets, they are, firstly, more tolerant of unexpected cost increases, and, secondly, apply a different 'net benefit calculus'. By this, Williamson means that the market applies a strict pecuniary net benefit calculus while internal organisation tends to be more tolerant of excuses if only because 'simple regard for human dignity demands that due process be respected' (1985, p. 151).

Thus in his comparison of two systems of justice (or decision-making processes), he poses the choice as being between, on the one hand, a better informed decision-making process while, on the other, a more highly motivated process. In the overall assessment, Williamson clearly feels that the characteristic of forgiveness so evident in the bureaucratic mode is a source of weakness rather than of strength. He also identifies other incentive problems stemming from the employment relation. For example, there tends to be a lack of reward for entrepreneurial activity since any system of special rewards is likely to damage the integrity of the employment relation.

Thus the essence of the internal allocation of capital is seem as deriving from the interaction between the 'labour process' and the 'investment process'. This interaction within the firm may be contrasted with the external capital market which 'has limited constitutional powers to conduct audits and has limited access to the firm's incentive and resource allocation machinery' (1975, p. 143).

3.2   Corporate governance, takeovers and the selection process

The above comparison looks at internal and external capital markets as essentially competing allocative mechanisms. Yet, Williamson does not see the relationship entirely in this light since he argues that there linkages of a more symbiotic character. In other words, where the internal market fails, the external comes to the rescue (and vice versa). There is a curious ambivalence in much of Williamson writing in this area which possibly reflects a more fundamental ambivalence concerning the efficacy of the takeover process. For example, in 'Markets and Hierarchies', Williamson (1975) argues that the capital market is a relatively crude mechanism for a number of reasons. Predators can exploit information impactedness concerning the internal conditions of the firm and the usual 'sorting out difficulties' to behave in an opportunistic manner (p. 142). Furthermore, it is difficult for outsiders to determine to what extent poor performance is due to managerial deviance from profit maximisation or whether it is due to exogenous economic events such as rivals' behaviour. In the former case, a takeover may be justified while in the latter, there would be little point. Even if opportunism can be detected, the predator must then convince the stockholders 'that a displacement effort ought to be supported'(p. 142)

These reservations on the efficiency of the market for control are difficult to reconcile with the later viewpoint that 'internal organisation and conventional capital market forces are complements as well as substitutes; the two coexist in a symbiotic relationship to each other' (p. 160). This blatantly panglossian statement seems to contradict earlier judgements on the inefficacy of the takeover mechanism! If the external market has problems monitoring the internal management of firms how can it be argued that the selection process, of which the market for control is an important part, will not actually reinforce (economically) damaging control systems as was argued in chapter four of this book?

Both the theoretical and empirical role of the M-form firm in the selection process seems ambiguous.[2] The diversified firm as an organisational form seems to play the part of predator and victim in the takeover process with equal facility. Case-by case evidence is contradictory. For example, while it is easy to find examples of conglomerates whose logic and coherence is hard to either justify or even identify, there are also some outstanding British examples of successful, diversified, predators. Companies such as Hanson and BTR are famed *both* for their decentralised, finance led management style *and* for an almost unique ability to make takeovers 'pay' (Goold and Campbell, 1987). Almost as well known is the criticism that they may be locked into a 'takeover syndrome'. In other words, since the organisational form makes *organic* growth difficult, in order to maintain growth, they must keep on finding new and ever larger victims. They are locked-in to a 'deal' → 'harvest' → 'deal' type of strategy. Of course, as I shall argue in the specific circumstances of the U.K. electronics industry, these strategies neatly illustrate the socially dysfunctional aspects of the takeover process since if takeovers were harder to accomplish such strategies and management styles would be impossible to sustain.

Goold and Campbell (1987) have conducted a recent survey of management styles in a sample of large, diversified British companies in which they assess the strengths and weaknesses of the 'Financial Control' management style. As they point out:

> It is not surprising that Financial Control companies miss opportunities for synergy between businesses or that they avoid businesses where coordination and cooperation are essential. As a result they have few global businesses requiring manufacturing, research and marketing in a number of countries simultaneously. The cell structure cannot respond

to the management complexity these businesses demand. The style appears to be more suited to simple, basic businesses or niche positions (p. 121).

The success or otherwise of this system depends partly on which indicators are looked at. For example, they suggest:

> Hanson's financial performance cannot be faulted. Although return on sales and return on capital and return on capital have been below that of the average of our sample during the period 1981-5, return on equity at 17% has been higher than all companies except Plessey ... Hanson is also top of the list in share price growth and earnings per share growth, the one blot on Hanson's performance record is organic growth. Between 1981 and 1985. Hanson averaged an annual decline of 9% in its ongoing fixed asset base, offset by an annual increase in assets of 66% from acquisitions net of divestments. It is this that has caused many observers to accuse Hanson of asset stripping (Goold and Campbell, 1987, p. 136).

Goold and Campbell's findings are significant in view of the model introduced in chapter four. Their study will also be drawn on in chapter nine where an analysis of management style and industry performance in the UK electronics industry will be presented.

Other recent criticisms of modern corporate governance have come from a surprising quarter. Jensen (1989) argues that the public corporation (and presumably, the M-form) is an institution which has failed in recent years to deliver the economic goods. Furthermore, it is being replaced by private companies formed by leveraged buy-outs which, he argues, have superior incentive and monitoring capabilities. He cites evidence which suggests that this long term trend has implications for the long term structure of corporate America. While he has his critics (Rappaport, 1990), his views actually introduce a variation in 'hierarchical decomposition' and corporate governance which is almost the norm in other major capitalist economies such Germany and Japan. These economies are sometimes called 'bank controlled'. These institutional arrangements have implications for internal management control and external reporting.

3.3   The external market: the question of the 'bank controlled economies'

The crucial role played by industrial banks in Japan and Germany was noted long before Jensen. Historically, the relationships go right back to the early days of industrialisation in these countries in the nineteenth century. While the stylised facts are well established, theoretically analysis has, until recently, been lacking.

In terms of the TCE paradigm, the problem is how to model these arrangements in terms of the internal/external market comparison. The arrangements are far more ambiguous than in the earlier comparison. For example, are the bank-controlled companies to be modelled as simple extensions of the *internal* allocation mode or are they *external* investors with many of the informational advantages possessed by *internal* managers? In this situation, a comparison must be made not on a simple 'market v hierarchy' basis but on a comparison between the internal decisionmaking of firms operating in markedly different relationships to capital market.

One of the few theoretical studies of the implications of industrial banking is provided by Cable (1985). He states that:

> As is well known, German companies make little use of their relatively undeveloped external capital market, and depend heavily on the banking system for their external finance. Moreover the banks not only supply or arrange access to investment funds, but are also extensively represented on the supervisory boards of companies, and in control of very large blocks of equity voting-rights. The system of industrial financing which results can be viewed as one of 'quasi-internal capital markets', with potentially important informational and transactions-costs implications (p. 119).

On the basis of his empirical research, Cable suggests that:

> ... there is a significant, positive relationship between the degree of bank involvement in leading industrial companies and their financial performance. This goes beyond what might be expected from market power enhancement or the provision of financial expertise alone, but is consistent with an internal capital markets hypothesis (p. 130).

Cable has argued elsewhere (Cable and Dirrheimer, 1983) that the M-form and bank control may be seen as alternative organisational adaptations to the same incentive problem- the representation of a 'proprietal interest' in the giant corporation. More recent research has developed along different lines, suggesting that bank control implies a more decentralised form of decision making (Aoki, 1990b). This latter approach will be pursued since it suggests an important development of the hierarchical model presented in chapter five.

4. An alternative approach to decentralisation

4.1 Tight and loose coupling

The hierarchical structures presented in chapter five suggested a system of control which combined incentive issues with decision making issues. Furthermore, the linkages were seen as being as equally stringent at the top and as at the bottom of the hierarchical systems. From an informational viewpoint, this was extremely significant because it suggested that the *same information could be used in decision-making and for incentives/reward systems.* Furthermore, the centralisation of the control system implied that the information gathered at the centre would tend to be highly aggregated and even misleading for purposes of economic allocation. This problem has been recognised by both Austrian economists (see chapter one) and recent researchers (see chapter eight). Some of these critics have suggested 'new measurements' (Kaplan, 1983). I submit that although improved measurements may be developed, the main solution has to be found in terms of structural and processional change in institutions. There has to be a process of organisational and informational 'decoupling'.

4.2 The decoupling of incentives and decisionmaking- the J-firm model

One form of decoupling has been presented by Aoki in his stylised model of the Japanese firm (J-firm). He argues that the 'internal organisation and financial control of the Japanese firm are duly characterised by weak-decision hierarchy and incentive-ranking hierarchy' (Aoki, 1990b, p. 18). His emphasis on *horizontal* flows of information implies an organisational form which is relatively tightly coupled to the product market but loosely coupled in a vertical decisionmaking mode. Paradoxically, his view of incentives relies on the sort of tightly coupled hierarchical mode which would be regarded as being very 'bureaucratic' to Anglo-American critics. Dore (1973) visualised this hierarchy in terms of finely layered triangle (see fig 6.2).

A further aspect of decoupling (as compared with the M-form) is the Japanese practice of sub-contracting which Aoki terms 'quasi-hierarchy'. Thus operations that under an Anglo-American type system would be co-ordinated through hierarchical modes (typically within an M-form) are organised via relational contracting in the J-firm. These characteristics may be observed in figure 6.2. This model may be compared with the system illustrated in figure 5.6. The contrast in structural terms is that in the latter case the main linkages are seen in vertical terms while in the former case vertical linkages are weak in an upward direction as compared with strong horizontal linkages.

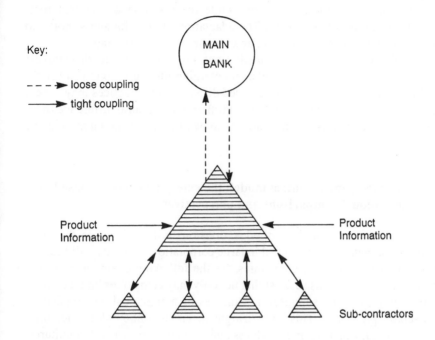

Figure 6.1   Bank co-ordination, incentive-ranking hierarchies and 'quasi-hierarchy'.

The structure illustrated in figure 6.1 helps to explain *some* of the stylised facts on differences in the importance of accounting in Anglo-American companies versus Japanese companies. For example, it explains the reduced focus on financial information within firms. It is less helpful, however, in terms of *external reporting* since Aoki suggests that Japanese banks rely on profitability measures and other familiar financial methods of appraisal. In this respect, one big difference that the diagram does *not* pick up is the bank appointed director. This convention gives the Japanese bank a more intimate knowledge of the firm than is possible for the external capital market implying a diminished reliance on published financial information. Yet, this phenomenon could just easily be linked to a model of tighter rather than the looser coupling suggested by figure 6.1.

One possible way out of this problem is to look at *process* as well as structure. Neither figure 5.6 nor figure 6.1 can satisfactorily distinguish all the differences in control mechanisms. The similarities in structural terms actually mask a fundamental difference in adjustment to crisis. To put it in Hirschmann's (1970) terminology, the response of the external controller in

127

figure 5.6 (the shareholder) is 'exit' while the response of the 'external' controller in figure 6.1 is 'voice'. The adaptation of Hirschmann's model to issues of corporate governance is at an extremely embryonic stage.

Although Japanese economic institutions probably provide the starkest contrast to Anglo-American models, an emerging literature reviewed briefly in the next section indicates that observed differences in practices may have a cultural as well as an institutional basis. Furthermore, cultural differences may be observed between Western countries as well as between Japan and the 'West'.

5. The management control model: the emerging evidence based on international comparisons and perspectives.

One of the criticisms of the orthodox divisionalisation thesis is that as a description of management control in large corporations it is only valid for US and to a lesser extent, UK companies. As the following examples indicate, international comparisons suggest that not only may companies be factored in different ways, but the supposed advantages of hierarchical decomposition may itself be questioned. This is not to argue that issues of bounded rationality, opportunism, information impactedness and so on disappear in other cultures. Rather, the suggestion is that there are other ways of coping with these problems which may be superior to the M-form solution. The debate is not only generated by international comparisons. As Goold and Campbell have shown, considerable differences in management style may be identified across UK companies (Goold and Campbell, 1987).

In his pioneering study of international comparisons of management control, Horowitz (1978) standardised for size and technology in order to focus on national differences. His study contributed towards what have become the stylised facts of management style. For example, German firms are more centralised and have more emphasis on production control rather than finance control than British firms. These findings not only question the standard divisionalisation thesis, they also show the culture bound nature of the distinction between what is 'strategic' and what is 'operational'!

Another example of an international *perspective* as well as comparison is offered by Lalanne (1990). She makes a distinction between Management Information Systems (MIS) and Accounting Information Systems (AIS). The former are defined as 'information systems which aim to give to the managers at all levels the tools and required information to make decisions and take corrective actions in their daily business' (p. 5). The latter are 'information systems presented in a financial or accounting form and which aim to create visibility for a company's performance' (p. 5). Using Goold and Campbell's concept of a Financial Control style (Goold and Campbell, 1987), Lalanne points out that while these companies are avowedly decentralised, the emphasis on AIS means that the focus of the managers is directed toward the 'centre' rather than towards the operating edge. The firm's vertical flows of information via the AIS dominate the MIS to such an extent that the apparent autonomy of the business unit is actually quite illusory. The financial control model of the firm which she describes is much closer to the agency rather than the TCE paradigm.

For example, Lalanne describes the budget in a financial control company in the following way:

> The short-range plan (budget) includes going through a process which is taken very seriously by managers. However, they do not emphasise it as an "action plan", a management tool, but as their *commitment*. Such an approach is .. in keeping ... with ... an American contractual logic: managers accept very easily- even wish- to be set precise, detailed objectives in a budget, because they feel as if they were in a "trade relationship" with their superior, as if they had a contractual commitment. Therefore they consider that it is fair that their boss feels interested in their results- this is something normal for a client- and appraises them against the objectives set in the budget. The budget is perceived as a *contract* by managers, not as a strategic instrument to plan the near future of the whole company (p. 6).

Lalanne is ultimately concerned to link management style and AIS/MIS to what she terms 'geocultural' matters. Thus her explanation of national differences is based on the work of researchers such as Hofstede (1987) who visualised Britain as being a 'village market' society. France is characterised as being an 'effectiveness driven country' while Britain is an 'efficiency driven country'. Of course, it is evident that such sociologically based explanations may be compared and contrasted with the explanation provided in chapter four which is more 'economics' based. Thus, in terms of economic determinism, observed cultural differences are superficial manifestations derivative of differences in economic systems.

Although many researchers (including this one!) refer sometimes to 'Anglo-Saxon economies/companies' as though there were no important cultural or institutional differences between them, this is not always the case. For example, there is some evidence of important differences between the UK and US divisionalised companies. This has largely been noted in the context of differences in multinational investment where US investment has been more of the direct/technology transfer type while UK investment has been more indirect or portfolio driven. For example, discussing her pioneering organisational approach to this area, Wilkins (1986) states that:

> The more research I did on European investment in the United States, the more I faced works by economists on capital flows that ignored the firm, put it in a peripheral role, or took it for granted (p. 81).

In her study of UK 'multinational enterprises' that invested in nineteenth century USA, Wilkins identified what she termed the 'free-standing firm' and came to these conclusions about their special characteristics:

> They were not existing UK domestic businesses that had extended themselves, nor were they family firms that had become international. None the less they were firms. They were the means by which capital was mobilised, *managed*, exported, and allocated ... They did not grow out of the needs of existing enterprises to become multinational. They did not build on existing UK operating entities that had knowledge, experience, technology, and goodwill; thus they did not benefit from the economies of internal management (p. 85 - 86).

Some of these differences will be looked again in a more contemporary context in chapter nine. Although the focus will be on the *UK* electronics industry, some contrasts will be noted between the performance of British and American owned companies.

6.   Concluding remarks

This and the previous chapter have begun the process of theoretical elaboration of a 'management control model' of the firm. While the raison d'etre of the firm is based on contractual theory as discussed in chapter three, the progressive elaboration of management control issues has resulted both in changes in emphasis and an emerging critique of 'hierarchical' and 'hierarchical decomposition' hypotheses. A holistic control theory was presented which showed that both firms and markets may be modelled within a common 'systems' framework.

The behavioural assumptions which lead to the emergence of hierarchy also point to the need for some form of 'hierarchical decomposition'. However, the design of that decomposition and, particularly, the alleged superiority of the M-form, may be disputed. In the remaining chapters, the focus will become more empirical as issues of testing and application of the theory become more pertinent. This process will in itself aid the more general aim of theoretical elaboration and refinement.

Notes

1. Reproduced from Levy, H. and Sarnat, M. *Capital Investment and Financial Decisions,* (1989) by permission of Prentice-Hall International.

2. See also chapter four.

7 The screw-driver and warehouse operation: The theory of the firm and value added accounting

In chapter four a theory was presented which argued that the selection of organisational forms in the UK private sector had weakened the ability of the UK economy to sustain the sophisticated structures necessary for the control and development of technology. More specifically, it was argued that selection pressures had led, not to the conventionally described 'deindustrialisation', but to the emergence of a population of organisationally 'degenerate' firms, journalistically known as 'screw-driver and warehouse' operations. In this chapter the theory is developed in two ways. Firstly, the nature of these firms is explored more deeply with an attempt to analyse their micro characteristics and their role in the wider economy. Secondly, an investigation is begun into the accounting and control characteristics of these firms with the aim of producing some definitions which enable the theory to be tested. In other words, if the theory predicts that the population of such firms is increasing then some attempt should be made to identify these organisations in terms of economic and accounting data.

Although other accounting data characterise these sorts of firms, it is argued that the concept of value added is particularly pertinent. This suggests a new role for value added accounting. The second section of the chapter chronicles the 'up and down' record of value added accounting and relates it to the various theories of the firm introduced in earlier chapters. Finally, some empirical evidence is presented which indicates how 'screw-driver and warehouse' operations may be identified with a particular focus on the UK electronics industry.

1. The screw-driver and warehouse operations: some qualitative characteristics

As I emphasised in chapter four, conventional neoclassical concepts may be of very little use in analysing economic *processes*. A commonly used unit of analysis such as the 'industry' is primarily concerned with the horizontal classification of economic activity which may lead to misleading interpretations of structural trends in the economy. For example, data on videos in the UK which indicates a growing output and export trade may easily mask the fact that the *control* of the industry is located overseas and that the technological capability for sustaining a competitive advantage in the industry also resides overseas. The key word is "control" - the issue of ownership is of less importance.[1] As Wilkins (1986) has shown (see previous chapter), legal ownership by overseas capital does not necessarily imply control of production by that capital.

It would seem that an adequate analytical framework must provide a perspective on vertical linkages as well as explicitly addressing the issue of the locus of control of the production process. Many of these issues have been looked at in the last two chapters. However, the organisational aspects of the phenomenon need to be related to the concept of *value creation* since, from an economics perspective, it is primarily on this criterion that institutional structures are judged. Of course, this does not preclude anxieties based on other criteria such as national or regional economic sovereignty.[2]

1.1   The screw-driver operation and value chain analysis

A particularly appropriate economics framework is provided by the concept of the *Value Chain* proposed by Michael Porter (1985). Originally developed as an analytical device in corporate strategy, it can also be used to model value creation in terms of geographical regions such as nation states.

In terms of the value chain approach, the *warehouse operation* is easily identified as a 'thin strip' cut out of the primary activities part of the chain. The simplicity of the operation means that few of the 'support' activities are likely to be of significance. The location of the 'strip' may vary. Literally speaking, a warehouse is mainly concerned with outbound logistics - the storing and dispatching of completed goods and spare parts. The inclusion of marketing and sales implies a far more sophisticated firm which may be able to control upstream activities even though it effectively subcontracts all manufacturing (e.g. Marks and Spencers). The *screw-driver operation* may be visualised as a 'thin strip' out of the 'operations' box. Once again the emphasis will be on 'primary' activities since technological development and procurement are intentionally located elsewhere. The human resource management and firm infrastructure may be more sophisticated than for the warehouse operation since even final assembly operations require quality control and process management.

This type of firm may, in fact, be organisationally complex with a highly sophisticated firm infrastructure, incorporating advanced human resource, technological development and procurement functions. Generally, the domain of this type of firm actually extends beyond its legal boundaries into its network of suppliers. If the purely legal boundaries of the firms are ignored, then it is probable that the relevant strip in the value chain is both 'thicker' and 'fuzzier'- reflecting the reality of a 'quasi-hierarchy'. It is able to obtain high mark-ups on its merchandise, have a relatively high return on capital and pay its employees premium wages for given grades of work. In short, as will be explained below, it is able to generate 'organisational rent'. Perhaps that is why it is best to confine critical associations to the word 'warehouse' rather than the word 'retailer'!

1.2 Value chains and economic rent

The value chain model can only capture some of the connotations implied by the expression. For example, to some there may be connotations that screw-driver operations can be equated with simple technology and a low level of skill in the labour force, reflecting low levels of human and physical capital. While this may be the case in isolated instances, I submit *that the real point of issue is concerned, not with the level of technology or investment, but its control since this will ultimately determine the locus of value creation. Indeed, as, will be shown in section three, both the final product and some of the production processes may be up to the best world standard and yet still be labelled screw-driver operations!*

As has been shown in previous chapters, the locus of control in production is not necessarily determined by locating the legal owners of the firm. These may simply be the suppliers of capital rather than 'owners' in the sense that they also manage (Putterman, 1988). Or, as Marglin (1984) emphasises, power lies with those who have knowledge of the organisation of production. A characteristic of a screw-driver operation is that although production may be taking place using state of the art technology, the knowledge of the organisation of production lies elsewhere. The firm is thus a 'transplant' rather than an organism that can reproduce itself.

Another characteristic often associated with the screw-driver firm is foreign ownership. This is understandable since it is then a simple matter to explain their existence in terms of the circumvention of trade barriers. In other words, in a world without trade barriers they would not exist. The problem with this explanation is that it sees the screw driver operation as being established at the initiative of an upstream multinational. However, it is also possible to find examples of screw-driver operations which have been established at the initiative of a *downstream operator* which has subcontracted most upstream activities overseas and yet still claims to control the value chain. A well known UK example is Amstrad which will be looked at in greater detail in section three. It could be argued (as the European Community (EC) often does!) that Amstrad's main motivation is the same as that of the non-EC multinationals, that is, to avoid external trade barriers. Alternatively, this may be far too simplistic since, as we have already noted, firms *may* have marketing skills, brand names and other controls over distribution channels which mean that the locus of control of the value chain *may* actually lie with the final 'producer' rather than with the sub-contractors.

1.3   Control and the locus of organisational rent

Theoretically, the markets and hierarchies literature and, in particular, the so called 'putting out' debate predicts that firms which rely over enthusiastically on subcontracting without possessing an adequate technical core may find that they run into the sort of problems associated with the old pre-factory manufacturing system (Williamson, 1985). Indeed, Amstrad has experienced some of these problems as has the Rover group which has become progressively more dependent on Honda for new models and technology. While the 'putting-out' debate is primarily concerned with the efficiency v control issue (Marglin, 1974), this issue is largely immaterial in the context of the value chain since the efficiency and control perspectives *both* indicate that the locus of control will determine where value will be added! As we saw in chapter five, Marglin's work serves as an example of how 'radical' views provide insights into the interplay between knowledge and power which are fundamental not just in distributional but also in efficiency terms.

This same logic can also be applied on a national basis. Thus organising ability is the basis of the power to create and appropriate economic rent for a national economy.[3] Indeed, some researchers notably Aoki (1984) have developed the notion of *organisational rent*, referring to the surplus generated by the formation of the firm. Aoki criticises the orthodox neoclassical view that organisational rent is the same as the profit accruing to the entrepreneur. He argues that the key to organisational rent is *firm specific capital* of which only a part may be under the control of the capitalist. In empirical terms, this perspective on the firm's surplus is more akin to a value added perspective involving the firm *as a team* in contrast to the neoclassical focus on profit accruing to the entrepreneur. As we have already seen with the value chain analysis, the strategy literature has developed insights on the interplay between vertical organisation and the appropriation of profit.

As an example of the role of organisation in controlling knowledge, Porter (1985) points out that firms go to great lengths to maintain proprietary control over the technology which creates appropriate value. They do this via organisational rather than legal devices. For example, technological leaders are 'often vertically integrated, building or modifying equipment in-house to protect technology, and are discrete in public disclosures' (p. 186). Firms that have a reputation for secrecy are frequently either technological leaders (or run by crooks!).

Thus from the point of view of the firm's search for economic rent, the role of technology in creating value is not just a matter of the *level of science* but also of proprietary control. This perspective is amplified by Hergert and Morris (1989) who, developing some of Porter ideas in the context of accounting, argue that many of the activities that firms engage in are necessary but not distinctive in the sense that they distinguish a firm from its rivals. The source of competitive advantage lies in 'those activities in which a firm has proprietary access to scarce resources (e.g. skills, patents, assets, distribution networks, etc)' (p. 178). Strategic analysis must, therefore, begin by identifying 'which activities are the actual or potential source of such rents' (p. 178).

These insights all help in the characterisation and identification of the screw-driver firm. Thus one way of looking at the screw-driver firm is to note the absence of economic rents rather than an absence of science and technology. Indeed, it is quite plausible that highly qualified/skilled workers may be employed in such plants as long as the organisation of production means that the level of organisational rent is low. In terms of Aoki's model, these workers will not be part of the firm's specific capital whatever the level of general human capital.

One aspect which the strategy literature neglects is that there may be a conflict between the generation of organisational rent and the appropriation of profit. This conflict is reflected in conventional accounting which, as we shall discuss next, is designed for the measurement of profit rather than organisational rent. For this reason, the rewards of organisational rent may have to be 'left where they lie'- attempts by one set of players in the production process to measure and then appropriate the entire surplus may jeopardise the value creating process itself.

1.4 The search for quantitative characteristics

The search for easily measured quantitative characteristics of screw-driver activities runs up against the same problems that corporate planners have run into in trying to make value chain analysis operational. The main problem is that there is neither an easy fit between value chain and accounting data nor a necessary correspondence between organisation structures and value creating activities. As Porter (1985) criticises conventional accounting systems because they can get in the way of strategic cost analysis. Much of his prescription reads like a call for activity based costing. For example, since conventional cost systems 'categorise costs in line terms such as direct labour, indirect labour, and burden' they actually 'obscure the underlying activities a firm performs' (p. 63). Costs are aggregated in a way that leads to the 'artificial separation of labor, material, and overhead costs related to the same activity (p. 63).

Similarly, Hergert and Morris (1989) have argued that the structural unit for analysis or SBU (strategic business unit) does not usually coincide with organisational structure since '(d)ynamic environments, proactive stances to strategy and a preference for only changing structures in the last resort, all contribute to misalignments ... (furthermore) ... accounting systems accumulate costs around products and organisational units' (p. 180).

There is an evident paradox here. The deficiencies or lack of correspondence between conventional accounting systems and the value chain perspective is seen as a *problem* for corporate strategists. Paradoxically, however, to the social scientists/economist it offers a *solution* - an explanation of differences in national/firm performance! However, an explanation of comparative performance based on a mismatch between accounting and organisational imperatives must almost inevitably run into the problem of lack of suitable data! As was pointed out in chapter four, the conventional deindustrialisation thesis may have its limitations but at least it has the advantage of a vast bank of published data on firms and industries!

One proposition has emerged from the above discussion which reinforces the arguments introduced in chapter four. Namely, there is a link between the aggregate level of national income and the organisational capability of firms within the economy. Inputs may be more productively employed within structures which nurture firm specific capital which, in turn, generate organisational rent. A second proposition, discussed in the next two sections, is that firm value added may be used as a proxy measure of organisational rent.

2. The screw-driver operation: value, value added or profit?

Curiously, perhaps, the founder of the Value chain approach is quite emphatic in rejecting value added as a basis for analysis because 'it incorrectly distinguishes raw materials from the many purchased inputs used in a firm's activities' (Porter, 1985, p. 39). Indeed, the concept of value added has had a roller-coaster record in terms of interest and acceptance, relating not just academic fads and fancies but also changing social and political forces (Burchell, et al., 1985). Although interesting, discussion of these forces is beyond the scope of this book. Attention, instead, will be focused on how the debate on value added accounting sheds light on number of issues concerned with the *economic* nature of the firm. The discussion also reveals how intimately such apparently practical issues as the definition and measurement of a firm's value added is bound up with fundamental theoretical issues concerning the boundary of the firm and the nature of economic surplus.

2.1 Value added accounting and the theory of the firm[4]

To many, politicians, perhaps, rather than economists, the goal of national economic growth seems desirable and relatively uncontroversial. However we might wish to distribute it or allocate it, higher national wealth would seem to imply an unambiguous potential increase in welfare. If wealth creation is such an acceptable national goal then surely, the argument goes, it must be a goal we can all aim for in our workplace. It follows apparently that firms should be maximising value added, not profit or sales or any other suggested goal. It is this sort of reasoning which ultimately seems to lie behind the sporadic interest in value added accounting (see Burchell, et al., 1985). If we wish to pursue value added maximisation then we must be able to define and measure it. Hence we see a macro-economic, national income accounting concept becoming the focal point of the performance of the individual firm.

Another source of stimulus to research in the area is international comparisons. For example, the industrial laggards of the West cast envious glances at the industrial performance of the Japanese but are sated by explanations based on cultural uniqueness. The search is on for management techniques and practices that can be transferred to firms operating in Western cultures. The temptation is to pinpoint a particular aspect and claim it as the 'alchemist's stone'.

Gregory (1985), while stressing the now familiar traits of teamwork and consensus in the Japanese firm, suggests that even Japanese accounting recognises the fundamental purpose of the enterprise in terms of value added creation. Gregory states that:

If the ultimate test and confirmation of the purpose of enterprise and its consistency with the shared values of its members is embedded in day-to-day practice, as manifested in physical demeanor and surroundings, it is also necessary to have a system of quantitative measurement to assure efficiency in the attainment of goals and give precision to the information from everyday life. Just as the profit-and-loss account provides the measure of performance for the profit-maximising enterprise, a method of measuring wealth creation through innovation is necessary.

For this purpose an elaborate system of value added accounting has been evolved and is widely employed in Japanese enterprise management as well as in public policy-making (p. 61).

A possible project seems to be indicated labelled 'a formal analysis of the Japanese firm' or alternatively, the 'Wealth (GNP)' maximising model of the firm based perhaps on a valued added approach. The implication is that formal neo-classical models of the firm which have long indicated how efficient production may be achieved via profit maximisation have left a gap. This section seeks to investigate the above gap by analysing the micro implications of the concept of value added. Firstly, the problem of defining value added is considered. Secondly, an answer is offered to the question 'What sort of firm (might) maximise Value Added?'. Finally, there is a discussion of the allocative and distributional consequences of pursuing such a goal.

2.2 The definition of value added

Much of the accounting literature on value added concerns itself with definitional and calculative problems. From an economics perspective, this may be regarded as perfectly understandable given the assumed professional pre-occupation of the accountant. It would be erroneous, however, for the economist to dismiss these problems as being outside his own sphere of interest. Indeed, it would seem that the definitional problems and undoubted ambiguities are to some extent the essence of the explanation for the neglect of the value added concept by economists.

Rutherford (1977) sums up the consensus view of accountants concerning the economist's interest in value added thus:

The economist's model of value added ... is designed primarily to yield aggregate data by summation, hence an individual entity's value added need not be precisely demarcated; all that is necessary is a 'consolidation adjustment' to avoid double counting (p. 217).

Value added then appears in economics as just one of the many issues in national income accounting. It also crops up in another macro-economic context; that is, incomes policies and value added incentive schemes (VAIPS). However, as Burchell, et al., (1985) argue:

> In discussions of VAIPS it is rare to find their merits presented solely in terms of their scope, self-financing character or measurement technology. In a number of different ways, the point was nearly always made that the effective functioning of these schemes presupposes a number of changes in the intra-organisational relations of the enterprise concerned (p. 396).

They go on to argue that issues of productivity measurement and efficient management were deliberately conflated with issues of employee participation and industrial democracy:

> Indeed, it became possible to completely invert the normal order of presentation and use the issue of industrial democracy as a springboard for advancing claims of VAIPS (eg. Marchington, 1977) (p. 397).

For this sort of project the equivocality of the concept of value added is a source of strength rather than weakness:

> The very ambiguity of value added might, in other words, be implicated in its emergence and functioning. Depending on the point at which the circle of reasoning is entered, value added may be seen as a determining factor in the process of social change, a harbinger of social change or a consequence of social change (p. 390).

While acknowledging the undoubted role of intentional 'fudge and mudge' in this area, there still remains a genuine conceptual difficulty in defining and calculating value added which ultimately lies embedded in standard neo-classical theory. This difficulty originates from the traditional vacuity of the concept of the firm which has been discussed in chapters one, two, three and five. As Jensen and Meckling (1979) put it:

> Most organisations such as the corporation are simply legal fictions which serve as a nexus for a complex set of contracts among individuals. Suppliers of inputs (labour, raw materials, capital, etc.) along with consumers of the product implicitly or explicitly enter into a set of contracts which delineate the rights and obligations of the respective participants in the activities of the organisations (p. 470).

This view of purchased inputs clearly informs Porter's perception and rejection of value added. As we have already seen, the conventional 'theory of the firm' is in fact a theory of the production function - we do not care who are 'insiders' or 'outsiders' or what the boundaries of the firm are - yet this is the real problem in calculating value added. The relevance of the markets and hierarchies literature to the concept of value added is that at least it is concerned with establishing a boundary between the 'firm' and the 'market'. It is only when this has been established that we can talk about "members" of the firm and non-members, between "in-house production" and "bought-in" production and all the issues which are highlighted through value added calculations.

Value added is often seen as representing the efforts of the firm acting as a team. But who is in the team? Are all employees team members regardless of their contractual relationship? What of the government or external debt-holders? Much of the diversity in calculation stems from differing views as to how to treat taxation (the government's contribution?) and depreciation (the capitalist's contribution?). Standard economic theory is unfortunately of little assistance in this area. The central feature of the standard theory is the production function which, as any introductory textbook emphasises, is a purely technological relationship. In this relationship the key distinguishing features of the inputs concern their degree of fixity or variability and this is determined by purely technological considerations and not on the basis of social relations. The convention has developed that capital is regarded as the fixed input while labour is regarded as variable. It is perhaps unsurprising that critics of neo-classical theory see this as an example of the implicit bias of the neo-classical system. In other words, critics argue that the fixity or variability of inputs *does* reflect *social relations* in production as well as technological considerations.

As has already been pointed out, the conventional production function is underspecified. As Jensen and Meckling argue:

> The maximum attainable output of the firm is then not purely a matter of 'physical' possibilities given the technology and knowledge; the production function depends on the contracting and property rights system within which the firm operate (p. 471).

A fuller specification, in their view, should include some explicit treatment of the 'internal rules of the game available to the firm' and of the 'contracting and property rights system within which the firm exists' (p. 471).

2.3 The 'ups and downs' of value added accounting

It would seem from the experience of the UK that as the perception of the production process changed through the 1970's and 1980's that interest in value added, correspondingly, waxed and waned. It would seem, however, that the emergence and decline of value added accounting was contingent on a change in the *social* and *political* environment rather than on any significant legal changes in British capitalism. For example, in the social and political climate of the 1970's, value added was seen as 'a performance criterion that put employees on a par with other interests in the enterprise' (Burchell, et al., (1985) p. 393).

In this climate of opinion, labour was perceived as a fixed, or at least quasi-fixed, factor of production. Value added thus became a focus of interest at the micro-level. There were, however, no fundamental changes in the rights structure of the firm, such as might have arisen, for example, out of the enactment of the Bullock Report. Thus, in the different (and from labour's point of view seemingly colder) climate of the 1980's, the labour force was 'disposable'; the only significant stakeholder is the claimant to the residual (the entrepreneur) and the only significant performance indicator is profit, with value added returning to its usual footnote significance in national income calculations.

Empirical evidence on the rise and fall of value added reporting is summarised by Burchell, et al., (1985) thus:

> Fourteen companies (out of 300) in the Institute of Chartered Accountants in England and Wales' Survey of Published Accounts included value added statements in their annual reports for the year 1975-6 (ICAEW), 1978). This figure grew to 67 for 1977-78, 84 for 1978-79 and 90 for 1979-80 before declining to 88 in 1980-81, 77 for 1981-82 and 64 for 1982-83 (ICAEW, 1980; Skerrat & Tonkin, 1982; Tonkin & Skerrat, 1983). Other surveys indicate that more than one-fifth of the largest UK companies produced value added statements in the late 1970's (Gray & Maunders, 1980, p. 386).

Changes in the structure of employment might be seen as an indication of a corresponding change in the relationship between the firm and its workforce. For example, recent and projected trends in occupational structure suggest that firms are turning to sub-contracting and work externalisation rather than developing in-house activities (see Rajan & Pearson (1986)). As we shall see shortly, this is precisely the sort of area where value added calculations lead to different results as compared with profit calculations.

2.4   Value added as a goal

The literature on profit seeking as a goal is voluminous and generally well known. From it we can deduce organisational forms and environments where goals other than profit become significant. The first necessary condition for alternative goal-seeking would seem to be less than perfect competition in product markets. In the theoretically well worked but empirically unlikely state of perfect competition, firms must not only pursue but also maximise profits as a condition of survival. The goals and conduct of the firm are dictated by the structure of the industry. As we have discussed in chapter two, discretionary behaviour requires some monopoly power plus some barriers to entry in the long run. These barriers may be a function of the product market, economies of scale, patents, advertising and so on. Internally, the additional requirement seems to be a degree of divorce of ownership and control based on the dispersion of stock ownership and the apparent control of a management team without a proprietary interest (Berle & Means (1932)). These are the usual conditions specified for 'managerialist' models. Seminal Managerialist contributions (eg. Baumol, (1959), Marris, (1964), Williamson, (1964)) all suggest alternative goals to short-run profit maximisation. None of them argue that management controlled corporations will explicitly pursue value added as an objective. Sales revenue, growth of sales, growth of assets may implicitly suggest concern with size and growth rather than profits and these goals may even subsume the pursuit of value added (see Seal (1986)). However, as shall be argued later, the adoption of value added as an explicit goal involves a significant change in the attitude of the management in the allocation of resources. For example, all of the above theories assume technical efficiency or, in other words, a given output will be produced at minimum cost. This cannot be assumed in the value added maximising firm.

2.5   Value added and the recent literature on the theory of the firm

Since at this stage we are solely concerned with the specification of the goals of firms, the most useful approach would seem to be that of Williamson (1964), who initially set up a general model of management utility maximisation (see chapter two). The approach has an appealing generality and provides a framework within which to consider which arguments are likely to feature in a management utility function. The two items which could lead to a form of value added mix are management emoluments and staff expenses. In other words, it is these elements which are regarded as fixed overheads rather than prime costs to be minimised. Cowling (1982) has argued that the growth of the M-form organisation has meant that this perspective is really only the prerogative of senior management. Management at divisional level is effectively monitored and controlled by the internal capital market. As he puts it:

> Ignoring the struggle within the managerial hierarchy, it is clear that management has a different attitude towards some costs than towards others. Williamson has characterised this as expense preference, and identifies staff and associated expenses as contributing directly to managerial utility. This leaves the minimisation of the direct costs of production as an objective of management, since profits are still desirable for their own sake and as a source of those elements of (overhead) costs for which management has an expense preference. Managerialism should therefore be identified with the adoption of profit-maximising rules with regard to short-run output - price determination, but also with the absorption of profits within various categories of overhead costs (p. 85).

From a behavioural perspective, the real loss of control may be more significant at plant level where the pursuit of sub-goals may be ineffectually controlled even with the M-form organisation (see chapter six). At this level, head office concern with profits, sales, market share, and so on, may seem insignificant compared with the enticing empires to be built at local level. For example, the utility of local management may be increased by the expansion of 'in-house production' even if it entails a higher cost than the bought-in product - a situation that, as we shall see below, has significant allocational implications.

Although we cannot easily discern an explicit goal of value added in this literature, we can at least being to identify the boundaries of the firm. The organisation takes on some substance in terms of 'team production' (Alchian & Demsetz, 1972) and 'internal labour markets' (Williamson, 1975). Here is some recognition that the simple 'production function' and 'limitless contracting' models fail to explain the existence of the giant corporation.

2.6 Value added and the Japanese firm

In the light of Gregory's observations on Japanese value added accounting, one apparently obvious line of investigation is the Japanese firm. In spite of a wealth of management literature and sociological studies, economists have until recently had trouble in modelling this important institution which in terms of formal legal rights seems almost indistinguishable from an American or British firm. We have already met Ouchi's concept of the 'clan' (Ouchi, 1980). Less well known is Odagiri's perspective which seems to view the Japanese firm in terms of 'everyone being a manager'. He argues that the usual distinctions between levels of management are, in the Japanese firm, very indistinct. He states that:

> The management we are concerned with is he or those who make decisions as to the variables under the control of the firm, for example, prices, recruitment, purchase of materials, finance, quality of the product, advertising, research and development, and investment. In its most strict sense, therefore, every member is participating in management in one way or another; ... The management, therefore, should be thought of as a team of personnel - perhaps from the bottom of the corporate hierarchy to the top - and not a single person (Odagiri, 1980, p. 39).

While to Western eyes this viewpoint seems to stretch the concept of 'management' so far as to become meaningless, it could, alternatively, be seen as an attempt to capture the peculiar form of Japanese teamwork known as 'vertical factionalism' that is often observed within the Japanese corporation (see, for example, Teasdale (1981)). As noted in earlier chapters, recent developments in the theory of the firm - bargaining models, managerial corporatism and the firm as a 'nexus of treaties', all suggest that for some type of firms in some economies, especially the Japanese, the firm 'as a team' is a plausible model. Many of the above theoretical developments can be attributed to Aoki (1984; 1986; 1990a; 1990b). As we have already seen, the relevant surplus emanating from these models of the firm is *organisational Rent* rather than profit. In this context the concept of value added has strong symbolic value even if the operational problems remain.

2.7   Value added and the labour managed firm

Moving away from the conventional corporation toward alternative ownership forms such as labour managed firms, self-managed firms, profit-sharing firms, partnerships, and so on, seems to bring us much closer to the sort of organisations which might explicitly and routinely pursue value added. Specifically, these firms generally have an identifiable membership. Secondly, labour is regarded as a semi-fixed cost. Decisions have to be made concerning the distinction between a fixed wage payment and a payment based on some notion of a 'surplus'. In Yugoslavian self-management, for example, the entire workforce is at least formally participating in the management via a democratic process. Indeed, the self managed firm is often explicitly modelled as maximising value added per member, (see eg. Dreze, 1976; Meade, 1972; Vanek, 1970).

While the status of labour seems assured in these organisations, the status of capital seems more ambiguous. Jensen and Meckling (1979) quote Meade's (Meade, 1972) definition of the labour managed firm as being:

> ... a system in which workers get together and form collectives or partnerships to run firms; they hire capital and purchase other inputs and they sell the products of the firm at the best prices they can obtain in the markets for inputs and outputs; they themselves bear the risk of any unexpected gain or loss and distribute the resulting surplus among themselves, all workers of any one given grade or skill receiving an equal share of the surplus; their basic objective is assumed to be to maximise the return per worker ... the workers may be hiring their capital resources either in a competitive capital market fed by private earnings or else from a central governmental organisation which lends out the State's capital resources at rentals which will clear the market (p. 476).

However, Jensen and Meckling then point out a number of unresolved problems, some of which do naturally impinge on the issue of value added calculation. In particular, they discuss the difficulty of defining 'net revenues' or, in our terminology, value added. They dub the problem 'the worker v the State' and put it as follows:

> The desire on the part of the Yugoslav state to limit the kind of claims that individuals can have on producer assets leads to the flaws outlined above, and these in turn lead to a labyrinth of other problems. If the state grants the firms unlimited authority to decide the total compensation package each year, it will in effect be giving authority to the workers to "eat up the assets of the firm". Employees would (with state blessings) be able to convert firm wealth into personal wealth via the annual vote on compensation.

> In an effort to prevent this practice the state lays down rules for computing the amount which will be available each year for distribution among employees and ordains that the firm must "maintain its capital". These rules define what we have called "net revenues" (1979, p. 495).

The calculation of value added in Yugoslav firm then depends not just on the internal rules of the organisation but also on the legal accounting standards laid down by the Yugoslav state. Jensen and Meckling acknowledge that the definition of income is in contention even under capitalism but argue that it is less crucial because there are internal incentives within the corporation to monitor the behaviour of management and workers.

A central role for labour in the production process and thus any consequent adoption of a value added goal may not necessarily require a significant change in legal form. For example, Cowling (1982) argues that, even in an 'orthodox' capitalist system, labour might be able to achieve "overhead" status through collective bargaining:

> By their actions workers would be converting themselves into an element of overhead or capacity costs rather than an element of direct or variable costs. Thus for appropriate changes in planned output (that is, output *reductions*) the appropriate definition of marginal costs would be simply materials costs (p. 122).

A similar, but slightly different proposal, is suggested by Weitzman (1983, 1984). He argues that workers should negotiate for a share in the company's profits. His proposal for profit sharing compensation seem to rely more on a change in attitude on the part of workers rather than a legal change. However, as with the self-managed variant there still seems the likelihood that concern will be with *average* value added maximisation rather than *total* value added with all the implications developed below.

2.8   Value added - some allocational issues

Some writers give the impression that the use of value added in company accounting is an innocuous and generally rather superfluous exercise. Rutherford (1977), for example, says:

> Although it (the statement of value added) contains a good deal of data, it adds little to the information content of an annual report ... The SVA, then, offers a fresh perspective rather than new scenery.

Burchell, et al., (1985) describe value added as:

> ... basically a very marginal calculative elaboration of existing accounting practice ... (p. 400).

Gilchrist (1971), on the other hand, is more forthright and bullish:

> To maximise Profit we need to maximise Added Value. This must be the objective, and all a company's policies should be directed to this

end, provided that it does not achieve the end at the expense of its social obligations (p. 12).

The marginality of value added depends crucially upon whether it is simply seen as information gather *ex post* via financial accounts or whether, *ex ante*, it becomes a goal of the firm or even an objective for maximisation. When accountants say value added accounting is marginal and innocuous they are correct in an *ex post* sense. The use of value added as a *goal* has, however, some fundamental allocational and distributional implications.

In the context of the standard theory of the firm, the usual issues are twofold. Firstly, at what level of output does the firm produce? Secondly, is the firm technically efficient in the sense of producing a given output at minimum cost? Most managerial theories assume that the firm will be technically efficient but that a degree of managerial discretion implies that a level of output can be chosen that reflects the interests of the management rather than the shareholders. This is certainly the approach adopted by Baumol (sales-revenue maximisation), Marris (long-run growth maximisation), and Williamson (management utility maximisation). All these models produce a determinate solution suggesting a level of output or rate of growth greater than that indicated by profit-maximisation. A similar approach with a value added maximising model would seem to be more problematic because the dichotomy between the output decision-making and cost decision-making seems harder to sustain. Making value added the *ex ante* goal of the firm has implications for both the choice of output and for the technical efficiency of the firm. More specifically:

(i) we cannot assume that with this goal the firm will be technically efficient.

(ii) we cannot determine value added without making some sort of assumption about the choices made with regard to fixed and variable costs and which goods and services to 'buy-in' as opposed to producing 'in-house'.

In a sense we have too many unknowns. We cannot calculate value added until we know the ratio between 'purchases' and other costs. On the other hand, an explicit goal of value added maximisation could have an effect on that very ratio!

Much of the accounting literature on value added seems implicitly to assume that *ex ante*, the firms profit-maximise (or, at least, cost-minimise). The value added figure then emerges as an *ex post* calculation. However, as Morley (1978) points out, the decision to pursue value added may result in higher unit costs if higher cost in-house production replaces cheaper bought-in materials and sub-contracted services.

If, on the other hand, we attempt to avoid this problem by assuming technical efficiency then the impact of the value added approach becomes so dissipated that it becomes subsumed by the sales-revenue or growth maximising models. In these models the ultimate source of managerial utility is *size* and, in this context, value added becomes just another indicator of a firm's size. Furthermore, given the undoubted controversies which surround even the *ex post* calculation, it is perhaps not surprising that most theorists (and practitioners) tend to prefer more easily ascertained size indicators such as turnover or market capitalisation.

2.9   Value added and the 'self-monitoring' hypothesis

It is evident that many advocates of the value added approach were looking for an improvement in economic performance based on a psychological impact rather than on any purely technical change in the allocation of resources. Even in this, the behavioural arena, the supporters of profit-seeking are unequivocal in their criticism of any alternative goals. A good example of this viewpoint is provided by Alchian and Demsetz (1972). In their highly influential article they view profits as the reward received by the 'monitor' whose role it is to minimise 'shirking' by members of the firm. Only profits provide an incentive to ensure that costs are minimised. As with many writers who come to this conclusion, they are sceptical concerning the productivity gains of self-monitoring, self-policing organisations such as the labour managed co-operative firm:

> An implicit "auxiliary" assumption of our explanation of the firm is that the cost of team production is increased if the residual claim is not held entirely by the central monitor. That is, we assume that if profit sharing had to be relied upon for all team members, losses from the resulting increase in central monitor shirking would exceed the output gains from the increased incentives of other team members not to shirk (p. 786).

Yet the enhancement of 'team spirit' and 'self-monitoring' was clearly one of the hoped for gains from the adoption of value added accounting. This point was made by Burchell, et al., (1985) thus:

> For in order for value added to be able to represent the company as a co-operating team, the company must first have been constituted as such. On further investigation, however, it transpires that value added is seen as being able to service as a means to this end. Value added

therefore does not simply represent the company as a co-operating team, it also is seen as playing a positive role in the creation of this co-operative harmony ... A change in accounting implies a change in what is seen and hence a change in action (p. 388)

The possibility of changing behaviour as a consequence of changing a technique raises peculiar methodological issues. The usual approach in comparing allocative outcomes is to assume that 'people stay the same' in terms of behavioural assumptions such as 'self-interest', 'rationality', and so on. Yet, as Burchell, et al., indicate, some writers seem to suggest that a change in technique can lead to the sort of change in behaviour that makes the more orthodox formal approach almost redundant.

There are several 'sources' of value added in the context of the firm. Some represent socially desirable output augmentation and some which are less desirable and make no net contribution to total output. The exploitation of monopoly power, vertical and horizontal integration all increase the firm's value added. They do not, however, imply any increase in national output. Wealth creation for the firm is not necessarily wealth creation for the nation.

2.10   Value added and distributional issues

The *distributional* implications of value added seem even more contentious than the allocational issues. This is probably because the representation of company accounts in value added form was supposed to promote a spirit of consensus. An implicit assumption behind this motive was the belief that the figures would reveal a satisfactory division of the cake. All members could see their contribution to the firm's output - they could also see the relative size of their reward. Burchell, et al., (1985) point out that this may have the unsolicited effect of increasing labour dissatisfaction and encouraging attempts to increase labour's share. In other words, it may be seen as a management trick. Citing Stolliday & Attwood (1978), they argue that:

> ... there is no obvious legal reason why the use of value added should not serve as a spur to workers in their attempts to totally eliminate the claims of others in its distribution. In this case value added still functions to reveal a "truth" about production, albeit a rather different one from production as teamwork. From yet another stand-point, the use of value added is viewed as a way of "misleading the workers" in an attempt to gloss "over the problem of profits" (see Hird, 1980; Labour Research, 1978). In this case value added serves as a device for misrepresenting reality. It presents a picture of a unity of interests in the financial performance of a given business organisation, whereas in fact

there exists a basic conflict of interests. Value added, it seems, is a distinctly equivocal social indicator (p. 389).

We should not, however exaggerate such equivocality. While it is true it may be used to represent unity where there is no reality conflict, the mere act of calculating value added puts the firm's labour force on a new and potentially stronger footing. It is saying to the workers that they are members of the firm. They may be downtrodden relative to the shareholders but at least they have become part of the bottom line. In this sense, value added accounting is far more radical than many writers seem to realise. Its abandonment in the 1980's in the United Kingdom was not simply a function of its 'marginality' as Burchell, et al., claim. Neither was it a function of its ambiguity. Rather, the *mode of thinking* introduced by the value added approach is potentially a barrier to the sort of fundamental restructuring that capitalism periodically requires and that has been so much in evidence in the United Kingdom in the 1980's. In this process of restructuring capital takes the initiative of hiring and firing labour at its convenience.

2.11   Value added accounting and the 'visibility' hypothesis

If, as has been argued, value added thinking treats the labour force not as just another input but as *part of the company* then value added accounting is a potential obstacle to the free manipulation of capital assets. Or, in other words, it is a perception of the firm which by implying both a contribution from and an obligation to several groups displaces the traditional primacy of the shareholder. Those who argue that accounting can have a pro-active role in organisational change usually illustrate this process in terms of extending the power of the capitalist/manager by focusing on the shareholder 'residual'. If this argument is consistent in its application then a technique which fudges this residual and emphasises collective efforts and rewards will presumably represent a new 'visibility' (Burchell, et al., 1980). From this perspective the many obituaries for value added accounting may have been premature. As the next section illustrates, new applications of the technique may be developed which do not require any changes in work relationships since we see accounting solely in its 'score keeping' role.

3.   Some empirical evidence for 'screw-driver' activity using value added data

In spite of the ambiguities and interpretative difficulties of using value added data noted above, some interesting results can still be obtained as long as the accounting data are accompanied by other *firm related* data. The use of value added data at the *industry level* in order to investigate 'screw-driver' activity is illustrated by a recent Lloyds Bank Economic Bulletin (1990) which uses data on net output to infer the possibility of 'screw-driver' type activity by Japanese firms in the UK. The bulletin notes that:

> The figures suggest that UK-based Japanese manufacturing industry achieve productivity levels worse than those of all UK industry. These figures are based on the value of net output. Figures for gross output per employee show Japanese levels second to none. In other words, Japanese industry in the UK was, in 1987, producing more per employee than any other group, but was buying in relatively large amounts of raw materials and semi-finished goods to do so, as shown in the table. Of course it is normal practice in Japanese industry to contract out the manufacture of many components. Nevertheless, the figures lend support to the argument that some Japanese plants in the UK are 'screw-driver' operations performing final assembly from parts possibly imported from Japan (pp. 1-2).

The data are shown below in table 7.1.

Table 7.1
Manufacturing production in UK by country of ownership, levels of net output and purchases as a percentage of output

	Net output/head (£)	Purchases as % of output
U.S.A.	34000	61
Canada	31000	59
Switzerland	24000	65
France	46000	47
Netherlands	27000	54
Germany	31000	56
Australia	53000	48
Japan	22000	79
Total foreign controlled	32000	60
Domestic controlled	21000	55

Source: Census of Production, 1987, Business Monitor PA 1002

One obvious determinant of value added per head is the type of industry. For example, retailing is bound to have a very high % of purchases. One way of eliminating this is to focus on one industry and then study the interfirm differences. Another determinant of value added is whether the firm is more concerned with manufacturing or with servicing. This distinction is especially important in the electronics industry on which I have chosen to concentrate in this book. This industry is frequently criticised for its lack of international competitiveness (see chapter nine) and for its apparent propensity to rely on screw-driver operations. Amstrad, in particular, has clashed with the EC commission over whether it can even be classified as a European manufacturer such is its extensive use of non-EC production.

In the table below (table 7.2) Amstrad is compared with three other firms in the UK electronics industry. The format is the same as in table 7.1 but the figures are not strictly comparable for a number of reasons. The Census of Production data is based on surveys conducted at the plant level. The firm data are estimated from company accounts. It thus includes overseas sales and overseas employees since companies do not now have to report on the number of UK employees separately. Furthermore, none of the companies have a value added statement or a 'net output' figure. Changes in stocks and work-in-progress were accounted for by averaging four years sales data. Fortunately, all the companies in the table used the reporting format which itemises 'Raw materials and consumables' and 'other operating charges'. These figures were summed over four years, averaged and deducted from the average sales figure for the same period. On this basis, the figures in table 7.2 are comparable with each other. Given the high rate of attrition in this industry plus the high level of concentration, the table actually portrays a surprisingly large chunk of UK owned electronics industry. The industry is dominated by GEC (1989 sales, £5,878m), STC (£2,607m) and Ferranti (£928m) with 17 of the remaining publicly quoted companies with turnovers of less than £250m. Thus the only large quoted company not in the table is STC which uses an alternative reporting format. Although a value added figure can be estimated, it would not be comparable with the others in the sample.

The Gross rather than Net Value Added figure has been calculated. As Morley (1978) has pointed out, there is little agreement between accountants on whether to include depreciation in the 'bought-in' component or not. The preference has been to report the gross figure. In any case, economists are generally happier working with GNP rather than NNP concepts!

Table 7.2

Net output/head and percentage of purchases in some UK quoted electronics companies

Company	Total Sales* (£'000)	Employment*	Net V.A. per head	'Purchases' as % output
Amstrad	516,924	1,118	72,504	84.0%
Ferranti	743,525	23,681	13,987	55.0%
GEC	5,483m	156,602	14,093	59.7%
Logica	119,220	2,831	30,927	26.6%

Source: 1986-89 company accounts/datastream
*4 year average figure based on company data.

The interpretation of the above data suggests that the key column is the final one. Both Amstrad and Logica have recorded high value added per head but, whereas the former has a 'buy-in-rate' of 84%, the latter is an extremely low 26.6%. These data reflect the different activities of the two companies. Amstrad is basically a marketing organisation while Logica is a software company. The two manufacturing companies, GEC and Ferranti are roughly comparable in terms of their 'buy-in rate' and in value added per head.

On the basis of the above data, Amstrad's claims to be a manufacturing company in the UK or anywhere seem flimsy. It could be argued that the company simply follows the normal Japanese of sub-contracting production. However, the Japanese model is one of 'quasi-hierarchy' whereby contractual relationships are longterm and intimate. Even Amstrad's own publicity does not suggest Japanese style contracts. On the contrary, the company extols the flexibility advantages of 'shopping around'.

The above comments are not intended to denigrate the real achievements of Amstrad. I am sure that I am not the only researcher who has benefited in having access to a low cost Amstrad word processor. Indeed, the high level of value added achieved by the company requires some explanation. It does not seem to easily fit in with the 'organisational rent' analogy since that model suggests an ability to appropriate a long term *equilibrium* surplus. The explanation probably lies with a Schumpeterian 'entrepreneurial' profit model whereby the company upsets equilibrium through the introduction of new products and the creation of new markets. The production process aspect of the Schumpetrian model has been left to Amstrad's Far Eastern suppliers. The sustainability of the company's success seems to hinge on the company maintaining its entrepreneurial vigour and on its suppliers being content to leave the marketing to others. The former seems to reside in the person of Alan Sugar while, in terms of the latter, there are signs that Far Eastern manufacturers are beginning to introduce their own brands in the West.[5] These developments will be further explored in chapter nine.

4. Concluding remarks

The conventional neoclassical paradigm with its production function approach cannot even begin to provide theoretical articulation of 'Screw-driver and Warehouse' types of firm. In contrast, the management control/new institutional literature does offer both a framework of analysis and a means of theoretically identifying such firms. The accounting literature on value added offers further insights since the definition of value added revolves intimately around the question of the nature and extent of the firm. It was shown that an analysis of value added, or more specifically, a firm's 'bought-in' figure, can help in the quantification of the issues both from an industry and from an individual firm perspective.

Notes

1. This is not to suggest that 'ownership does not matter'. As was pointed out in chapter five, ownership does matter but the exercise of the owners' control function may take different forms with different consequences for economic development.

2. Some of these anxieties relate to the 'branch' economy syndrome which is often discussed in the context of British regional imbalance.

3. The notion of 'GB Ltd' has been the butt of satirists for nearly two decades. Yet, the idea that there are close analogies between wealth creation and appropriation by the firm and by the nation is an idea whose time seems to have come - witness the interest shown in Porter's most recent book (Porter, 1990).

4. Most of the material in sections 2.1 - 2.11 has been published in Seal (1987b).

5. The recent problems of Amstrad and Alan Sugar further support the above suspicions!

8 The economic consequences of management accounting

One of the basic premises of this book is that economic calculation cannot be taken for granted. Cognitive problems are endemic. Allocative decisions are driven by information flows and calculative routines as well as by resource constraints and the preferences of economic agents. In this sort of world, institutions matter. In particular, institutions which are directly involved in economic calculation such as, in the UK, *management accounting,* matter. Yet this viewpoint is neither the basis of orthodox neoclassical economics nor even accepted by many management accountants themselves.[1] The chapter explores the role of management accounting in terms of an 'economic consequences' approach. The aim is to indicate both a theoretical and an empirical line of analysis.

While the 'Economic consequences' approach is more usually associated with financial accounting as in the analysis of links between financial reporting and share prices, it may also be applied to investigate the links, if any, between internal and external performance indicators. Just as the economic consequences model may be used to appraise the usefulness of financial reporting, it may also contribute towards the debate over the relevance or otherwise of modern management accounting as initiated by writers such as Kaplan and Johnson (Kaplan, 1983;1984, Johnson and Kaplan, 1987). The issues raised in Johnson and Kaplan's book are especially pertinent to this book for the three reasons.

Firstly, the general connection that Johnson and Kaplan (J&K) have made between accounting and economic performance is an important theme of the book. Secondly, J&K have conveniently couched their arguments within the markets and hierarchies paradigm which is generally the preferred framework in this book. Finally, they provide both evidence of, and explanations for,

156

'mistakes' in economic allocation. This critical aspect is particularly useful in support of a natural selection model as outlined in previous chapters where it is argued that resources are misallocated at least partly on the basis of *miscalculation* rather than as a result of resource *manipulation*. To put it in Aldrich's (1979) terminology, the selection process (which in J&K is implicit rather than explicit) is oriented toward the environment as an 'information flow' rather than a 'resource flow' (Aldrich, p.110).

1. The 'Relevance Lost' debate

The ideas in 'Relevance Lost' (J&K, 1987) and expounded in a number of other articles by Kaplan have had a profound impact in the academic accounting literature with reviews and counter arguments still pouring out (Bromwich and Bhimani, 1989; Ezzamel et al., 1990). The emotional response to the Kaplan thesis reveals a certain ambivalence. On the one hand, Kaplan is criticising both the academic development and the practice of management accounting. On the other, he is ascribing to these erroneous accounting theories and practices a far greater economic influence than is usual. Accounting is projected as being far more than 'score keeping' - it is seen as affecting long and short-run economic decision making within firms and between firms and the market. As Kaplan puts it in his 1983 article:

> ... While accounting cannot play the key role in initiating or implementing technological innovations and organisational change, the accounting system should provide incentives for improving manufacturing performance and measurements to evaluate progress toward this goal (p. 689).

1.1 The 'Kaplan thesis': a brief summary

According to Johnson and Kaplan (J&K,1987) a misallocation of resources is occurring in the US economy because of mistakes in economic calculation. These mistakes are due to a combination of both faulty information and unsatisfactory decision rules. More specifically, the data provided by management accounting are too late, too aggregated, and too distorted. According to J&K, modern management accounting fails to measure actual increases or decreases in economic value. This has three main consequences:

a. Management accounting reports do little to help reduce operating costs or increase productivity.

b. Management accounting fails to accurately cost products.

c. Management accounting encourages 'short-termism'.

Not only are operations poorly controlled but long term mistakes are made in terms of product pricing, make-or-buy decisions, and capital investment.

J&K chronicle a history of the development of management accounting as it accompanied *technological* changes in industry and transport as well *organisational* changes such as vertical integration and divisionalisation. Since about 1925, they suggest, the subject has not only failed to progress as a useful tool of economic management but has actually 'lost relevance'. J&K are critical of an evident undue focus on performance indicators such as RO1 and earnings. The sin is one of commission and omission - the error of the 'missing measurements'. As they point out:

> A company's economic value is not merely the sum of the values of its tangible assets, whether measured at historic cost, replacement cost, or current market prices. It also includes the value of intangible assets: the stock of innovative products, the knowledge of flexible and high quality production processes, employee talent and morale, customer loyalty and product awareness, efficient distribution network, and the like
> ... In earlier years, when companies gained competitive advantage mainly through economies of scale and low cost production, the accounting model defect was not significant. But for contemporary organisations, the intangible assets may be the most critical. Therefore, recent overemphasis on achieving superior short-term earnings performance is occurring just at a time when such performance has become a far less valid indicator of changes in the company's long term competitive position (p. 202).[2]

1.2   A critique

The 'validity' of these measures may actually depend upon the viewpoint adopted. As will be seen shortly, the relevance or otherwise of accounting measures can be, and has been, empirically investigated. Other limitations of the J&K approach have been looked at in other chapters. For example, in as much as measurement changes behaviour, it might change it in undesirable directions (the Human Relations critique of Taylorism). Secondly, Kaplan seems reluctant to confront the institutional obstacles to his call for improved manufacturing performance. In particular, his criticisms of the role of the Stock Market, especially the 'market for control', are too oblique to be effective. From this perspective, Kaplan's ideas seem under developed rather than incorrect. His reluctance to develop many of the ideas he introduces may stem from a distaste for further conjecture. Alternatively, inhibitions may stem from a reluctance to push the ideas to the point which his readers would regard as being too radical.

Bromwich and Bhimani state that acceptance of the J&K thesis 'suggests either laxity or lack of managerial ability on the part of corporate executives for over five decades in blindly allowing financial reporting obligations to determine internal management information priorities' (Bromwich and Bhimani, 1989, p. 47). There is an alternative explanation which is critical, not of managerial laxity or lack of ability, but rather of the structure of incentives in the environment in which managers operate. Thus the natural selection model already outlined argues that the 'mistakes' identified by J&K may be explained in terms of a perfectly rational[3] adaptation to the prevailing selection process. Any imperfections in the system must be traced to the selection process which, as I have already argued, favours a 'financial control' style of management.

Just as Kaplan's explanation is only partial is proposed solutions, particularly the discovery (or rediscovery) of the 'missing measurements', may be, at best, a partial solution and, at worst, aggravate matters through a reversion to the ethos of 'scientific management'. For example, in his 1983 article, Kaplan looks at three areas of management control-quality, inventory and productivity improvement - where Japanese practices have been so favourably compared with American practices. While he argues for new measurements to improve matters, the real 'solution' lies in the more fundamental issue of the internal relationships between the firm and its workers and the external relationships with suppliers. In transactions cost parlance, changes in the 'measurement branch' may be necessary but they are unlikely to be sufficient without change in the 'governance branch'.

Hiromoto (1988) argues that it is the *interpretation* of accounting data rather than any technical elaborations that distinguishes the Japanese approach from American practice. He states that:

> Japanese companies seem to use accounting systems more to motivate employees to act in accordance with long-term manufacturing strategies than to provide senior management with precise data on costs, variances, and profits. Accounting plays more of an 'influencing' role than an 'informing role (p. 22).

One of the best examples of Kaplan's critique of modern US business methodology is provided by his comparison of US and Japanese approaches to inventory. The US approach is generally characterised by the usual textbook models of stock control. In contrast, the Japanese approach is characterised by a pragmatic attempt to eliminate uncertainty and thus the need for inventory. This is clearly the aim of the well known 'just-in-time' system of supply. The ingredient missing in the UK/US is not primarily appropriate performance indicators but a radically different management and business style. The likely obstacle in the UK environment is an 'arms-length' tradition of management exacerbated by a class system which further breaks up the team-work of the Japanese firm (Dore, 1973, Aoki, 1986). Furthermore, as described in chapter six, the Japanese deliberately foster 'networks' of related firms. Long-term links help to develop the co-operation required to run a just-in-time system. A very different tradition has developed in, for example, the UK motor industry where the philosophy is to keep suppliers 'on their toes' by requiring frequent re-negotiation of contracts. Of course, the reliance on trust in a long term relationship is characteristic of the Japanese firm's attitude to both its suppliers, its customers, and its workers.

Given the central importance of incentive systems in all theories of social organisation, Kaplan seems particularly wary in his comments on the existing incentive structure in US manufacturing industry. For example, he suggests that it is:

> ... (L)ess well understood is why senior managers' incentive plans should rely so heavily on financial measures of performance (e.g. earnings per share, return on capital in excess of a minimal rate of return) rather than operating measures more consistent with the long-term health of the firm (1983, p. 697).

Clearly, Kaplan is indicating a research agenda focused on analysing the incentives for gathering particular data and basing rewards on it. More specifically, research on management compensation systems would seem to be suggested. There is, indeed, a growing literature in this area which, significantly, is appearing in the accounting and finance journals.[3] Much of this literature is critical of compensation practices in US companies which is somewhat surprising given that the theoretical basis of much of the research is the supposedly panglossian agency paradigm (see especially Baker, Jensen and Murphy, 1988).

In terms of other environmental pressures, Kaplan is mildly critical (see below) of the US financial system but believes that any problems may be reduced by good public relations. He recommends 'an active programme of investor communications ... (which) ... could be implemented by firms committed to a long-term strategy of product and market leadership' (p. 699). In other words, although he exhibits an understandable mistrust of the investment community he suggests that 'investor education' provides adequate safeguards for the innovating manufacturer. Similar views have been expressed by other writers who have argued that manages can influence, even manipulate, their environments. This important 'strategic choice' perspective will be looked at in more detail in the next chapter in the specific context of the UK electronics industry.

In spite of the above criticisms and qualifications of the 'Kaplan thesis', I have to confess that Kaplan's general approach as exhibited in his 1983 article was an early source of inspiration for this book. Thus, whatever detailed reservations I have subsequently acquired concerning his arguments, his boldness and scope as well as his critical tone encouraged me to explore the economic influence of accounting practices. Thus the gaps and/or errors in his analysis, should be regarded as a stimulus for fresh research. In general terms, the problem with many of the 'missing measurement' or 'short-termist' type arguments is the inadequacy of the conceptual framework surrounding management accounting. In particular, as has already been pointed out in previous chapters, there has been a failure to integrate the control of the labour process and the control of the investment process. The latter is generally modelled in terms of a stock approach (the PV rule) while the former is modelled in terms of a flow approach. These issues will be addressed below.

2. The 'short-termist' debate

2.1 Is the problem 'information inefficiency' or myopia?

As we have seen, Kaplan adds his voice to those (in the UK and the US) who are critical of 'short-termism'. Although his discussion is focused mainly on internal performance evaluation, his criticisms have obvious relevance concerning the impact of the external monitoring role of the stock-market. He argues that there is some evidence to suggest that 'there was apparently less pressure for short-term financial performance in the 1920s and 1930s than exists in the 1970s and 1980s' [Kaplan, 1984, (p. 411)]. The clear inference is that 'short-termism' leads to poorer decision-making.

There may be, for example, a failure to monitor the performance of a company or division over the whole cycle or a failure in spotting 'opportunistic' management behaviour. Although this book is obviously sympathetic in general terms concerning the possible social inefficiencies of capital markets in the UK and US, it has already been suggested in earlier chapters that criticisms based on short-termist type arguments are not always quite as easy to sustain as might be thought.

2.2 'Short-termism': a definition

Suppose the firm is visualised as a bundle of n projects. Then its economic value is the sum of the net present values (NPV) of these projects as determined by cash flows and discount rate(s). That is

$$NPV = \sum_{i=1}^{n} NPV_i \qquad (1)$$

This perspective on the firm shows that it is not always clear what critics of stock markets in the US and UK mean when they talk about 'short-termism'. Do they mean that markets do not recognise the future cash flows of a company or that they tend to discount them too heavily? The second alternative suggests that there is a 'correct' social rate of time preference and an 'incorrect' market rate of time preference. Or, more specifically, the investors rate of time preference is greater than the socially optimal rate of time preference.

It is beyond the scope of this chapter or book to do full justice to the huge literature on the socially optimal discount rate (see Layard, 1972, for a good selection of classic articles). A strict adherence to Paretian principles would rule out crude criticisms of a market determined rate of discount based on straightforward charges of myopia since such a criticism involves an appeal to 'unscientific' arguments such as the Pigovian "defective telescopic faculty". There are, however, sophisticated discussions of external effects, 'isolation' paradoxes and other capital market imperfections which suggest that, in fact, the social discount rate should be less than the market discount rate. The context of the discussion is, however, the appropriate rate of discount for public expenditure projects and is not concerned directly with formulating policies for the private sector.

The existing industrial policy debate is not usually couched in the rigorous framework of Paretian welfare economics. Grand issues of Social Choice versus Individual Choice are usually transmuted into more modest concerns such as the often expressed view that Japanese and German banks take a longer term view than UK and US shareholders and fund managers. Evidence is often anecdotal (see e.g. the account of the Deutsche bank's tolerance of the early problems of the Mannesmann Company [Eatwell, 1982]). The inference seems to be that banks in these countries are more 'patriotic' than British or American shareholders who rarely reveal preferences whereby personal profit is sacrificed for the sake of national economic growth. While there is an understandable reluctance to ascribe differences in national economic growth rates to such academically unfashionable concepts as nationalism, it is often hard to avoid the feeling that ultimately some writers would fall back on such explanations if only they could square it with their professional and ethical sensibilities. Of course, the real problem with the literature is that, as was argued in chapter six, it is only recently that the heavier economic journals have taken institutionalist and comparative approaches at all seriously.

2.3 'Short-termism' in planned economies

In terms of the comparative systems literature, it has long been noted how non-market or planned systems can exhibit 'short-termist' type problems. It has frequently been observed that (pre-Perestroika) Soviet managers are (were?) reluctant to introduce new products or new manufacturing technology. To some extent, this is explained by the lack of incentive in that, unlike the owners in the capitalist firm, Soviet managers cannot appropriate the rewards for such innovation. Recent advances in institutional economics (Williamson, 1985) have shown that these problems are not confined to planned economies. Salaried managers in *both planned and market systems* have incentives to behave opportunistically and *both* suffer from similar disincentives to risk failure in meeting short-term targets. The Soviet manager may find that inevitable 'teething' problems mean that new products and new processes could result in non fulfilment of short-term output targets. Paradoxically, this is a very similar problem to that facing the capitalist manager who may fear that similar technical problems may damage short-run profitability thereby affecting bonuses or even a hostile takeover. As Williamson points out, if these drawbacks were not general to *all* hierarchical systems then there would be no difficulty in organising the economy in one huge firm (Williamson, 1985). Couching the argument in terms of comparative systems, it seems that *both* Soviet planners and capitalist investors have difficulty in monitoring and rewarding managers who excel at operational efficiency and enterprising technological innovation.

2.4 Short-termism and the managerial labour market

Kaplan's solution is to reform and supplement the conventional monitoring techniques and, as such, is, presumably, relatively 'systems-neutral' in that similar reforms could improve Soviet performance. Of course, as has already been pointed out, Kaplan also argues that a major source of difficulty in using conventional performance and incentive systems is the increased mobility of managers in the managerial labour market. With lower mobility, managerial performance will be assessed far more on the basis of long term operating efficiency and innovation and less on short term financial indicators and 'paper entrepreneurship'. The benefit of monitoring efficiency may of course be added to other benefits stemming from the increased congruence of interest between human and firm capital (see Section 3.2).

163

Given the frequent and extensive criticisms of the 'bundle of projects' perspective on the firm expressed in this book, it may seem odd to call upon the model in the context of the short-termist debate. It does, however, illustrate that the task of making accusations of short-termism stick is theoretically quite difficult. Jensen (1988), for example, argues quite convincingly that while managers *may* be short-termist, markets are not.

Alternative performance criteria provide a solution. Thus, it is actually far more satisfactory to re-cast the 'short-termist' debate in a broader paradigm which looks at economic performance as comprising *more* than just discounted cash flows - a paradigm in which Kaplan's missing measurements viewpoint would seem to have some resonance. For example, as we shall see in chapter nine in the context of the UK electronics industry, there may be a conflict between success in the product market and success in the market for control which is relatively easy to empirically observe. As both this section and the next illustrate, in spite of its many limitations the neoclassical approach will always offer the distinctive benefits of analytical rigour.

3.   The 'micro-micro' economics of supply

Kaplan's general argument suggests that there is a link between microanalytical economic calculation and the overall competitiveness and efficiency of an economy. In this section a theory is developed which forges such a link. The obvious starting point is the well known neoclassical theory of supply which not only links micro decisions on production to a general equilibrium model of the economy but also has well known welfare properties (Bator, 1957). Since, however, it posits a world where perfect knowledge removes the need for firms, let alone management accounting, it cannot be expected to provide much guidance on issues such as the boundary between financial and non-financial control.

3.1   The neoclassical theory of supply

In the neoclassical theory of supply the technical domain is separated from the economic domain via assumption. There is a clear distinction between technological efficiency and economic efficiency. The former is exogenously provided by the *production function:*

$$Q = g(L,K........) \qquad (2)$$

According to Baumol, the 'existence of such a function already presupposes a set of optimality calculations on the part of the company's engineers or production managers' (1965, p.251). This useful analytical device means that with given prices for inputs, cost curves can be derived.

Alternatively, the impact of different relative input prices can be studied using iso-quant analysis. If w and r are the prices of L and K respectively, then the costs of production are given by the following equation:

$$C = wL + rK \qquad (3)$$

The production problem is solved through the maximisation of profit subject to the above cost function. The theory throws up familiar marginal rates of substitution between factors of production and, by extension, between products. Yet, from a management accounting perspective, most of the key problems have simply been assumed away! Of course, as has already been stated in this book, an analysis of internal allocation of resources within the firm or the 'task of management' has never traditionally been the purpose of the theory of the neoclassical theory of supply. It was designed to predict how supply responds to changes in, for example, prices of inputs and outputs or to exogenous technological change. In comparative institutional terms, the theory *does* demonstrate how the price system *can* allocate resources in a decentralised economy. It does not, however, enable us to compare institutional arrangements between economies which are similarly based on market allocation and private property but which vary in terms of combinations of market and hierarchy or different management control practices.

Before introducing an explicitly institutionalist approach, we should note the contribution of some dissenting economic voices who have qualified the production function approach. For example, as modified by Alchian (1959) and Alessi (1967), the analysis of the firm may be conducted in stock rather than flow terms. Costs are defined as 'the change of equity caused by the performance of some specified operation (Alchian, 1959, p.160). The choice of input combination can be expressed as a question of intertemporal choice where 'the individual firm is hypothesised to adjust the quantity and the form of each input it uses until the present value of the marginal stream of outlays is equal to the present value of the marginal stream of receipts for each input' (Alessi,1967, p.1135). However, this perspective can cut both ways. Alessi and Alchian clearly expect that the value of equity will reflect the discounted net cash flows of the firm. The direction of causation is from the firm's costs and revenues to the value of its equity. As will be discussed later in this chapter, a 'reverse causation' may be hypothesised by which an 'incorrect' value for the equity impinges on the firm's operations in a dysfunctional manner - cash flows may be miscalculated due to incomplete markets or the discount rate may be 'incorrect' as discussed in the previous section. However, this chain of events requires the abandonment of the neoclassical dichotomy between the *technical* and the *economic* - a recognition that production functions may be imperfectly specified.

3.2   Enter 'X-efficiency'

The impossibility of completely specifying the production function was the starting point for Leibenstein's (1966) theory of 'X-efficiency'. Leibenstein argued that 'microeconomic theory focuses on allocative efficiency to the exclusion of other types of efficiencies that, in fact are much more significant in many instances. Furthermore, improvement in "non-allocative efficiency" is an important aspect of the process of growth' (Leibenstein, 1966, p. 392).

According to Leibenstein, X-efficiency is concerned with three elements ... 1) intra-plant motivation, (2) external motivational efficiency, and (3) nonmarket input efficiency. He argued that inputs cannot be transformed into predetermined outputs due to incomplete labour contracts, incomplete markets for other factors, incompletely specified production functions and tacit co-operation and imitation between firms. Although critical of the production function paradigm, Leibenstein did not develop his argument in terms of *cognitive problems* but argued that - efficiency was a function of competition. In other words, *motivation* was all important and more competition = more effort. Subsequent contractual models based on information impactedness or information asymmetries between principal and agent suggest that the effort issue is really more complicated. Indeed, recent work by Holmstrom and Ricart I Costa (1986) suggests that problems may arise even when effort is assured. They suggest that given conflict between firm capital and human capital, managerial effort may be misdirected rather than absent. Holmstrom and Ricart I Costa (H&R) argue that there is a misalignment of incentives. As they put it:

> ... Divergent preferences arise from the dissonance between the financial value of present performance and its reputation value. In effect, decisions influence two separate capital returns, one human and one financial. Absent explicit incentive schemes, a manager is concerned only about his human capital stream; while owners are concerned only about the financial returns. To bridge the preference gap some form of contracting is essential (p. 837).

Interestingly enough, H&R point out that the problem could be solved if manager could sell himself to firm. They naturally rule this out as being inconsistent with contemporary conventions on property rights. An alternative solution is offered by the Japanese lifetime employment system which so effectively resolves the conflict between the firm's capital and the manager's human capital.

166

These emerging developments in agency theory suggest a real breakthrough since the source of the agency problem is more related to *multimarket conflicts* as described in chapter four than on the earlier 'effort' models. In other words, the emphasis is less on *managerial shirking*. Managers are assumed to be industrious but are concerned with the value of their lifetime income stream. As remarked earlier, much of the literature on management compensation is surprisingly 'unpanglossian' even with work associated with Jensen (Baker et al., 1988). The overwhelming theme of their paper is the extent of the gap between contracting theory and actual compensation systems in the US. In particular, they find that '(t)he empirical relation between the pay of top executives and firm performance, while positive and statistically significant, is tiny' (p.611). By 'contracting theory' they are obviously alluding to the principal-agent version rather than the transaction cost version in which the 'anomalies' have been explained in terms of incomplete contracts and contrasts between internal and external labour markets. Paradoxically, this new perspective in agency theory on the *misdirection* rather than the *absence* of managerial effort actually meets some of the criticisms that Kaplan has expressed on the applicability of agency theory to management accounting!

As has been discussed extensively in chapters five and six, not only is the firm more than a production function, it is also, *pacé* Alchian and Alessi, more than a project or bundle of projects. In a first best world of full or costless information, the stock approach has much to commend it. In a second or even third best world of limited/costly information and bounded rationality, first best optimality rules such as those suggested by the present value rule may actually take the firm and the economy further away from economic efficiency.

In the context of this debate, the contingency (as opposed to a universalist) approach to management control takes on a new resonance. Thus, for example, when Ouchi (1977) suggests that control methods will differ depending on the availability of suitable output measures and/or a knowledge of the 'transformation process', these distinctions may be interpreted as representing differential knowledge of the production function. This knowledge would seem to be a function partly of output ambiguity (incomplete markets) or technological inseparability. Ouchi's examples tend to focus on extremely differentiated types of organisations (foreign embassies versus tin can factories). Yet it seems plausible that similar differences, in degree, if not in kind, can be identified between manufacturing firms on the basis, for example, of new product technology versus mature product technology.

3.3 A transaction cost perspective on management accounting.

Much of the contracting literature emphasises the contrast between the production function view of the firm and the contracting perspective. As Riordan and Williamson point out '(B)oth approaches, however, maintain an economising orientation. And plainly production and transaction costs both need to be taken into account in any effort to realise a broadly economising result' [(1985)p. 366]. This section draws on their approach in order to provide the theoretical link between microeconomic calculation and wider economic performance highlighted by Kaplan. With some additions and modifications, the TCE framework generates results which suggest the sort of dysfunctional role for management accounting alluded to by Kaplan and Johnson.

3.4 Asset specificity and the cost of production

The importance of asset specificity has already been discussed as has an heuristic model in which asset specificity is shown as an *independent* variable helping to determine in which circumstances *internal* organisation or *market* organisation is the least cost mode. The model assumes that 'both modes produce the same level of output and that the optimal level of asset specificity is the same for each' Riordan and Williamson, 1985, (p. 369-370). An alternative heuristic may be contemplated where asset specificity (A) is a *dependent* variable being a function of governance costs (G) such that:

$$A = A(G) \qquad (4)$$

where $dA/dG < 0$

Production costs are assumed to be a function of asset specificity such that:

$$C = C(A) \qquad (5)$$

and $dC/dA < 0$

The relationships are illustrated in figure 8.1. In this model, asset specificity is the link joining exogenously induced changes in governance costs to changes in productive efficiency.

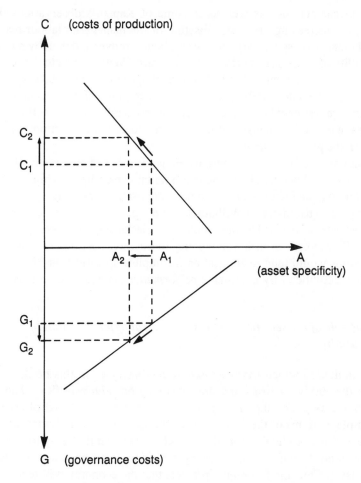

Figure 8.1   Increase in governance costs leads to fall in productivity and rise in production costs

A rise in governance costs ($G_1 \rightarrow G_2$) causes a fall in asset specificity ($A_1 \rightarrow A_2$) and thence a fall in conventionally measured productivity. Thus rises in governance costs cause a reduction in the overall performance of the economy. Of course, the rise in governance costs may also cause a change in the balance between market and internal organisation but this cannot be expected to fully compensate in productivity terms.

The above model begs two questions. Firstly, why might governance costs increase? Secondly, why are production costs a function of asset specificity? The first question is easily related to the model of the selection process outlined in chapter four as well as to some of Kaplan's observations. For example, the increasing professionalisation of the managerial labour market reduces human asset specificity, increases labour turnover and thereby reduces the reliability of managerial performance measures. With respect to the second question, it could be argued that technological options are reduced if specific assets cannot be adequately protected against premature termination of agreements. Investment takes place in general assets rather than specific assets reducing the general propensity of the economy to earn organisational rent as outlined in the previous chapter.

One limitation of the above approach is that it is based on a reconciliation with the traditional neoclassical production function paradigm. While it is true that 'technological features of economic organisation are ... relegated to a secondary role' (Riordan and Williamson, 1985, p. 365) a strong neoclassical flavour persists. In particular, the production relationships are assumed to be fully specified when, in a thoroughgoing transaction cost model, cognitive imperfections would tend to suggest an incomplete specification. Or, as we saw earlier, activities vary in terms of *performance ambiguity* as well as asset specificity.

3.5 The role of the selection process: a reversal of the direction of causality

Another limitation which has been extensively analysed in this book is that although the surviving firms and practices may be *relatively* fitter than the others, they may not be the *fittest* in terms of a more absolute set of criteria. For example, in terms of the performance ambiguity model, activities may be chosen where the production function is well known and thus easy to manage via output controls, but which, almost by definition, focus on mature products and processes. Thus the full model predicts that the economy will tend to be technologically unprogressive if output measures become the dominant mode of control. Of course, financial control systems tend to be output orientated. The selection model outlined in chapter four suggested that this mode may be chosen because of its survival properties in an environment dominated by an active market for control. The theory of supply is thus turned on its head! The direction of causation flows down from the top of the hierarchy rather than emerging from a quasi-technical marriage of economics and production engineering as envisaged in the neoclassical theory of supply outlined in Section 3.1.

4. Empirical testing: towards an 'economic consequences' model of management accounting

The wider hypothesis which emerges from the discussion in this and earlier chapters is that, if there is a crisis in management accounting then the culprit is not that incompetent management decision making is leading to an inappropriate choice of performance indicators. It is rather that the selection of control techniques is determined by the environment of the firm which has selected the techniques of modern management accounting as representing the best 'fit'. Furthermore, as has already been discussed at length, good fit does not imply any absolute superiority. The implication of this analysis is that changes in practices must be contingent on changes in the firm's environment.

This hypothesis lends itself to a research design which is, in principle, quite straightforward. Once the external criterion for selection 'success' is identified, the researcher focuses on the internal performance indicators in order to test the degree of correlation. It is not even necessary to establish causality between *ex ante* decision rules and *ex post* outcomes. If there is a correlation then managers and investors will tend to infer a causal link whether it exists or not. In the context of the 'Relevance Lost' arguments, it is no good arguing that measurements such as RO1 and earnings have no economic meaning if meaning is given by stock market. In the criteria of the *economic consequences* literature, information has relevance if it affects a firm's stock market valuation. This, in itself, may be a flawed valuation but, from a survivalist viewpoint, it may, in a US or UK context, be the only valuation that matters.

4.1 Accounting returns and shareholder returns

The theoretical work on the relationship between accounting measures of return and 'true yields' has a long pedigree (see Solomon, 1966). The debate has been revived by advocates of shareholder wealth maximising approaches to management (see e.g. Rappaport, 1986). This approach sometimes referred to as 'strategic financial management' is predicated on an apparent lack of theoretical and empirical association between accounting numbers and stock market valuations. The approach has been enthusiastically pedalled by academics/consultants who argue that firms interested in 'creating shareholder value' should measure success with the right indicators. The 'right' indicators are derived from a valuation model which indicates the internal 'value drivers' and which should therefore inform management decision making.

The aim of the empirical work outlined in this chapter is to investigate the degree of association between firm value and a number of 'internal' performance indicators. These are chosen by reference to the literature on management accounting and strategy rather than from the finance literature. Thus the aim is *not* to build a valuation model or to test existing models such as the Arbitrage pricing or Capital asset pricing models. The theoretical and empirical strengths and weaknesses of these finance models are the subject of a literature which is already so large that even decade-by-decade surveys present monumental tasks. The 'economic consequences' literature is similarly immense (Lev and Ohlson, 1982). The aim in this particular literature is frequently to investigate the economic impact of *financial* reporting whether as a test either of market efficiency or of the economic relevance of financial accounting. Thus posing the issues in terms of *management accounting* is a relative rare endeavour. This may be because the interpretation of findings is even more problematic than in the literatures cited above. For example, one of the difficulties in testing the efficient markets hypothesis (EMH) and the Capital Asset Pricing Model (CAPM) is the so-called 'dual hypothesis problem' (Roll, 1977). In other words, in order to test the CAPM the stock market must be assumed to be a 'fair game'. There is a similar 'dual hypothesis' problem in the study presented below in so far as an economic interpretation of internal performance indicators using the firm's stock price as an external bench mark requires the assumption that the market be 'semi-strongly' efficient.

4.2 The hypotheses

a) Accounting measures of performance are chosen and used as a basis of corporate control and executive incentive because they will improve economic wealth of corporation's shareholders.

b) Management control techniques such as financial control ratios are chosen in order to protect existing managers from loss of office via a hostile takeover. In this study it is assumed that the main requirement for survivability is that shareholders are satisfied by the level of return so as to avoid takeover or any other form of threat to the incumbent management.

4.3 The data

The data are drawn from a cross sectional study of the companies listed on the UK stock market as being in the electronics industry. The issue of industry classification is discussed in the next chapter. There are theoretical problems in looking at firms in the same industry. For example, profitability may to some extent be seen as a 'zero-sum' game. However, unlike the usual industrial economics studies, the aim of this study is not to explain the levels of profitability in the industry but see whether conventional internal measures of performance reflect *ex post* external performance. The industry has been chosen as the main empirical reference point throughout the book. The aim is not to present a comprehensive analysis of the industry but use it as a testing ground for the theoretical approach developed in the book. Thus the empirical results generated in this chapter also have relevance for chapter nine.

The results are summarised in tables 8.1 and 8.2 below.

Table 8.1
Correlation ratios

MTB > CORRC2-C2   C3   C4   C5   C6

	C2	EPS89	EPS	C5
EPS89	0.541			
EPS	0.261	0.849		
C5	0.097	0.673	0.646	
C6	0.374	0.735	0.633	0.877

Table 8.2
Regression results

The regression equation is:
C2= 28.4 + 0.953 EPS89 - 0.661 EPS - 2.22 C5 + 2.51 C6

Predictor	Coef	Stdev	T-ratio	P
Constant	28.41	19.42	1.46	0.163
EPS89	0.9533	0.3076	3.10	0.007
EPS	-0.6611	0.4131	-1.60	0.129
C5	-2.2178	0.7887	-2.81	0.013
C6	2.508	1.215	2.07	0.055

s = 21.10   R-sq = 62.2%   R-sq(adj) = 52.7%

The definition of the variables is as follows:

C2 = actual annual return in 1989;
EPS89 = % change in earnings per share in 1989;
EPS = four year average % growth in EPS;
C5 = return on capital employed in 1989;
C6 = return on shareholder equity in 1989.

[Sources of data: Returns - LBS 'Beta Book', accounting data - Datastream].

4.4   An interpretation of the results

It should be emphasised that further refinement of the model is required. In particular, table 8:1 shows evidence of extensive multicollinearity. In spite of this, there is a statistically significant relationship between annual stock market returns and annual change in earnings per share. This result conflicts with evidence cited by Rappaport (1986) that, in the US there is no correlation between these variables. It is an interesting result in view of Kaplan's criticism of the use of earnings-per-share numbers in managerial compensation packages since it suggests that boosting EPS also boosts shareholder wealth. Further refinement of the model is clearly required looking at other years and eliminating the highly correlated independent variables.

5.   The Japanese 'Cure'

5.1   Management accounting and national culture

In their recent review, Ezzamel, Hoskin and Macve (E,H&M)(1990) describe how J&K's work has 'deservedly been greeted as one of the most significant monographs on the history of accounting published to date' (p.153). They are, however, critical of the interpretation of history implied by J&K as well as sceptical of what they term the 'Japanese Cure'. It is regrettably beyond the scope of this book to comment on the first point. The question of the 'Japanese Cure' has already been introduced in previous chapters and merits further discussion.

EHM are rightly critical of the notion of 'grafting' Japanese business practice onto American business cultures. They are also right in pointing out that much 'Japanese' management is simply well known good management practice. As they suggest in connection with Japanese reward systems:

One is almost excused for thinking that such humanly oriented behaviour is a Japanese invention, whereas in fact it is its absence in many American and Western organisations that is perplexing, given the rich and insightful organisational and behavioural accounting literatures which have accumulated over the last six decades ... (p. 162).

They then proceed to criticise J&K for proposing the adoption of Japanese practices as being hopeless because of the absence in the West of the unique cultural and behavioural context in which these practices have developed and thrived. There seems to be a contradiction here. On the one hand, good management is presented as having a *universal* character. On the other, it is seen as a *culturally relative* phenomenon! The latter approach would seem to suggest a sort of contingency approach whereby management accounting and other aspects of management control may be tailored to the cultural specifics of each national culture.

Economic competition on a global scale is less tolerant. Competitive advantage in whole industries is driven by organisational factors which mean that either the best organisational form is chosen or it is wiped out. In the next chapter, the decline of the U.K. electronics industry illustrates these imperatives. The arguments in this book are generally deterministic but on an economic and institutional basis rather than a cultural one. I agree with EHM that good management practices, whether they are 'Japanese' or not, cannot just be grafted on to existing business structures.

That is clearly the message of the natural selection approach. However, the choice is very stark since, in a world of contestable markets, the source of organisational rent is embedded in the organisational structure. This latter point is well made by Aoki in his paper on the 'The Participatory Generation' of Information Rents and the theory of the firm (Aoki, 1990a). Here, he explicitly rejects the cultural 'cul-de-sac' implied by EHM:

> I speculate that the participatory mode is not just an Oriental cultural phenomenon, but that it also reflects a rational response of universal relevance by competing firms to their changing environment: increasing educational and intellectual achievements of employees and their democratic aspirations, the unprecedented development and accessibility of communication and information processing technology at the grassroots level, ever intensifying global competition in which quick adaptation to market signals and continued introduction of innovation are becoming crucial conditions for their survival, and so on (p. 27).

Aoki's remarks are particularly pertinent in the context of the electronics industry which will be looked at in the next chapter.

6   Concluding remarks

The relevance of management accounting has been demonstrated both theoretically and empirically. Strictly speaking, it is only *irrelevant* in a neoclassical world of perfect information where production functions are perfectly specified and all economic problems are simply 'priced out'. Of course, the modern critics of management accounting such as Johnson and Kaplan are not concerned with such theoretical pedantries. They are more concerned with the possibility that, far from being irrelevant, "incorrect" management accounting practices can potentially damage companies and, by extension, whole economies.

Notes

1. This was certainly a popular viewpoint held by many participants at a recent CIMA sponsored research workshop at Manchester University.

2. From Johnson, H. Thomas, and Kaplan, Robert S., *Relevance Lost: the Rise and Fall of Management Accounting*, Boston, Mass: Harvard Business School Press (1987).

3. I am using the expression 'perfectly rational' in its colloquial meaning. As we have already seen, the general behavioural assumption is one of bounded rationality.

4. See, for example, a series of articles in the 1985 volume of the Journal of Accounting and Economics (Murphy, 1985; Healy, 1985).

9 Rational versus natural selection: Strategy and management control in the UK electronics industry

The theory of organisational failure presented in chapter four argued that, given the selection process as prevailing in the UK economy (especially in the market for control), widespread structural problems could be expected. The chapter cited the electronics industry to illustrate these problems. In this chapter the industry is analysed in greater detail focusing on the performance, management control and strategy of some of the major players.

By examining the interrelationship between strategy and management control the aim is to illustrate the pivotal role of the latter in determining long run competitiveness. At a higher level of abstraction, the industry may be viewed as a useful illustration of the issues raised in the debate between the *natural* and the *rational* selection views of organisational control. In other words, to what extent has the development of the industry and the emergence of certain dominant firms been a result of *ex ante* strategic choice and to what extent have dominant firms with specific management control styles emerged through a process of natural selection peculiar to the UK? The answer to this question is important because many commentators (including the authors of a NEDO study which will be drawn on extensively in this chapter) imply that a change of strategy and management style turns primarily on the preferences of the senior management in the industry.

The chapter is both an application and an elaboration of the theoretical framework introduced in chapter four. The aim is to demonstrate the heuristic value of the 'efficiency and selection' methodology. However, as well as exploring some of the 'stylised facts' of the industry, it also reviews the contrasting explanations and solutions suggested by the natural and rational selection frameworks revealing in the process some difficulties which are sometimes overlooked in the new institutionalist literature.

The stylised facts indicate that a far from panglossian outcome characterises the industry - firms may 'fit their environments' but yet offer poor performance records in terms of innovation, product development and competition for market share. Indeed, given the well known predilection for 'management by numbers' in the industry, it seems to offer itself as a supreme example of the sort of failures discussed in the previous chapter. Alternative explanations have been offered, such as a poor educational and scientific infrastructure, or too much reliance on easy defence contracts. However, the conventional wisdom has also commented on an inappropriate management style. Using both theoretical and empirical methods, the chapter seeks to establish if a single management style can be distinguished, whether it is appropriate or not and whether it is the result of conscious management choice or the result of natural selection pressures.

1. The 'stylised facts' of management control and economic performance in the UK electronics industry

1.1 Defining the industry

The term 'stylised facts' implies that there is a body of generally accepted data based on an equally well accepted analytical concept such as the 'industry' or the 'market'. Although these concepts are not without their critics (Auerbach, 1988: Seal, 1990) industry analysis is so prevalent among economists and so institutionalised in terms of official statistics that it does not seem unduly heroic to try to identify a body of stylised facts.

If we accept, *in arguendo*, that the industry is an acceptable unit of analysis, the problem then emerges of satisfactorily defining the industry in terms of available statistics. For example, Soete and Dosi (1983) emphasise the difficulties in distinguishing between electrical and electronic industries as well as determining how such a widespread technology as electronics can be corralled into a single sector. Once the definitional issues are resolved then examples of 'economic effectiveness' data may easily be obtained from published sources. It is, indeed, contended that there is a body of 'stylised facts' concerning at least some socioeconomic outcomes. For example, sales growth, market shares and employment data all may be used to monitor the socioeconomic effect of industrial and organisational change. It is, however, a more contentious matter to relate these facts to specific 'causes' such as organisational structure and management control.

1.2   Sources of data

In the UK, the national Economic Development Office (NEDO) has an Electronics Industry Study Sector Group. They have commissioned a recent study (NEDO 1988) which includes seven sectors: defence and aerospace electronics, computers and automation, electronic components, software, consumer electronics, telecommunications equipment and instruments. This study serves not only as a useful source of data but also as an important example of conventional wisdom concerning the problems facing the sector.

The study noted that a strong growth of demand in the UK market has been accompanied by a deterioration in both the balance of payments in electronics products and a loss of domestic market share by indigenous companies. Given the past concentration of UK companies in the defence and 'protected' telecom sectors, it is likely that the end of the Cold War and the privatisation of telecom will see a further weakening of the UK companies' position. The poor performance of British companies may be contrasted with the relative success of non-UK companies based both in the UK and abroad. This seems to rule out the conventional 'explanation' of international trade theory which would suggest that the UK lacks a comparative advantage in the industry. It does not however, rule out a 'reinterpretation' of comparative advantage which focuses on *organising capability* rather than on the more traditional preoccupation with the price and quality of inputs (see Seal, 1990).

The term 'poor performance' applies when measuring performance in terms of market share. In terms of financial indicators, such as profitability, UK companies did as well if not better than many of their overseas rivals in the past decade. The study also notes a significant move into cash over the same period reflecting both high profitability and a reluctance or inability to develop new investment projects. This paradoxical evidence will be explained and reconciled later.

There are few non-financial or non-economic aspects of performance such as scientific or technical excellence to compensate for this record. Even in the so-called 'soft' markets of defence and telecom, products have generated a significant volume of technical criticisms (Foster, 1989).

2.   Major players, industry structure and survivorship: some perspectives on management control and strategic choice

The NEDO report concentrated on eight companies: British Aerospace, Ferranti, GEC-Marconi, Plessey, Racal, STC-ICL, Thorn EMI, Logica. Of these companies, Plessey has been taken over by GEC since the report was published. Indeed, the growing dominance of GEC relative to other UK firms has been a feature of the industry for nearly three decades! The company is not only been a 'survivor' but an important 'predator'. This is true not only of the well publicised mega mergers involving the other major players but also in terms of the steady ingestion of small electronics companies. The company is an industry leader - not certainly in terms of product innovation and development but rather in terms of ownership and control of the UK electronics industry. As will be argued later, the management control style of this giant has become both directly, an important component of UK performance in electronics but also, indirectly, an influence on the selection environment for the other firms in the industry.

2.1   Organisational and management control data

The reservations which may be held concerning the industry data are relatively insignificant when compared with the conceptual and empirical difficulties in establishing stylised facts concerning management control and organisational structure. The problem is not just that organisational data are inherently more ambiguous and subjective than economic data but the issue of theoretical spectacles is more controversial. A variety of typologies of organisational style management control and strategic goals are on offer which affect not only the interpretation of facts but their initial selection.

While the NEDO study is a useful source of industry economic data it is less useful as a source of organisational and management control data. A source of this sort of data for some of the key domestic players in the UK electronics industry is provided by Goold and Campbell (G&C) (1987). G&C include in their sample of companies GEC, Ferranti, Plessey, and STC. These companies are chosen because they are *diversified* rather than because they are electronics companies. The focus of the study is on management style and, in particular, the role of the 'centre' in a diversified company. This focus has influenced their classification of companies into categories based on 'strategic management styles' where the main identifying dimension is the form of control exercised by the centre.

Their framework generates three main categories - *Strategic Planning, Strategic Control* and *Financial Control*. As the titles suggest, there is no separation between organisational style and strategic style. Indeed, the categories have been established in terms of the relationship between the two dimensions of management control (flexible, tight strategic, and tight financial) and 'planning influence' (ranging from largely corporate to largely business unit). Although quite logical in terms of the objectives of their own study, G and C's approach creates difficulties in terms of resolving the natural versus rational selection issue. For example, if a company is called a 'Strategic control' company then the question - 'Is the control style appropriate to strategy? - seems to have been already ruled out by the inextricable intertwining of the two dimensions. In contingency terms, the firm's strategy is not seen as an independent factor which can be used to explain organisational form or management process. Other theoretical ambiguities are apparent such as the approval of *both* Chandler's structure following strategy approach (Chandler, 1962) and also Williamson's approach to the M-form. Although the latter was heavily influenced by Chandler's work, his own work stresses the role of 'unintended consequences' almost as much as conscious strategic planning (Williamson, 1975;1985).

Of the electronics companies in Goold and Campbell's sample (i.e. companies which also overlap with the NEDO study), STC is classified as being a Strategic Planner, Plessey is in the Strategic Control group while Ferranti and GEC are Financial Controllers. As mentioned earlier, the fortunes of the sector have, as expected, further declined. The loss of captive markets has resulted in further restructuring. Plessey has finally been taken over by GEC. Ferranti has been decimated by a disastrous acquisition while STC has sold ICL, the only British owned mainframe computer manufacturer, to Fujitsu. Ironically, STC now finds itself in the cash rich situation of GEC, in spite of a different strategic approach. Unlike GEC, whose management style discourages the development of technological interdependences, STC made an attempt to exploit the supposed technological convergences between telecommunications and computing.

STC's bailout strategy does have interesting implications for the natural versus rational selection debate. Unlike Plessey it is still independent. In terms of a natural selection model it has survived. In Mintzberg's terminology (Mintzberg, 1978), its *intended* strategy may have failed but its *realised* strategy has left it free to choose its own partner(s). Ferranti, in contrast, has all but lost its independence due to a single disastrous acquisition. Since G&C argue (p.138) that Ferranti have historically relied on *internal* growth it could be argued that the company was a victim of its own inexperience of growth through acquisition.

In G&C's typology, Plessey represented that hybrid of strategic planning and financial control - the Strategic Control style. G&C are highly critical of this model for Plessey. Describing the poor response of the company to the recession of 1985 and the bid from GEC, G&C suggest:

> It can be claimed that the Strategic Control style adopted by Plessey was not ideally suited to coping with these problems. Decentralisation did not make it easy to develop an integrated corporate view of the business in which Plessey was competing; or for the centre to devise imaginative,

aggressive strategies to deal with the company's difficult competitive position. At the business level, a strong corporate emphasis on financial control targets did not encourage bold long-term moves; it may even have led to some sacrifice of competitive position. Moreover, central concern with the underlying long-term strategy of some businesses was easily rebuffed by those business managements who could demonstrate a strong recent profit record, who were more closely knowledgeable about the details of their business, and who did not wish to make fundamental changes (p. 105-6).

With the success of the GEC bid for Plessey it would seem that the style which was unambiguously triumphed in the British electronics industry is the Financial Control style! Yet, as I argued in chapter six, it is precisely this style which is so frequently criticised as being particularly inappropriate for an industry such as electronics!

GEC's management style is actually easier to discern than many companies since it has never disguised its combination of decentralisation and rigorous financial control. Indeed, as many authors point out, this structure and information system was regarded as 'state of the art' in the seventies. Recent strategic moves into joint ventures may seem superficially to indicate a change of direction into global markets and production. Critics remain sceptical, pointing out that such changes are more likely to be motivated by 'poison pill' considerations. For example, according to Manley and Lloyd (1989), GEC now resembles 'a heavily armed corporate crab', with eight claws but no legs, capable of full perimeter defence but quite unable to move (p. 25).

The industry seems to offer itself as a supreme example of the sort of failures identified by researchers explaining the loss of competitiveness of US manufacturing industry (Johnson and Kaplan, 1987). If it is accepted that the main problem is one of an inappropriate management style then the issue then becomes one of trying to determine whether this management style has come about as a result of strategic planning or as a result of natural selection type processes.

3.   A natural selection theory of organisational change

The version of natural selection theory presented in this section is essentially an application of the theory presented in chapter four to the particular circumstances of the UK electronics industry. In that chapter a number of empirical examples were cited which included the UK electronics industry. The theory does seem to explain many of the above facts. However, as will be seen in the next section, both empirical and theoretical problems have emerged. These problems have not, however, damaged the main objectives of the chapter which were to establish the importance of organisational factors in explaining broad economic developments such as 'deindustrialisation' and also to show how natural selection paradigms need not inevitably produce panglossian theory.

3.1 The model and the UK electronics industry

As explained at length in chapter four, the theory is based on disequitibrium selection and a multi-market approach. Each market requires certain adaptations which conflict with the adaptations appropriate in other markets. In terms of organisational theory, the model is based on a version of contingency theory where the best 'fit' in each market conflicts with the best fit in the other markets. The outcome for the firm is determined by how it resolves these conflicting pressures. Firms are pushed towards a 'generalist' type of structure and control system regardless of *task* contingencies which require contractual relationships to protect specific assets. In the long run inappropriate adaptation and population change mean that the task becomes the 'victim' rather than the driving force of the system as it is in 'conventional' contingency theory. In the particular instance of the UK electronics industry, an easy non-competitive environment in product sector coupled with a harsh environment in market for control has resulted in a most 'degenerate' organisational form. The only source of rent is one based on 'artificial' market power rather than competitive advantage won through product innovation. The vulnerability of this basis is then exposed by changes in political conditions and increasing competition from global players.[1]

As stated in chapter four, biologists usually argue that any particular organism will represent a compromise in terms of the different functions that it has to fulfill in order to survive and reproduce. However, some environments may be more pressing than others. Thus, in the model of the firm proposed in this section, it is suggested that the imperative on one environment (the market for control) effectively dominates efficient adaptation in other, socially more significant markets such as the product market.

4. A rational selection interpretation

4.1 Empirical and theoretical weaknesses in the natural selection model

The above model may be described as being a natural selection theory which conceptualises structures and behaviours in terms of contracting categories and which views the environment in both resource and information flow terms

(Aldrich, 1979). In still more general terms, it illustrates the capacity of the transaction cost framework to synthesize economic and behavioural aspects of the selection process. Furthermore, it helps to organise the stylised facts as outlined in section one. In particular, it explains the relative success of Japanese and European firms vis à vis UK firms. In this instance there is a marked difference between the former's bank dominated 'takeover free' capital markets and the UK's stockmarket orientated system (NEDO, 1988). However, the NEDO study contends that environmental determinism works less well in explaining the relative success of US electronics companies:

> European and Japanese companies have until now operated within a financial system which provides more freedom from perceived short term performances pressures than that which exists in the US or the UK ... (p. 55)
> ... There is no inherent reasons why the UK companies should be more short term focused than their US counterparts. The greater short term pressures in the UK, we believe, have resulted more from the way in which companies have structured their businesses and communicated with the markets, rather than from fundamental differences in financial market behaviour (p. 58).

This latter position is supported by a comparison of the volatility of price/earnings rations which the NEDO study uses to argue that the share price of UK companies is more related to earnings than is the share price of US electronics companies. As I shall argue shortly, the empirical evidence offered by the NEDO study is unconvincing.

Setting aside the validity or otherwise of the stock market evidence, the above quotation raises the possibility of managerial discretion. The possibility arises that managers may release themselves from the determinism of the natural selection model. It is more supportive of the 'Strategic choice' model of Child who argues that a positive association between contextual variables and organisational structure does not mean the former determines the latter (Child, 1972). Child's views are critical of several aspects of natural selection models since he argues that power holders may make 'strategic choices' which affect the context, performance standards and structure. Even the definition of the environment is a function of the goals of the organisation since '(o)rganisational decisionmakers normally perceive themselves as operating only in certain 'markets' and utilising selected sources of inputs; they regard success in these areas as particularly vital for the organisation's survival' (p. 9).

4.2 Some responses to the strategic choice model

Aware of these criticisms of the natural selection approach, Aldrich (1979) partly accommodates the strategic choice argument by introducing the notion of the *rational selection* model which he describes as follows:

> The rational selection model places heavy reliance on *active* alternative generation and search procedures as sources of variation. Planned variations, such as tactics and strategies in competitive situations, are emphasised, as is the socially constructed nature of organisations. Variations are selected in terms of their fit with a specific criterion, and it is assumed that structural and behavioural patterns are selected, discarded, or modified on the basis of their contribution to the organisations's goals (Benson, 1971). *Choice* characterises rational behaviour in organisations, and even though there are severe limits to cognitive rationality (March and Simon,1958), the burden of choice is still on people as decision makers and generators of alternatives (p. 107, original author's emphasis).

However, Aldrich argues that there are limits to managers' strategic choice such as barriers to entry and even limitations on the ability of managers to perceive opportunities due to their socialisation. Other contextual changes have tended to further limit the exercising of strategic choice particularly if a lengthy gestation period is required. Certainly, a strategic change directed towards the nurturing of a 'clan' type company would require an extremely long term planning horizon. In this respect, it could be argued that the globalisation of production and the deregulation of world capital markets have constrained managers' freedom of action far more than Child could have envisaged in 1972. In an era of leveraged mega bids, corporate size alone does not offer the same security to managers as it did in the US and UK economies of the seventies. International competition in the producer market is also much fiercer.

4.3 Difficulties in making a distinction

One further problem with the both natural and rational selection models is that the same outcome may be explained by both approaches. For example, in the case of the UK electronics industry, it is quite difficult to distinguish empirically between a rational and a natural selection approach since both the interests of the dominant management groups and the imperatives of the financial environment seem to converge. There is no need for a change in either the structure of the organisation or a modification of the processes of management accounting under either models. The recent moves by GEC towards joint ventures with overseas companies *may* suggest that the ultimate demise of the financial control strategy occurs when the predator finally runs out of (domestic) prey. An alternative interpretation is that, as has already been noted, the company is seeking to strengthen its defences against hostile bids rather than moving into a new strategic phase.

The rational selection position (RSP) would be easier to sustain if there was at least *one* major British electronics company which was successfully pursuing a highly integrated product-led strategy. It would also help the RSP if the financial control style was not quite so prevalent right across British industry (Armstrong, 1987). The retention of the financial control form is, as we have already noted, buttressed by examples from other 'successful' firms in the UK and by the institutionalisation of the practices by professional groups. There is also an internal dynamic in the system. The role of the control system is not merely one of passive adaptation. As Dent (1990) points out:

> ... it is customary to think of control system changes following strategic changes in a passive reflective way... Hopwood (1987) has argued the case for viewing accounting as constitutive and not merely reflective of organisational endeavour. Hopwood (1987) notes how accounting systems initiated for one purpose, can become suggestive of new possibilities for organisational action, shaping the trajectory of organisational development. Accounting systems become implicated in wider processes of organisational perception, governance and strategic mobilisation, he argues (p. 19).

In terms of the multimarket model, the proactive role of accounting systems is evident in reinforcing the success in the market for control at the expense of failure in the product market. Thus, a system of control that began as a prudent restraint on overzealous innovation has culminated in a stagnant technological and scientific culture.

4.4   Is a distinction necessary?

Perhaps the whole 'natural versus rational selection' debate is somewhat overblown in the literature. Indeed, some organisational researchers argue that there is no pressing need on theoretical grounds to choose between 'choice' and 'determinism'. Hrebiniak and Joyce (1985) argue that:

> The important research issue of voluntarism versus determinism is the relationship between them and how their interactions and resulting tensions culminate in changes over time. The issue is how choice is both

a cause and a consequence of environmental influences, as cause and consequence interact and conflict to result in noticeable organizational adaptations (p. 337).

They propose a typology of organisations based on the relationship between strategic choice and environmental determinism. This raises the possibility of an organisation combining both high strategic choice characteristics and high environmental determinism. The 'multiple niche' model seems to fit the highly diversified GEC up to a point. However, a straight application of their typology is problematical since their 'multiple niches' refer to product markets only rather than to the multimarket pressures described above.

As I will argue below, there is some mileage to be gained from distinguishing between natural and rational selection models. In particular, the outcome of such a debate helps to determine the scope for significant change via management education versus change via a more drastic manipulation of the firm's institutional environment.

4.5   Strategic choice, performance ambiguity and 'efficiency-based' theory

One benefit of considering the strategic choice model is that it does highlight the general difficulty of using contingent factors such as performance ambiguity. In particular, it emphasises that if goals may be a matter of management choice then so are organisational performance indicators. Performance ambiguity takes on a political rather than a purely technical hue- ambiguity that may be obvious to a research scientist or even an accountant may not be quite so evident to a shareholder!

The relationship between goal congruence and performance ambiguity becomes crucial. For example, the clan's ability to efficiently organise transactions in situations of performance ambiguity depends on its ability to reduce goal incongruity. Yet organisational performance can only be technically determined where goal congruence is high. As Child (1984) has pointed out, organisational performance is both an *input* and an *output* in organisational design.

The strategic choice approach actually pinpoints a weakness in the whole methodology of 'efficiency-based' organisational theory. As Rueschmeyer (1977) puts it:

> There is, however, a more fundamental problem that plagues all arguments about increased efficiency or 'adaptive capacity' in the operation of collectivities. Any judgement about efficiency hinges on a given set of ranked goals and on a given evaluation of alternative means to reach these goals. What is efficient in terms of one preference

structure may be wasteful by other criteria. Not only different cultures, but lord and serf, entrepreneur and worker, executive and employee, as well as many other social categories, differ fundamentally in their evaluation of the price paid and the advantage gained with a new arrangement of their social relations; and since preference structures and cost-benefit calculi vary, what efficiency means is always and inevitably determined by varied interests and value commitments (p. 5).

Of course, these points have been made in contexts which make no reference to Strategic choice. The latter model does, however, increase the prominence of the interplay of goals and performance measurement which can sometimes be submerged behind the technicist language and concepts so typical of the new institutionalist literature. Such criticisms do not, in my judgement, invalidate the *heuristic* value of the new institutional approach. They do, however, emphasise that prescription should follow a comparative institutional path rather than be based on a social welfare paradigm. Such a path will be illustrated below.

5. Alternative institutional responses to 'organisational failure'

5.1 The natural selection response

Given the acceptance of the basic hypothesis that the main problem with the UK electronics industry is one of organisational failure, how may this failure be remedied? The natural selection response suggests that change is contingent on changes in the features of the UK economic environment which influence organisational design and management control characteristics. An 'ecological' problem requires an ecological type solution. Thus if we wish to encourage a rare species of deer we have to first nurture the correct habitat by planting a protective tree cover. Of course, this approach is not new. For example, the 'infant industry' argument has formed the basis of many protectionist pleas over the centuries (List, 1966). The novelty lies in emphasising the role of competition in non-product markets. Thus in terms of the familiar multimarket diagram, it is suggested that product and capital markets should be as competitive as possible. The desired protection of organisational structures will be achieved through modifications on competition in the markets for control and markets for labour (especially managerial labour) as indicated in figure 9.1.

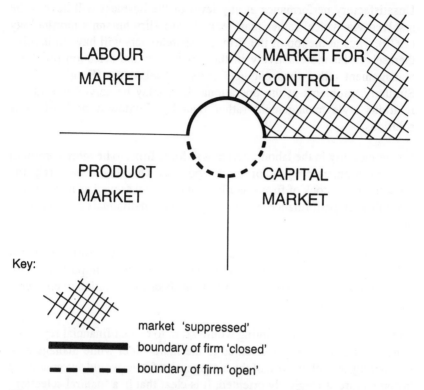

Figure 9.1   The multi-market model with resource 'lock-in' modifications

Before considering the non-trivial problems of how these changes may be engineered, it is important to indicate the sort of organisational responses that might be expected.

a.   The main general result is to increase organisational stability. Stakeholders - managers, shareholders and employees are all 'locked in' to a far greater extent than in the usual neoclassical world. This has a number of corollaries. Managers will find it much harder to renegotiate internal contracts and restructure businesses. At the minimum, managerial effort will be channelled into competition in the product market. This will have the effect on the management control system both in terms of structure and process. Customers, especially at the retail end of the value chain are not locked in. Overall, the emphasis will be directed toward long term objectives such a market share and product development and away from financial entrepreneurship.

b. Unsatisfactory performance at any level of the business will have to be resolved via 'voice' rather than 'exit' to use Hirschmann's terminology (1970). Thus at the top of the firm, the shareholders will have to involve themselves far more actively in the monitoring and selection of senior management rather than engineer exits and takeovers (Berglof, 1990). Similarly, problems at the operational level may be solved via human relations style management rather than by shutdowns or MBO-type solutions.

c. Lower mobility in the labour market will force firms to be more careful in their selection, training and promotion policies. This should encourage the build up in the stock of firm specific human capital as well as improve the reliability of performance monitoring of both individuals and business units.

d. The firms would be expected to improve the horizontal flow of information. As was seen in earlier chapters, this is an important factor contributing to the both innovation and the efficient resolution of emergent operating problems.

e. The implications for accounting would seem to be that financial reporting would be less exclusively oriented to the shareholder while management accounting, as with the rest of the management focus, would automatically become more strategically oriented. It is clear that in a 'natural selection' world, accounting is seen as a relatively passive instrument which records and monitors data dictated by organisational imperatives rather than developing an agenda of its own.

5.2 The Japanese 'Cure' revisited

As readers will recognise, many of the organisational changes listed above amount to a sort of 'Japanese Cure' as discussed in earlier chapters. The suppression of the market for control and the dominance of internal over external labour markets are well known features of the Japanese firm and economy. As has already been pointed out, the resulting firm has strong similarities with the familiar 'managerialist' model. There are, however, some differences with the model as it was developed in the early and mid sixties (see Chapter Two).

Aoki (1984) in one of his numerous works on the Japanese firm describes a 'Corporative Managerialist' model. These terms do not have the connotations of the word 'corporatist' as it is frequently used in British political debate where it is used (generally perjuratively) to summarise the state sponsored corporatism of the 1970's. The aim is rather to suggest a 'stylised' model of the firm where a relatively neutral management 'makes decisions to integrate and mediate the interests of S(shareholders) and E(employees)' (p. 126). As may be seen in figure 9.2, Aoki proposes three other stylised models. He discusses models 1) 2) and 3) quite extensively but is relatively perfunctory in his treatment of the 'Managerial discretionary Model'.

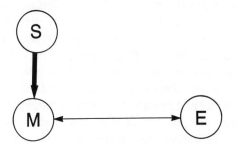

(1) The Shareholders' Sovereignty-cum-Collective Bargaining model

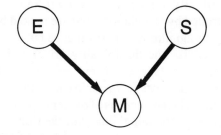

(2) The Co-determination model

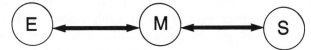

(3) The Corporative Managerialism model

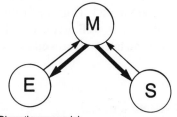

(3a) The Managerial Discretionary model

Figure 9.2   Stylised decision-making models of the firm (after Aoki, 1984, p.127)[2]

Interestingly, this model seems to characterise the Strategic choice/rational selection model developed in this chapter.

In a recent survey article, Aoki (1990b) proposes three 'Duality Principles'. The first duality principle postulates a deliberate asymetry between a hierarchical, rank based system of incentives combined with both horizontal co-ordination via information sharing and strong localised problem solving capability. Both the all round virtuosity of the workers and their willingness to share information are generated through a carefully managed internal labour market accompanied by an external labour market which focuses on new entrants to the labour market rather than mid-career movers.

The second duality principle postulates that '(t)he internal organisation and financial control of the Japanese firm are dually characterised by weak-decision hierarchy and incentive-ranking hierarchy' (p. 18). This refers to the bank oriented financial control system whereby banks hold stock and operate as main bank but do not intervene unless a company runs into problems. Aoki argues that this allows managers autonomy, stabilises ownership and virtually eliminates takeover raids. Managers are not hierarchically controlled by shareholders but are ranked by their profit levels. Banks are expected to monitor firm performance but not intervene unless the company runs into crisis. The third duality principle is that 'the corporate management decisions of Japanese firms are subject to the dual control (influence) of financial interests (ownership) and employees' interests rather than to unilateral control in the interests of ownership' (p. 20). It is on this basis that he has developed a 'bargaining' model of the firm.

Aoki's comparison of his two stylised models - the Hierarchical (H-) firm and the Japanese (J-) firm has a strong contingency flavour. For example, if the environment is either highly stable or highly unstable then the H-firm has some comparative advantages. If, on the other hand, the environment is less extreme then the J-firm is superior. As with most contingency arguments, Aoki concentrates only on the product market. Yet the general argument clearly may be applied in a multimarket model. Thus the H-mode, which is so apparent in the UK electronics industry, is well adapted to both a stable and protected product market (defence and telecom) as well as the highly unstable market for control.

6.   The rational selection model

6.1   Rational selection as 'managerial discretion'

Aoki talks about his 'managerial discretion' model as being a 'degenerate' version of the 'corporative managerial' model. Whether this is because managers are deemed to be less 'neutral' and possess their own objective function, or whether it is because the constraints on management are weaker, is not absolutely clear in his discussion. In terms of the traditional managerial discretion literature (see chapter two), there is usually an assumption that some degree of market power pertains in the product market. Similarly, it is argued that the market for control may be manipulated to extend and protect managerial interests rather than serving as a device to discipline managers.

In terms of the UK electronics industry, apart from the declining defence sector, there is little evidence of market power - it is after all the loss of market share that is the main object of concern! There is, however, some suggestion that senior management do have some discretion over the way they structure their businesses and in the way they communicate to the stock market. If, as has been argued, the emphasis is on vertical rather than horizontal communication, on financial control rather than non-financial control and on short term earnings rather than long term viability then these are all characteristics are deemed to result, not from selection pressures, but from *managerial choice*. Illustrating these issues in figure 9.3, the firm is seen to be a relatively robust institution able to manipulate the market for control and the labour market but relatively weak in the product market. Traditionally, many managerial discretion/strategic choice models have tended to depict a greater level of discretion/opportunity for choice in the product market as well (Cowling, 1982; Child, 1972).

6.2   An empirical test of the rational selection model

As already mentioned, some of the support for a rational selection interpretation comes from NEDO's comparative analysis of UK and US stock market behaviour. Thus, while accepting the conventional view that the UK industry faces a different financial environment from that of the Japanese or continental industries, the NEDO study argues that managers can change the basis of the market's perception of their performance. The suggestion is that economic systems with similar shareholder oriented financial systems may nevertheless evaluate companies in different ways according to the way the companies are structured and according to the way managers communicate to the market. The study argues that British Electronics companies apparently invite the market to evaluate their performance according to earnings while the US companies encourage the market to evaluate according to non-accounting information.

This interesting proposition deserves empirical investigation. NEDO's own empirical support is unconvincingly based on some highly confusing graphs which purport to show that the UK stock market reacts to the earnings of UK

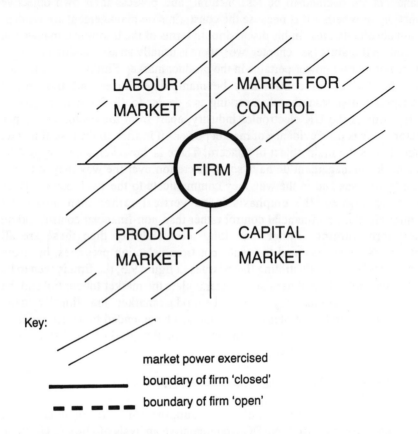

Figure 9.3 The Multimarket Model: a rational selection perspective

electronics companies more than the US market does to the earnings of its own electronics companies. The idea behind the test seems plausible even if the graphical evidence is unsatisfactory. Following a quantitative rather than a pictorial approach, I looked at the variation of P/E ratios for a number of large UK and US electronics companies over the past six years. The results are shown in table 9.1. Although the sample is limited both in terms of the number of companies and the length of the time series, the data so far produced do not support the conclusions of the NEDO study.

As can be seen, Racal, STC, Amstrad and Logica all show greater volatility of P/E compared with the three US companies. Perhaps significantly, GEC shows the greatest stability of the UK companies but even it is more volatile than Rockwell.

Table 9.1
A comparison of the volatility of P/E ratios's in selected US and UK electronics companies - annual range of P/E and six year mean

Year	1986	1987	1988	1989	1990	1991	Mean Range
Company							
Martin Marietta	5.3	5.6	5.4	5.0	4.6	1.8	4.6
Rockwell	3.6	7.3	2.6	2.0	2.3	2.3	3.4
IBM	3.3	10.8	3.0	4.2	8.3	4.6	5.7
GEC	5.4	6.7	1.9	4.2	3.4	2.4	4.0
RACAL	10.0	12.7	11.3	17.7	10.4	5.1	11.2
STC	37.1	24.0	6.6	6.0	4.1	0.4	13.0
AMSTRAD	23.4	12.4	5.8	6.9	15.6	4.4	11.4
LOGICA	4.6	18.9	9.7	7.9	8.9	6.3	9.4

Source: Datastream

It is clear that further work needs to be done on comparing US and UK stock markets as well as testing the general notion that managements can (legally) manipulate the stock market. Recent events at Phillips and Bull suggest that Western electronics industries are all suffering from Far Eastern and, particularly, Japanese competition. However, the problems of the UK industry seem far deeper and intractable. Weighing up all the above evidence together with the continuing inability of British companies either to hold market share or even preserve their independence, I prefer to adhere to a natural rather than a rational selection interpretation.

7.   Some theoretical prospects and policy conclusions

Child argues that too much contingency research has concentrated on task contingency and consequently advocates a *political* contingency approach. The above two theories certainly go beyond considerations of task - ownership and control, labour markets and capital markets all influence management control. In the rational selection model, managers have sufficient discretion in order to make strategic choices which also affect structure and control. Though less ambitious in their macro-societal scope than Lalanne (1990) who includes geo-cultural context in her model, they do seem to explain the industry's development somewhat better than the traditional international trade/factor endowment theory or the less orthodox/neo-Keynesian theory of 'cumulative causation' (Eatwell, 1981). Additional research is indicated in two areas. Firstly, more data are required on structures and management control on a comparative basis. Lalanne's study is clearly a contribution in this area. Secondly, more work needs to be done on the relationship between company structure and stock market valuation since this was seen to be a vital aspect of the NEDO analysis. The illustration of this particular strand of empirical work presented above certainly did not confirm the NEDO submission.

The policy significance of the natural v rational selection interpretation lies in the quite different remedies implied by the two theories. A natural selection interpretation suggests that the problems of the electronics industry are both deep seated and are likely to be observed across a wide range of UK industry. A rational selection interpretation suggests that the apparent weaknesses are more the result of past management failures which are both isolated in terms of the whole economy and relatively easy to remedy given a change strategy by the senior management of the main players. Major changes in institutions and culture are unnecessary - the solution lies as a 'gift' of senior management. As I have already indicated a preference for the natural selection version of events, I find this solution implausible.

Notes

1. GEC may be seen as a firm which epitomises the 'generalising' approach to survival (Hannan and Freeman, 1977, p. 949). This gives the company an advantage in the unstable or 'coarse-grained' market for control.

2. Diagram reproduced from *The Co-operative Game Theory of the Firm* by M. Aoki (1984) by permission of Oxford University Press.

10 Conclusions

1. General theoretical implications

As I discussed in my introduction, one of the most famous articles on economics and accounting characterised the two subjects as being "uncongenial twins" - sharing a common terminology and subject matter but little else (Boulding, 1962). I submit that in this book I have shown that the degree of uncongeniality can be reduced by proposing changes in both accounting and economics. If the economic problem is seen in terms of cognitive difficulties and *information* flows rather than in the more traditional 'unbounded rationality' and *resource* flow terms and if accounting is seen as an *economic* institution, then a shared paradigm may be constructed.

The shared paradigm is based on a version of the new institutionalist economics. It is a version which deduces both the institution of the firm and of accounting from the same problematic of incomplete contracts. The *ex ante* script is incomplete - new information may arise causing readjustments. The approach is more *process* oriented than in some contractural theories with a far more explicit treatment of selection mechanisms. Problems arise both from the *path* of equilibrium and from the conflicting requirements of different markets.

One way of assessing the enormous importance of the new institutionalist approach on the perception of accounting is to consider a 'pre-institutionalist' theory of accounting as proposed by Chambers (1966). This admirable piece of work has helped me a great deal both in terms of its general approach and in terms of its content. It would, indeed, be interesting to see how a similar endeavour would turn out with the benefit of drawing on the developments in economics which have occurred since 1966.

197

Accounting has become endogenous in the new institutionalist paradigm. It is not just an exogenous source of data as it was in the old structure-conduct-performance paradigm. Thus weaknesses in the data may now be explained in terms of an economic model rather than just anguished over as in the earlier 'theories of the firm'. As we have seen, questions directed toward the correctness of the accounting data are part of a more general critique of old style industrial economics.

Although accounting was presented as being *codeterminous* with other institutions of post contract completion, it was emphasised that other institutions were also codeterminous. As the management control/OFF paradigm shows, there are other equally valid sources of 'economic' information. Indeed, it may even be argued that under some circumstances accounting measurement of financial information may lead to a dysfunctional focus. Just because accounting can be reconciled with the theory of the firm does not necessarily give it any greater significance than other sources of information or calculative routines.

Indeed, one of the 'unintended consequences' of the inquiry has been a realisation that an 'accounting theory of the firm' has proved to be an illusion. Not only does the accounting system fail in all the traditional ways (backward looking, arbitrary, etc.) but the institutionalist approach actually stresses the crucial decision-supporting role played by informal and tacit economic information. Furthermore, the new emphasis on process does not displace the influence of structure. Or, to use transaction cost terminology, explicit and extensive analysis of the measurement branch reinforces the importance of the governance branch especially in situations where output indicators are unreliable.

1.1   Normative implications

The apparent strength of the traditional neoclassical paradigm is its ability to generate normative theories and decision rules both for managing the firm and for looking at wider welfare problems. The new institutional paradigm cannot offer the same 'box of tools'. Indeed, as we have seen, the tendency is to question the validity of many of the 'market-like' techniques of management such as the PV rule.

The 'Principal-Agent' literature does propose some highly stylised 'optimal contracts'. This 'complete contracts' version of institutional economics was not regarded as being the most useful for the purposes of this book (see especially chapter three). The main problem is that 'the theory tends to lead to very complex fee functions ... (W)e do not find such complex relations in reality' (Arrow, 1985, p.48).

Arrow's contribution here (as elsewhere in his work) is to recognise the limits of the economic approach. He recognises the importance of what he calls 'socially mediated rewards' (p. 50). In retrospect, I submit that much of the normative thrust of this book is concerned not so much with dismissing existing techniques or developing new ones but in analysing the circumstances in which particular techniques are appropriate. It is, to put it another way, about 'drawing boundaries' - between the market and the firm, between financial and non-financial information and even between the 'economic' and the 'non-economic'.

Thus the solutions proposed in this book are often as critical of the 'neoclassical numbers' proposed by some advocates of 'Strategic financial management' accounting as they are of traditional accounting numbers. Indeed, as was argued in the previous three chapters the 'answer' to many management problems is not new numbers but either fewer numbers or a different interpretation of the old numbers.

1.2 The pivotal role of selection processes

Many have interpreted this normative approach in terms of a 'Japanese Cure' because the empirical demonstration of these principles so often manifests itself in Japanese companies. Yet the natural selection model presented in the book focuses less on cultural imperatives and more on economic selection pressures. Managers may have difficulty in practising the 'best' management methods because of the economic environment rather than the cultural one.

1.3 Participation, management control and economic efficiency

One 'unintended outcome' of the book is the surprising (to me) congruence between economic efficiency (as measured in terms of sustainable economic growth) and the more participatory modes of corporate governance. This finding was coupled with the confirmation that accounting is a more willing servant of the authority relation than of the economic collective. More specifically it is more useful in 'top down' control than in creating economic wealth.

Of course, this finding would come as no surprise to those analysts who base their whole research programme on conflictual assumptions. Yet I submit that is rather more rewarding and persuasive to deduce the efficiency properties of democratic/participatory modes of organisation. This tradition is demonstrated by some radical writers cited in this book such as Marglin and Putterman.

2. Empirical issues

Although the book has been predominately a theoretical endeavour some progress made with empirical issues. Originality can derive from the discovery of 'new facts' and/or a new arrangement of existing facts. Thus the theory introduced in chapter four represents the creation of new framework in which to place stylised facts of institutional/industrial and organisational change. Indeed, as has been pointed out on several occasions, selection models are essentially heuristic, serving as a guide to further research, more refined theories and new data. Again, one difficulty encountered was that data may be readily available for testing conventional economics theories but that *organisational data* is both much sparser and much more difficult to aggregate and summarise.

Empirical work thus involves the use of more 'partial' data and also a need for cautious interpretation of results. If, however, the selection process focuses on the 'market for control' and if success in this market depends on shareholder wealth then it seems that quite conventional models 'economic consequences' type of research is appropriate (see chapter eight).

Slightly less conventional is the attempt to correlate 'standard' economic data with organisational data as in chapter nine. As was pointed out, there are difficulties in obtaining data and even in classifying such data as exists. It is unsurprising that the call is for more case study type research. Yet, the methodological issues raised by case study research suggest that it is not just a matter of adding to a notional 'bank' of data as writers such as Kaplan and Williamson suggest (Williamson, 1985: Kaplan, 1983;1984).

3. Economy wide implications

The great strength of the conventional neoclassical theory of the firm is that there is a clear link between the allocative decisions made by the firm and changes in the wider economy. Indeed, it is well known that the so-called theory of the firm is actually more the theory of the industry such is the conventional lack of interest in the internal processes of the firm. A new theory of the firm must also link into the wider economy. The theory proposed in this book does not link into the economy in the usual additive sense. The linkage is visualised not in output and input terms but rather in terms of populations of organisations possessing *qualitative* rather than *quantitative* characteristics. There is an *indirect* link with output and particularly output growth. Unlike in conventional production economics, production has to be managed. This helps to determine both the level of organisational rent and its rate of change.

Agency theory offers yet another economy wide perspective since it sees the economy not in terms of populations of firms ("legal fictions") but as a web of interlocking contracts. For reasons explained, this perspective was rejected in favour of the firm-market distinction.

3.1   Short-termism

Much current debate revolves around the so-called short-termism of stock market driven economies. It was argued that seeing structural issues in terms of short - or long horizons was theoretically problematical since there are difficulties in specifying the 'correct' rate of time preference. It was argued that an alternative way of confronting basically the same issues focused on differences in management style rather than hypothesised differences in time preference.

3.2   The Japanese 'Cure'

Closely associated with both debates about short-termism and management style is the theory of the Japanese firm. As I stated in the introduction, one of the original motives for this enquiry was based on a desire to try to elaborate such a theory. In this respect the contribution of Aoki has to be acknowledged. Like him, I prefer to see the firm less in terms of national characteristics and more in terms of universalistic concepts such as participation, hierarchy and so on.

Aoki is beginning to explicitly consider the environmental impacts on the firm (Aoki, 1990b). His focus still seems to be a traditional emphasis on the *product* market although there is some evidence of an emerging literature looking at a more multi-environment model as outlined in chapters four and nine in this book.[1] [2]

4.   Concluding remarks

It is customary at this point in a research programme to point out that "further research is necessary". Indeed, there have recently been some interesting advances both in the theory of the firm and in research on the organisational context of accounting . There has, however, been relatively little progress in following the theoretical synthesis proposed in this book.

As I outlined at the beginning of the book, the ultimate aim of the theoretical development is to contribute to the debate on economic policy. In this respect, it is interesting to contrast the current differences between the US and the UK. In the former, a new administration has just appointed an economics team which represents a more 'institutionalist' perspective than would probably emerge simply by selecting from the mainstream of US academic economics. In the UK, criticisms of economic policy making have persuaded the government to consult former 'outsiders'/mavericks. The focus still, however, reflects the traditional Treasury fixation on *macroeconomic management*. There is little sign of a search for a coherent, *domestically* based solution to the structural and long term problems of the UK economy. It is this set of problems which is addressed by the ideas outlined in this book.

Notes

1. Porter's recent book (1990) illustrates the limitations of focusing almost entirely on the product market. Thus while he effectively describes successful industrial structures in various countries, his explanations for these different structures seem incomplete.

2. This emerging literature is illustrated in Aoki, et al. (1990).

References

Alchian, A. (1950), 'Uncertainty, evolution and economic theory', *Journal of Political Economy*, 58 (June): 211-21.

_____ (1959) 'Costs and Outputs' in *The Allocation of Economic Resources* by Abramovitz, M. et al., Stanford: Stanford University Press.

_____ (1984) 'Specificity, specialisation, and coalitions,' *Journal of Economic Theory and Institutions*, 140 (March): 34-49.

_____ , & Demsetz, H. (1972), 'Production, information Costs and Economic Organisation', *American Economic review*, 62, pp.777-795.

Aldrich, H.E. (1979) *Organisations and Environments,* Englewood Cliffs: Prentice Hall.

Alessi, de L. (1967) 'The Short Run Revisited', *American Economic Review*, June, pp. 450-461.

Alexander, S. (1950) *Five Monographs on Business Income,* New York: Study Group on Business Income, AI(CP)A.

Anthony, R.N. (1965) *Planning and Control Systems: A Framework for Analysis,* Boston: Harvard Business School.

_____ , and Dearden, J. and Bedford, N. (1984) *Management Control Systems,* (5th edition), Homewood: Irwin.

Antle, R. (1989) Intellectual Boundaries in Accounting Research, *Accounting Horizons*, June, (vol. 3, no. 2).

Aoki, M. (1984) *The Co-operative Game Theory of the Firm.* Oxford: Clarendon Press.

_____ (1986) 'Horizontal vs Vertical Information Structure of the Firm', *American Economic Review,* December, vol. 76, no. 5: 971-983.

_____ (1990a) 'The Participatory Generation of Information Rents and the theory of the firm' in Aoki, M., Gustafsson, B. and Williamson, O.E. (eds) *The Firm as a nexus of Treaties*, London: Sage.

_____ (1990b) 'Towards a Theory of the Japanese Firm', *Journal of Economic Literature,* vol. XXVII (March), pp. 1-27.

_____ Gustafsson, B. and Williamson, O.E.(eds)(1990) *The Firm as a nexus of Treaties.* London: Sage.

Armour, H.O. and Teece, D.J. (1978) 'Organisational Structure and Economic Performance: a Test of the Multidivisional Hypothesis,' *Bell Journal of Economics,* (Spring), pp. 106-122.

Armstrong, P. (1987) 'The Rise of Accounting Controls in British Capitalist Enterprises', *Accounting, Organisations and Society*, vol. 12, no. 5, pp. 415-436.

Arrow, K.J. (1948) *Individualism and Economic Order*, Chicago: University of Chicago Press.

_____ (1978) 'The Future and the Present in Economic Life', *Economic Enquiry,* vol. XVI (April): 157-169.

_____ (1985) 'The Economics of Agency' in *Principals and Agents: the Structure of Business* edited by Pratt, J W and Zeckhauser, R. J., Cambridge, Mass: Harvard Business School Press.

Auerbach, P. (1988) *Competition: the Economics of Industrial Change.* Oxford: Basil Blackwell.

Baiman, S. (1990) 'Agency Research in Managerial Accounting: a second look', *Accounting, Organisations and Society*, vol. 15, no. 4, pp. 341-371.

Baker, G.P, Jensen, M.C. and Murphy, K.J. (1988). 'Compensation and Incentives: practice vs Theory', *The Journal of Finance*, vol. 63, no. 3 (July).

Ball, R. (1989) 'The Firm as a Specialist Contracting Intermediary: Application to Accounting and Auditing', *University of Rochester Discussion Paper*.

_____ (1990) 'What Do We Know About Stock Market "Efficiency"? *University of Rochester Discussion Paper*.

Barry, N.R. (1979) *Hayek's Social and Economic Philosophy*. London: Macmillan.

_____ (1988) *The Invisible Hand in Economics and Politics; a study in the two conflicting explanations of society: end-states and processes.'* London: Institute of Economic Affairs.

Bator, F.M. (1957) 'General Equilibrium, Welfare and Allocation', *American Economic Review*, (March), pp. 22-59.

Baumol, W.J. (1959), *Business Behaviour, Value and Growth*. London: Macmillan.

_____ (1965) *Economic Theory and Operations Analysis*. Englewood Cliffs: Prentice-Hall International.

_____ Panzar, J.C. and Willig, R.D. (1982). *Contestable Markets and the Theory of Industry Structure*. New York: Harcourt Brace Jovanvich.

Beaver, W. (1981) *Financial Reporting: an Accounting Revolution*. Englewood Cliffs: Prentice Hall.

Benson, J.K. (1971) 'Models of Structure Selection in organisations: On the limits of Rational perspectives'. Paper presented at the *Annual Meeting of the American Sociological Association*, Denver, Colorado.

Berglof, E. (1990) 'Capital Structure as a Mechanism of Control: a Comparison of Financial Systems', in Aoki, M., Gustafsson, B and Williamson, O.E. (1990) *The Firm as a Nexus of Treaties*. London: Sage.

Berle, A.A. & Means, G.C. (1932), *The Modern Corporation and Private Property*. New York: Commerce Clearing House Inc.

Bertalanffy, L. Von (1968) *General Systems Theory*. Harmsworth: Penguin.

Birnberg, J. (1980) 'The Role of Accounting in Financial Disclosure', *Accounting Organizations and Society*, vol. 5, no. 1, pp. 71-80.

Bloch, H. (1974) 'Advertising and Profitability: a reappraisal', *Journal of Political Economy*, (March-April), pp. 267-286.

Boland, L. (1982) *The Foundation of Economic Method*. London: Allen and Unwin.

Boulding, K. E. (1962) 'Economics and Accounting: The Uncongenial Twins', in Baxter, W.T. and Davidson, S. (eds.) *Studies in Accounting*. London: Sweet and Maxwell.

Braverman, H. (1974) *Labor and Monopoly Capital: The Degradation of Work in the Twentieth Century*. New York: Monthly Review Press.

Bromwich, M. (1990) 'The Case for Strategic Management Accounting: the role of Accounting Information for Strategy in Competitive Markets', *Accounting Organisations and Society*, vol. 15, no. 1/2, pp. 27-46.

Bromwich, M.(1992) *Financial Reporting, Information and Capital Markets*. London: Pitman.

_____ and Bhimani, A. (1989), *Management Accounting: Evolution not Revolution*. London: CIMA.

Buchanan, J. M. (1969) *Cost and Choice: an inquiry in economic theory*. Chicago Markham.

_____ and Thirlby, G.F. (1973) *L.S.E. Essays on Cost.* London: L.S.E.

Buckley, W. (1968) 'Society as a Complex Adaptive System', in Buckley, W. (ed) *Modern Systems Research for the Behavoural Scientist*. London: Aldine.

Burchell, S., Chubb, C., Hopwood, A., Hughes, J. (1980) 'The Roles of Accounting in Organisations and Society,' *Accounting, Organisations and Society*, vol. 5, no. 1 pp.5-27.

Burchell, S., Chubb C., & Hopwood, A.G. (1985), 'Accounting in its Social Context:Towards a History of Value Added in the United Kingdom', *Accounting, Organisations and Society,* vol. 10, no. 4, pp. 381-413.

Cable J. (1985) 'Capital Market Information and Industrial Performance:the Role of West German Banks', *The Economic Journal* 95 (March), pp. 118-132.

_____ and Dirrheimer, M.F. (1983) 'Hierarchies and Markets: an empirical test of the multidivisional hypothesis in West Germany', *International Journal of Industrial Organisation*, vol. 1, pp. 43-62.

Canning, J. (1929) *The Economics of Accountancy.* New York: Ronald Press.

Casson, M. (1987) 'Multinational Firms', in Clarke, R. and McGuinness, T., *The Economics of the Firm.* Oxford: Basic Blackwell.

Chambers, R. (1966) *Accounting, Evaluation and Economic Behaviour.* Englewood Cliffs: Prentice-Hall.

Chandler, A. (1962) *Strategy and Structure:Chapters in the history of Industrial Enterprise.* Mass: MIT press.

_____ (1977) *The Visible Hand: The Managerial Revolution in American Business.* Cambridge, Mass: Harvard University Press.

Child J. (1972) 'Organisational Structure, Environment and Performance: The role of Strategic Choice', *Sociology*, pp. 1-22.

_____ (1984) *Organisation: a guide to problems and practice* . (2nd edition) London: Harper Rowe.

Christenson, C. (1983) 'The Methodology of Positive Accounting', *Accounting Review*, 58 (January): 1-22.

Chua, W.F., Lowe, E.A. and Puxty, A. (eds) (1989) *Critical Perspectives in Management Control.* London: Macmillan.

Clarke, R. and McGuiness, T. (1987) *The Economics of the Firm.* Basil Blackwell: Oxford.

Coase, R. (1937), 'The Nature of the Firm', *Economica* 4, pp. 386-405.

_____ (1990) 'Accounting and the Theory of the Firm', *Journal of Economics and Accounting*, vol. 12, pp. 3-13.

_____ (1990) 'Accounting and the Theory of the Firm', *Journal of Accounting and Economics*, vol. 12, pp. 3-13.

Comanor, W.S. and Wilson, T.A. (1967) 'Advertising, Market Structure, and Performance', *Review of Economic Statistics*, vol. 49, no. 4, pp. 423-40.

_____ (1979) 'On Advertising and Competition', *Journal of Economic Literature*, vol XVII (June).

Cooke T.E. (1986), *Mergers and Acquisitions*. Oxford: Basil Blackwell.

Cowe, R. (1990) 'Stuck with a large cash cache and the problems of what to do with it', *The Guardian*, July 31.

Cowling, K. (1982) *Monopoly Capitalism*. London: Macmillan.

Demsetz, H.H., (1969) 'Information and Efficiency: Another viewpoint', *Journal of Law and Economics*, 12 (April): 1-22.

_____ (1974) 'Two systems of belief about monopoly', in Goldschmid, H., Mann, H. and Weston, J., *Industrial Organisation: the New Learning*. Boston: Little, Brown.

_____ (1983) 'The Structure of ownership and the Theory of the Firm', *Journal of Law and Economics,* vol. 26: 375- .

Dent, J.F. (1990) 'Strategy, Organisation and Control: some possibilities for Accounting Research, *Accounting, Organisations and Society*, vol. 15, no. 1/2 pp. 3-25.

Diamond, P.A. (1967) 'The Role of the Stock Market in a General Equilibrium Model with Technological Uncertainty', *American Economic Review* 57, no. 4, pp. 759-776.

Dimaggio, P. and Powell, W. (1983) The Iron Cage Revisited: Institutional Isomorphism and Collective Rationality in Organizational Fields. *American Sociological Review,* vol. 48 (April) pp. 147-160.

Dore, R. (1973) *British Factory - Japanese Factory.* Berkeley: University of California Press.

Dréze, J.H. (1976) 'Some theory of Labour Management and Participation', *Econometrica*, 44(6), pp. 1125-1139.

Eatwell, J. (1982) *Whatever Happened to Britain?* London: Duckworths/BBC

Edwards, E. and Bell, P. (1961) *The Theory and Measurement of Business Income*. Berkeley: University of California Press.

Emmanuel, C. and Otley, D. (1985) *Accounting for Management Control*. London: Van Nostrand Reinhold.

Ezzamel, M., Hoskin, K., Macve, R. (1990) 'Managing it all by numbers: a Review of Johnson & Kaplan's "Relevance Lost", *Accounting and Business Research*, vol. 20, no. 78, pp. 153-166.

Fama, E. (1980), 'Agency Problems and the Theory of the Firm', *Journal of Political Economy*, vol. 88, no. 2, pp. 208-307.

_____ and Laffer, A.B. (1971) 'Information and Capital Markets', *Journal of Business*, vol. 44, pp. 289-298.

Flamholtz, E.G. (1983) 'Accounting, Budgeting and Control Systems in their organisational Context: Theoretical and Empirical Perspectives', *Accounting Organisations and Society*, vol. 8, no. 2/3, pp.153-169.

_____, Das, T.K., and Tsui, A.S. (1985), 'Towards an integrative Framework of organisational Control', *Accounting, Organisations and Society*, vol. 10, no. 1, pp. 35-50.

Foster A. (1989) 'How Bad is GEC?' *Management Today*, January, pp. 40-45.

Gilchrist, R.R. (1971), *Managing for Profit*. London: George Allen & Unwin.

Goold, M. and Campbell, A. (1987) 'Strategies and Styles'. Oxford: Blackwell.

Grabowski, H. G. and Mueller, D.C. (1978) 'Industrial research and development, intangible capital stocks, and firm profit rates', *Bell Journal of Economics*, pp. 328-343.

Gray S. I. & Maunders, K.T. (1980), *Value Added Reporting: Uses and Measurement*. London: Association of Certified Accountants.

Gregory, G. (1985), 'The Dynamics of Japanese Innovation', *Journal of Japanese Trade and Industry*, no. 1, pp. 59-61.

Hannan, M. and Freeman, J. (1977) 'The Population Ecology Model of Organisations', *American Journal of Sociology*, vol. 82, no. 5, pp. 925-964.

Hart, O. (1988) 'Incomplete contracts and the Theory of the Firm', *Journal of Law, Economics and Organisation*, vol. 4, no. 1 (Spring).

Hay, D.A. and Morris, D.J. (1979) *Industrial Economics: Theory and Evidence*. Oxford: Oxford University Press.

Hayek, F. (1945) 'The use of Knowledge in Society', *American Economic Review*, 35 (September) pp. 519-30.

Healy, P. (1985) 'The effect of Bonus Schemes on the selection of accounting Principles', *Journal of Accounting and Economics*, pp. 81-108.

Hergert, M. and Morris, D. (1989) 'Accounting Data for Value Chain Analysis', *Strategic Management Journal*, vol. 10, p.175-188.

Hicks, J. (1946) *Value and Capital*, 2nd edition. Oxford: Oxford University Press.

Hird, C. (1980) 'Beware of Added Value', *New Statesman*.

Hiromoto, T. (1988) 'Another Hidden Edge - Japanese Management Accounting', *Harvard Business Review*, July - August, pp. 22-26.

Hirshleifer, J. (1958) *Investment, Interest and Capital*. Englewood Cliffs: Prentice Hall.

_____ (1977) 'Economics from a biological viewpoint', *Journal of Law and Economics*, p. 1-52.

_____ and Riley, J.G. (1979) 'The analytics of uncertainty and information - an expository survey', *Journal of Economic Literature*, vol. XVII (December), pp. 1375-1421.

Hirschmann, A. (1970) *Exit, Voice and Loyalty*. Cam, Mass: Harvard University Press

Hofstede, G. (1980) *Culture's Consequences: international differences in work-related values*. Beverley Hills: Sage.

Holmstrom, B. and Ricart-Costa, J. (1986) 'Managerial Incentives and Capital Management', *Quarterly Journal of Economics*, pp. 835-60.

Hopwood, A.G. (1987) 'The Archaeology of Accounting Systems', *Accounting, Organizations and Society*, vol. 12, no. 3, pp. 207-234.

Horovitz, J.H. (1978) 'Management Control in France, Great Britain and Germany', *Columbia Journal of World Business*, Summer, pp. 16-22.

Hrebiniak, L.G. and Joyce, W.F. (1985) 'Organisational Adaptation: Strategic Choice and Environmental Determinism', *Administrative Science Quarterly*, vol. 30, pp. 336-349.

Hymer, S.H. (1976) *The International Operations of National Firms*, Lexington Books.

Ijiri, Y. (1978) 'Cash Flow Accounting and its Structure', *Journal of Accounting, Auditing and Finance* (Summer), pp. 331-348.

Institute of Chartered Accountants in England and Wales (ICAEW), (1980), *Survey of Published Accounts 1979*, ICAEW.

Itami, H. (1975) 'Adaptive Behaviour: Management Control and Information Analysis', *Studies in Accounting Research*, no. 15, American Accounting Association.

Jensen, M. (1978) 'Some anomalous evidence regarding market efficiency', *Journal of Financial Economics*, vol 6 (2-3): pp. 95-101.

_____ (1983) 'Organisation Theory and Methodology', Accounting Review, 50 (April): 319-39.

_____ (1988) 'The Takeover Controversy: Analysis and Evidence' in *Knights, Raiders and Targets*, Coffee, J., Lowenstein, L., and Rose-Ackerman (eds). Oxford: Oxford University Press.

_____ (1989) 'The Eclipse of the Public Corporation', *Harvard Business Review*, September - October, pp. 61-75.

_____ and Meckling, W. (1976), 'Theory of the Firm: Managerial Behaviour, Agency Costs and Ownership Structure', *Journal of Financial Economics*, 3, pp. 305-360.

_____ (1979) 'Rights and Production Functions: an Application to Labor-Managed Firms', *Journal of Business,* 52, pp. 469-506.

Johnson, H. (1983) 'The search for gain in markets and firms: a review of the Historical emergence of Management Control Systems', *Accounting, Organisations and Society*, vol. 8, no. 2/3, pp. 139-146.

Johnson, H. T. and Kaplan, R. S. (1987) *Relevance Lost: the rise and fall of Management Accounting*. Boston: Harvard Business School.

Kantor, B. (1979) 'Rational Expectations and Economic Thought', *Journal of Economic Literature*, vol. XVII, (December), pp. 1422-1441.

Kaplan, R.S. (1983) 'Measuring Manufacturing Performance: A New Challenge for Managerial Accounting Research'. *Accounting Review*, Oct, vol. LVIII, no. 4: 686-705.

_____ (1984) 'The Evolution of Managerial Accounting', *Accounting Review* vol. LXI, no. 3: 390-418.

Keynes, J. M. (1936) *The General Theory of Employment, Interest and Money*. London: Macmillan.

Labour Research, (1978), *Value Added*, (February).

Lachman, L. (1956) *Capital and its Structure*. London: London School of Economics.

Lakatos, I. (1978) *Philosophical Papers* (2 vols). Cambridge: Cambridge University Press.

Lalanne, H. (1990) 'Preliminary Findings on the Roles of Accounting and Management Information Systems in different Management styles and different national contexts', paper presented at the *European Accounting Association*, Budapest.

Langlois, A. (1986) *Economics as a process*. Cambridge: Cambridge University Press.

Layard, R. (ed.) (1972) *Cost-Benefit Analysis*. Harmondsworth: Penguin.

Leibenstein, H. (1966) 'Allocative Efficiency vs, "X-Efficiency", *American Economic Review*, vol. 56, pp. 392-415.

Leijonhufvud, A. (1968) *On Keynesian Economics and the Economics of Keynes*, Oxford: OUP (1986) 'Capitalism and the Factory System', in

Economics as a Process, Langlois, A., (ed). Cambridge: Cambridge University Press.

Lev. B and Ohlson, J.A. (1982) 'Market Based Empirical Research in Accounting: a review, interpretation, and extension' *Journal of Accounting Research,* vol. 20, (supplement) pp. 249-322.

Levins, R. (1962) 'Theory of Fitness in a Heterogenous Environment, 1. The fitness set and Adaptive function', *American naturalist,* 96 (November-December), pp. 361-78.

Levy, H. and Sarnat, M. (1990) *Capital Investment and Financial Decisions.* (4th ed) Englewood Cliffs: Prentice Hall.

List, F. (1966) *The National System of Political Economy.* New York: Kelley.

Lloyd T. (1987) 'A one man Band? If it is, its a big one', *Financial Weekly,* October 1, pp. 32-38.

Lloyds Bank Economic Bulletin (1990) No. 138 (June).

Loasby, B.J. (1976) *Choice, Ignorance and Complexity.* Cambridge: Cambridge University Press.

Lowe, E.A. Puxty A.G. and Laughlin, R.C. (1983) 'Simple Theories for complex Processes: Accounting Policy and the Market for Myopia', *Journal of Accounting and Public Policy* 2: pp. 19-42.

_____ and Machin, J. (eds) (1983) *New perspectives in Management Control.* London: Macmillan.

Luria, S.E., Gould, S.J. and Singer, S. (1981) *A View of Life,* Menlo Park: Benjamin/Cummings.

Manes, R.P., Chen, K.C. & Greenberg, R. (1985) 'Economies of Scope and Cost-Volume-profit analysis for the multi product firm', *Journal of Accounting Literature,* pp. 77-111.

Manley, J. and Lloyd, T. (1989) 'A Deal Too Far?' *Financial Weekly,* April 20, pp. 24-29.

Manpower Services Commission, (1986) *Annual Report.* H.M.S.O.

March, J.G. and Simon H.A. (1958) *Organisations*. New York: Wiley.

Marchington, M.P. (1977), 'Worker Participation and Plant-wide Incentive Systems', *Personnel Review*, pp. 35-48.

Marglin, S.A. (1974) 'What do bosses do? The origins and functions of hierarchy in capitalist production', *Review of Radical Political Economics*, 6: 33-60.

_____ (1984) 'Knowledge and Power', in Stephen, H. (ed) *Firms, Organisations and Labour*. London: Macmillan.

Marris, R. (1964), *The Economic Theory of Managerial Capitalism*. London: MacMillan.

McGuinness, T. (1983) 'Markets and Hierarchies: a suitable framework for an evaluation of organisational change?' in Francis, A., Turk, J. and Willman, P. (eds), *Power, Efficiency and Institutions: a critical appraisal of the Markets and Hierarchies Paradigm*. London: Heinemann.

Meade, J.E. (1972) The Theory of Labour-managed firms and of profitsharing, *Economic Journal*, 82, pp. 402-428.

Mintzberg, H. (1978) 'Patterns in Strategy Formulation', *Management Science*, pp. 934-948.

Mises, von L. (1949) *Human Action*. London: William Hodge.

Morley, M.F. (1978), *The Value Added Statement: a review of its use in Corporate reports*. London: Gee & Co.

Murphy, K. J. (1985) 'Corporate Performance and Managerial Compensation: an Empirical Analysis'. *Journal of Accounting and Economics* (April) pp. 11-42.

Muth, J. (1960) 'Optimal Properties of Exponentially Weighted Forecasts', *Journal of American Statistical Association*, (June), vol. 55 (290), pp. 299-306.

_____ (1961) 'Rational Expectations and the Theory of Price Movements', *Econometrica*, (July) vol. 29 (3), pp. 315-335.

National Economic Development Office (1988) *Performance and Competitive Success: strengthening competitiveness in UK Electronics*. London: National Economic Development Office.

Nelson, R. and Winter, S. (1982) *An Evolutionary Theory of Economic Change*. Cambridge: Harvard University Press.

Odagiri, H. (1980), *The Theory of Growth in the Corporate Economy: An Inquiry into Management Preference R & D and Economic Growth*. Cambridge University Press.

Otley, D. and Berry, A.J. (1980) 'Control, Organisation and Accounting', *Accounting, Organisations and Society*, vol. 5, no. 2, pp. 231-46.

Ouchi, W. (1977) 'The Relationship between Organizational Structure and Organizational Control', *Administrative Science Quarterly*, vol. 22, pp. 95-112.

_____ (1980) 'Markets, Bureaucracies and Clans' *Administrative Science Quarterly*, (March) vol. 25:129-145)

Parker, R. and Harcourt, G. (1969) *Readings on the concept of the measurement of income*. Cambridge: Cambridge University Press.

Paton, W. (1922) *Accounting Theory*. Chicago: Accounting Studies Press.

Phillips, A. (1976) 'A Critique of Empirical Studies of Relations between Market Structure and Profitability', *Journal of Industrial Economics,* vol. XXIV, no. 4, pp. 241-249.

Pike, R. (1982) *Capital Budgeting in the 1980's: a Major Survey of the Investment Practices in Large Companies*. London: ICMA.

_____ (1983) 'The Capital Budgeging Behaviour and Corporate characterisitics of capital-constrained firms', *Journal of Business Finance and Accounting*, vol. 10, no. 4: pp. 663-671.

_____ (1985) 'Owner-manager conflict and the role of the pay-back method', *Accounting and Business Research*, Winter, pp. 47-51.

_____ and Ooi, T. (1988) 'The Impact of Corporate Investment Objectives and Constraints on Capital Budgeting Practices', *British Accounting Review*, vol. 20, no. 2, pp. 159-173.

Porter, M. (1980) *Competitive Strategy.* New York: Free Press.

_____ (1985) *Competitive Advantage.* New York: Free Press.

_____ (ed) (1986) *Competition in Global Industries.* Harvard: Harvard Business School Press.

_____ (1990) *The Competitive Advantage of Nations.* Basingstoke: Macmillan.

Putterman, L. (ed) (1986) *The Economic Nature of the Firm: a Reader.* Cambridge: Cambridge University Press.

_____ (1988), 'The Firm as Association versus the firm as Commodity', *Economics and Philosophy*, vol. 4, pp. 243-266.

Puxty, A.G. (1985), Critiques of Agency in Accountancy, *Strathclyde Convergencies.* Glasgow.

Rajan, A. & Pearson, R. (eds) (1986), *UK Occupation and Employment Trends to 1990: An Employer-Based Study of the Trends and Their Underlying Causes.* London: Butterworths.

Rappaport, A. (1986) *Creating Shareholder Value: the new standard for Business Performance.* New York: Free Press.

_____ (1990) 'The Staying Power of the Public Corporation', *Harvard Business Review*, January-February, pp. 96-104.

Reeves, T.K. and Woodward, J. (1970) 'The Study of Managerial Control,' in Woodward. J (ed) *Industrial Organisations: Behaviour and Control.* London: Oxford University Press.

Ricketts, M. (1987) *The Economics of Business Enterprise: new approaches to the Theory of the Firm.* Brighton: Wheatsheaf.

Roll, R. (1977) 'A Critique of Asset Pricing Theory's Tests', *Journal of Financial Economics*, March.

Ross, S. (1987) 'The Interrelationship between Economics and Finance', *American Economic Review*, (Papers and Proceedings), vol. 77, no. 2, pp. 29-34.

Rueschmeyer, D. (1977) 'Structural Differentiation, Efficiency and Power', *American Journal of Sociology*, vol. 83 no. 1.

Rutherford, B.A. (1977), 'Value Added as a Focus of Attention of Financial Reporting: Some Conceptual problems', *Accounting and Business Research*, pp. 215-220.

Salter, M. and Weinhold, W. (1988), 'Corporate Takeovers: Financial Boom or Organisational Bust?' in *Knights, Raiders and Targets*. Coffee, J., Lowenstein, L., and Rose-Ackerman (eds), Oxford: Oxford University Press.

Schotter, A. (1981) *The Economic Theory of Social Institutions*. New York: Cambridge University Press.

Schumpeter, J.A. (1942) *Capitalism, Socialism and Democracy*. London: Allen and Unwin.

Seal, W.B. (1986) 'Should Firms Maximise Value Added?' *Department of Economics and Public Administration Discussion Paper*, Trent Polytechnic.

_____ (1987a) 'The Measurement of Manufacturing Performance and the Efficient Markets Hypothesis: Some Thoughts on the Limits to Accounting in Different Economic Systems.' *E.P.A. Occasional Paper in Economics and Politics*, no. 87/2, Trent Polytechnic.

_____ (1987b) 'Value Added and the Theory of the Firm: on Mirages and the fallacy of Decomposition', *British Accounting Review*, vol. 19, pp. 145-159.

_____ (1990) 'Business Organisation and Deindustrialisation:an institutionalist critique of the Natural Selection Analogy,' *Cambridge Journal of Economics*, vol. 14, pp. 267-275.

Shubik, M. (1988) 'Corporate Control, Efficient Markets, and the Public Good', in *Knights, Raiders and Targets*, Coffee, J., Lowenstein, L., and Rose-Ackerman (eds). Oxford: Oxford University Press.

Simon, H. (1978) 'Rationality as Process and as Product of Thought', *American Economic Association Papers and Proceedings*, Richard T. Ely Lecture, May, vol. 68, no. 2.

_____ (1983) *Reason in Human Affairs*. Stanford: Stanford University press.

Singh, A. (1975) 'Takeovers, Economic Natural Selection, and the Theory of the Firm: Evidence from the Postwar United Kingdom Experience', *The Economic Journal*, 85 (September), pp. 497-515.

Skerratt, L.C.L. and Tonkin, D.J. (1982) *Financial Reporting 1982-83: A Survey of U.K. Published Accounts*. Institute of Chartered Accountants in England and Wales.

Soete, L. and Dosi, G. (1983) *Technology and Employment in the Electronics Industry.* London: Frances Pinter.

Solomon, E. (1966) 'Return on Investment: The Relation of Book Yield to True Yield; in Jaedicke, R., Ijiri, Y. and Nielson, O. (eds) *Research in Accounting Measurement.* Chicago: American Accounting Association.

Spicer B.H. and Ballew, V. (1983) 'Management Accounting Systems and the Economics of Internal Organisation' *Accounting, Organisations and Society,* vol. 8, no. 1: 73-96.

Spicer, B. (1988) 'Towards an Organisational Theory of the transfer pricing Process', *Accounting, Organisations and Society*, vol. 13, no. 3, pp. 303-322.

Steer, P. and Cable, J. (1978) 'Internal Organisation and Profit: an empirical analysis of Large U.K. companies', *Journal of Industrial Economics* (September) pp. 13-30.

Sterling, R. (1970) *Theory of the Measurement of Enterprise Income.* Lawrence: University of Kansas Press.

Stiglitz, J.E. (1981) 'The Allocation Role of the Stock Market: Pareto Optimality and Competition', *Journal of Finance*, vol. XXXVI, no. 2, pp. 235-251.

Stolliday, I. & Attwood, M. (1978), Financial Inducement and Productivity Bargaining, *Industrial and Commercial Training*.

Teasdale, A. (1981), 'The Paradoxes of Japanese Success', *Personnel Management*, November, pp. 29-33.

Thompson, S. and Wright, M. (eds) (1989) *Internal Organisation, Efficiency and Profit.* Oxford: Philip Allan.

Thornton, D. (1979) 'Information and Institutions in the Capital Market', *Accounting, Organisations and Society*, vol. 4, no. 3, pp. 211-233.

Tiessen, P. and Waterhouse, J.H. (1983) 'Towards a descriptive theory of management accounting', *Accounting Organisations and Society*, vol. 2/3, pp. 251-267.

Tinker, T. (1988) 'Panglossian Accounting Theories: The Science of Apologising in Style, *Accounting, Organisations, and Society*, vol. 13, no. 2 pp. 165-189

Tonkin, D.J. and Skerratt, L.C.L. (1983), *Financial Reporting 1983-84: A Survey of Published Accounts*. Institute of Chartered Accountants in England and Wales.

Underdown, B. and Taylor, P. (1985) *Accounting Theory and Policy Making*. Heinemann: London.

Vanek, J. (1970) *The General Theory of Labour Managed Market Economies*. Ithaca, Cornell University Press.

Watts, R. and Zimmerman, J. (1979) 'The Demand and Supply of Accounting Theories: The Market for Excuses', *Accounting Review 54*, (April) pp. 273-305.

_____ (1986) *Positive Accounting Theory*. Englewood Cliffs: Prentice-Hall International

Weber, M. (1947) *The Theory of Social and Economic Organisation*. London: William Hodge.

Weiss, L. (1969) 'Advertising, Profits and Corporate Taxes', *Review of Economic Statistics* vol. 51, no. 4 pp. 421-30.

Weitzmann, M. (1983), 'Some Macroeconmic Implications of Alternative Compensation Systems', *Economic Journal* vol. 93, pp. 763-783.

Weitzmann, M. (1984), *The Share Economy: Conquering Stagflation*. Cambridge, Mass.: Harvard University Press.

Wilkins, M. (1986) 'Defining a Firm: History and Theory,' in Herter, P. and Jones, G. (eds) *Multinationals: Theory and History*. London: Gower.

Williamson, O.E. (1964) *The Economics of Discretionary Behaviour. Managerial Objectives in a Theory of the Firm.* Englewood Cliffs: Prentice-Hall.

_____ (1970) *Corporate Control and Business Behaviour: an inquiry into the effects of Organisational Form on Enteprise Behaviour.* Englewood Cliffs: Prentice-Hall.

_____ (1975) *Markets and Hierarchies: Analysis and Antitrust Implications.* Free Press.

_____ (1985) *The Economic Institutions of Capitalism.* The Free Press, New York.

_____ and Riordan, M.H. (1985) 'Asset Specificity and Economic Organisation', *International Journal of Industrial Organisation*, vol. 3, pp. 365-373.

_____ (1987) 'Transaction-cost Economics the Comparative Contracting Perspective', *Journal of Economic Behaviour and Organisation*, vol. 8, no. 4.

_____ (1988) 'Corporate Finance and Corporate Governance', *The Journal of Finance,* vol. XLVIII, no. 3 (July) pp. 567-591.

Wiseman, J. (1973) Uncertainty, Costs, and Collectivist Economic Planning. [first published in *Economica* (May, 1953)] reprinted in *L.S.E. Essays in Cost* edited by Buchanan, J.M. and Thirlby, G.F., London: Weidenfeld and Nicolson.

Index

incomplete markets contd. 43-44, 116, 166-168
information flows
  horizontal 12, 109-110
  vertical 110

Japanese Cure 12, 109, 176, 190, 199, 201

labour markets 10, 56, 82-83, 85-87, 106-107, 109, 120-121, 144, 164, 168, 171, 190, 192-193, 195

managerialist theory 10, 45, 49
market for control 6, 10-11, 30, 45, 78-79, 82, 84, 86-88, 104, 123, 159, 165, 172, 177, 183, 186, 190, 192-193, 196, 200
market power 9, 34-38, 40, 45, 53, 61, 71, 125, 183, 193

natural selection 5, 12, 53, 58, 60, 73-80, 82, 89, 157, 159, 176-178, 181-185, 188, 190, 196, 199

organisational failures framework 4, 6, 9-10, 52, 64, 66, 68, 71
organisational rent 12, 134-137, 145, 154, 171, 176, 200
ownership 10-11, 34, 45-46, 71, 81, 84, 92, 104-105, 113, 133, 135, 143, 145, 152, 155, 180, 192, 195

power 14, 20, 45-46, 54, 89, 104-107

process 5-6, 11, 85, 92, 198
profit
  measurement of 36, 41-42, 49
putting-out 84, 106-107, 135

quasi-hierarchy 126-127, 134

rational expectations 8-9, 14-15, 18, 22
rationality 5, 18, 24-26, 49, 51, 62, 87, 94-95, 150, 185
'Relevance Lost' debate 157

screw-driver firm 1, 7, 135-136
short-termism 7, 12, 79-80, 158, 161, 163-165, 201
strategic management accounting 3
systems theory 95, 98-99, 110

transaction cost economics
  governance branch 57, 91, 114, 159, 198
  measurement branch 3, 10, 26, 58, 63, 71, 91, 111, 114, 159, 198

uncertainty
  active response 27
  event 20-21
  market 20-21

value added 12, 132, 136-155
value chain analysis 133, 136-137

X-efficiency 53, 167